Student Reviews from the Class of 2011:

"This book should be THE book you read if you are planning to go through the recruitment process in consulting and want to know how to survive every step of the process. Not only did it provide detailed tips, the book was in every aspect highly relevant and accurate."

- L.E.K. Consulting Associate*

"This is the only book in the business that comes from a student's perspective. It's very helpful for someone who doesn't have any background in how to get a consulting job. "

- McKinsey & Company Business Analyst

" Great way to familiarize yourself with the consulting recruiting process, especially if you do not have anyone to walk you through it."

- BCG Associate

"Great comprehensive introduction to the consulting [recruitment] process from someone who has been through it before. Candid and honest advice that will get you in the right mindset to face the grueling process of interviews."

- Oliver Wyman Consultant

"Any consulting question that I had lingering in my mind, this book answered it."

- Deloitte Technology Analyst

"Great overview of consulting and helps significantly in positioning yourself to earn an offer with a great consulting firm."

- Booz & Company Consultant

College2Consulting

The Complete Insider's Guide to the
Consulting Recruitment Process

Charles Benkendorf

Reed Walker

Edited by Shannon Clark

Copyright

ISBN-13: 978-0-615-53153-3

Printed in the United States of America.

Acknowledgements:

Behind anything of significance stands a supportive team of people. Without these people, this book never would have been completed. I'd like to thank Shannon Clark and Allison Clark for their excellent work in editing and designing this book.

Thank you to Professor William White, Patricia Crisafulli and Bob Reiss for their advice & guidance throughout the publishing process.

Thank you also to Shannon Clark, Alexandra Hallas-Button, Asaf Elani, Ewelina Lewandowska, Hossam Tewfik, Ilya Trakhtenberg, John Le, Kiran Pookote, Lee Ettleman, Marissa Benson, Michael Sachaj, Rafal Ciechowski, Jeff Bartow, Laura Gravley, Kevin Fishner, and Royce Dalby for directly (or indirectly) contributing content to this book.

Thank you to Irene Liang, Sandeep Kini, Kim Swertfager, Melissa Holmes, Rhonda Mann, and Keira Sagner for reviewing the manuscript.

Finally, thank you to Julie Shen for encouraging me to look at a career in consulting in the first place, and then helping me practice dozens of cases when I decided to pursue management consulting.

Authors' Note

For most students, deciding what they want to do after graduation is quite daunting. We recommend management consulting for many reasons. Most importantly, management consulting gives you options later in life. Consulting is an extremely rewarding job and will provide the fundamental skills to succeed in business. You may find after being a consultant for a few years that advising CEOs and flying around the world solving challenging problems really isn't such a bad life. You might even make a career out of it! However, before you get there, the recruitment process stands in your way.

At times, recruitment becomes almost unbearable. Preparing for case interviews, going to info sessions, and modifying your cover letters can require twenty-plus hours per week on top of your regular classes. We remember that well. But we promise, the reward is worth it!

The tools in this book will set you up in a way that no other resource can. We will prepare you for the twists and turns in the process and give you the best possible chance of landing that job. After watching so many of our friends struggle through recruitment and struggle to get a job, we noticed who ultimately succeeded and who failed. This insider's guide will put the process in perspective for you so that you won't fail where our friends did. In this book, you will benefit from the advice of dozens of other consultants who now work for the world's most respected consulting firms.

We wish you the best during recruitment.

Sincerely,

Contents:

1   Ch. 1: Introduction

Part 1 Introduction to Management Consulting

5   Ch. 2: What is Management Consulting?

11   Ch. 3: What is Strategy Consulting?

25   Ch. 4: Why Do Companies Hire Management Consultants?

29   Ch. 5: Why Management Consulting? I have a Million Career Choices!

33   Ch. 6: What Are Management Consulting Firms Looking For?

Part 2 The Recruitment Process

41   Ch. 7: Learn About Consulting and the Firms

49   Ch. 8: Pre-Recruitment Networking

59   Ch. 9: Build Up Your Business Acumen

63   Ch. 10: GPA Cutoffs

67   Ch. 11: Resume Experience

75   Ch. 12: Writing a Resume

85   Ch. 13: Writing Cover Letters

93   Ch. 14: Getting You to Apply

107   Ch. 15: Preparing for Recruitment

Part 3 The Interviewing Process

119   Ch. 16: Introduction to Fit and Case Interviews

123   Ch. 17: The Case Interview

147   Ch.18: The Fit Interview

163   Ch 19: First and Second Round Interviews

169   Ch. 20: Thank You Letters

171   Ch. 21: Dealing with Rejection

177   Ch. 22: Please Accept Our Offer!

Part 4 Case Studies

195   Ch. 23: How to I Master Case Interviews?

213   Ch. 24: How do I Practice Framework Creation ?

241   Ch. 25: Practice Cases

287   Appendices and Sponsor Profiles

Dedicated to all those i-bankers working 100 hour weeks who should have read this book.

1

Introduction

Welcome to College2Consulting – an insider's guide on how to land your dream job in management consulting. It's brought to you by dozens of consultants who recently made the transition from prestigious universities to the world's most respected consultancies.

Management consulting is a very attractive first career choice. Consultants advise senior executives from Fortune 500 companies, they travel the world solving today's most challenging business problems, and they are (usually) rewarded handsomely. The skills management consultants develop are applicable to almost every industry, and the experience provides an unmatched foundation from which to build a career – even if you decide to leave consulting for something else entirely.

Unfortunately, precisely because of its attractiveness, finding a consulting job is very competitive. The competition is even more intense at the top few firms, with these firms estimated to average a *2% nationwide acceptance rate.* It can be easier to gain acceptance to Stanford Business School or Yale Law than getting the consulting job of your dreams. While a few students are "naturals" and receive an offer with little preparation, most students who receive offers work extremely hard to prepare for the recruitment process. Most students who do not effectively prepare do not receive an offer.

And it's only becoming more competitive. As each class of recruits builds on the knowledge they glean from the preceding class, the bar continues to rise. It's no longer enough to simply ace the case interview or practice a few behavioral questions. You need knowledge of the world of management consulting, a solid understanding of what recruiters seek, and a holistic understanding of recruitment. This is what the best candidates do to succeed.

College2Consulting will show you how to be the best candidate you can be, leaving nothing to chance. You can learn from our successes and failures and get a leg up on the competition. We will walk you through each step of the recruitment process, pointing out ways you can stand out and be multi-faceted at every turn, as candidates with little substance to them will inevitably fail. To be successful, you need to smooth out rough edges and be impressive from start to finish. *This book is a one-stop-shop for taking you from college to consulting.*

Now, let's dive in and land you a management consulting job!

PART 1: INTRODUCTION TO MANAGEMENT CONSULTING

It is crucial to understand a number of key concepts before applying to management consulting firms. The most critical questions include:

- What is management consulting?
- What is strategy consulting, and what is the difference between "strategy" and "management" consulting?
- Why do companies hire management consultants?
- Why should I pursue management consulting?
- What qualities do I need to display in order to attract management consulting firms?

2

What is Management Consulting?

You may have heard that a management consultant "counsels CEOs" or "gets paid to travel around the world." People love talking about the great perks associated with this exciting career path, but what does management consulting really entail?

Let's begin by defining the term "consulting." Consulting is advising; to be a consultant, someone must become aware of your ability to render specific guidance prior to making a decision of consequence, small or large. A consultant must take time and energy to become educated on a situational basis. Once educated in the matter at hand, the consultant helps the client to come to terms with an informed and viable decision. As you could imagine, this lends itself to countless possibilities! Consider these examples which appear when googling the term "consultant":

- Customer Service Consultant
- Political Consultant
- Stock Consultant
- Education Consultant
- Magic Consultant

Clearly consultants are not just limited to management, and the scope of consulting can get even broader. You have probably been a consultant many times throughout your life already. You are a relationship consultant when your friends ask you for help with their latest girlfriend/boyfriend trouble, you are a computer consultant if you have ever diagnosed a friend's computer problem, and you are a food consultant when you suggest a recipe for a co-worker's get-together.

While you may have been a consultant already, management consulting takes the same idea; however, it supports the advice with significantly more data and analysis to increase confidence in the recommendation. There are profits, jobs, and the futures of companies on the line. This "focus on data" has always been a significant part of management consulting from its very beginning.

History

Management consulting emerged when scholars began to study successful companies and apply their findings to less efficient companies. MIT professor Arthur D. Little founded the first management consulting firm in 1886 by integrating analytical studies and professional services. Before that time, it was uncommon for an external agency to improve one business through the analysis of other businesses.

The firm began by offering chemical analysis, but by the early 1900s, the firm had branched into offering its expertise in coal, lubrication, biology, textiles, engineering, and forest products, as well. As an innovator in the fledgling field of management consulting, Little's firm built its expertise by tackling tough problems.

In 1914, Edwin Booz founded the first firm to serve both industry and government clients. It later evolved into Booz Allen Hamilton and then Booz & Co.

William McKinsey started McKinsey & Company in 1926 with the theory that management consultants could benefit not only inefficient companies, but also prosperous ones.

Services Offered Today

Today, management consulting firms are hired to perform a variety of projects focused on improving the performance of their clients' businesses. History has shown that there are seemingly unending methods for improving a business. As such, the range of service offerings is extensive. Here are common examples of services offered by management consulting firms:

1. Change Management – Providing a structured approach to transitioning individuals, teams, and organizations from a current state to a desired future state. Change is complicated because organizations are constantly in motion. For example, suppose you work at McDonalds, and you're in charge of installing a replacement fryer. Assuming that you have some mechanics available and an instruction manual, it seems like a straightforward task. But now imagine that this restaurant has a busy, 24/7 operation, and the manager is not willing to slow down business. The change is now much more complex to execute. In many situations, firms will bring in consultants with experience to help develop a change plan and assist in execution.

2. Customer Relationship Management – Developing a system for managing and nurturing a company's interactions with customers and sales prospects. Such a system can help a company to provide better customer service, more accurately target customers with relevant marketing messages, and track marketing effectiveness.

3. Human Resources Management – Developing a strategic and coherent approach to the management of a company's employees. This can include minimizing healthcare spending, developing a benefits package to attract the right employees, and optimizing executive compensation to incentivize optimal performance.

4. Process Management – Process customization for optimization. In other words, a consulting firm can restructure the client's business model (process) to become more efficient. Process management often times includes both human and technological components

for maximum effect. The goal is to create a malleable process that organically changes to maximize efficiency at any given stage.

For example, suppose a supply chain for Company A includes three internal locations, each with separate IT solutions. This likely leads to inefficiency because translation is needed for the systems to communicate. This may be achieved through additional code or manual input. To improve efficiency, a consulting firm could reorganize and integrate the human and technical processes into one seamless system.

5. Risk Management – Understanding the nature of risk, prioritizing risk, and determining appropriate solutions. Sometimes the solution is simply a process that monitors risks. The technical steps involved in risk management are solidified in an easy-to-remember framework.

    a. Identification of risks

    b. Analysis of risks

    c. Mitigation of risks

6. Supply Chain Management – Managing interconnected processes and businesses and ultimately enabling the timely delivery of a final product or service to the end consumer. The purpose is to improve the performance of individual businesses in the supply chain as well as the supply chain as a whole. Often, this involves logistical optimization and efficiency improvement.

    A good way to understand supply chain management is to pick an end product, such as potato chips, and imagine how they got into your hands.

    First, identify the raw materials at the beginning: potatoes, salt, and vegetable oil. Second, consider the businesses involved in creating each of the raw materials. Third, think about aggregating the raw materials and all relevant distribution networks. Fourth, think about the manufacturing of the chips and packaging them. Then, after the chips are created and packaged, consider the network that distributes the packaged chips to your local grocery. Finally, you buy them.

If any one of those steps is disrupted, the bag of chips won't be on the shelf for you to buy, and the entire supply chain suffers. While there are a number of businesses and moving parts involved here, this is still a simple example. You can imagine how complex and cumbersome some supply chains can become and why a consultant would be hired to optimize them.

7. Strategy Consulting – Advising executives on their strategy. "Strategy consulting" is often used interchangeably with "management consulting." However, strategy consulting is actually a niche within the overarching realm of "management consulting." Due to its great importance, complexity, and diversity of meaning, the next section will delve deeper into this branch of management consulting.

3
What is Strategy Consulting?

Strategy consulting is a more recent invention jump-started by the Boston Consulting Group (BCG) in 1965. BCG was already a few years old at that point and needed to create a distinctive niche to survive against the larger and better known management consulting firms. They debated and analyzed numerous ways to differentiate themselves before "business strategy" came up. At least one person in the room felt it was too vague, but founder Bruce Henderson shot back, "That's the beauty of it; we'll define it." Henderson set forth to define and develop strategy consulting as BCG's distinct specialty within management consulting.

Thus, strategy consulting was born as the specific art of advising CEOs and other decision makers as to their strategy. Since then, strategy consulting has become a widely accepted function of management consulting firms, similar to supply chain, customer relationship, human resources, process, risk, and change management.

But which firms offer "strategy" consulting and which offer "management" consulting?

The two terms are often used interchangeably because referring to your firm as a "strategy" firm seems to get students to perk up their ears more. A firm that calls itself a "management consulting" firm on its website may tell recruits that it is a "strategy" firm in its information sessions.

Let's try to distinguish between these two terms. You can rest
assured that any business consulting firm to which you apply is a
"management consulting" firm. The added terms "business" or
"management" before consulting differentiate these management
consulting firms from all the other companies and individuals calling
themselves consultants (e.g., "magic consultant").

Common Problems in Strategy Consulting

The following pages examine different types of problems a strategist
might encounter. These problems and their solutions are important
to understand; you may encounter derivatives of these problems
during the recruiting process in the form of business case interviews
(see chapter 17). Presumably, you will find these business issues
interesting. If not, strategy consulting might not be for you.

There are different approaches that strategy consultants can take.
A top-line approach increases a client's revenue by combining
organizations (inorganic growth) or by growing the organization from
within (organic growth). A bottom-line approach aims to cut costs to
increase a client's profit. As expected, there are hybrid approaches as
well.

Top-Line Focus

1. Inorganic Growth – Inorganic growth indicates expansion by
    means of combining multiple organizations. More specifically,
    inorganic growth is the process of expanding a business via
    buying a company (acquisition), merging multiple firms, or
    creating a joint venture between organizations. A consultant could
    have a variety of roles within the inorganic growth process, from
    the initial recommendation all the way through to integrating and
    improving the new and larger company.

    1.1. Merge or acquire another company – A company can either
    merge with another company or acquire them outright. Both
    of these topics, or "M&A," are particularly contentious topics
    among CEOs, because it is difficult to predict whether a merger/

acquisition will succeed. While it is clear to the business world that many mergers/acquisitions fail, it is much less clear why some succeed. Each consulting firm has their own theories and corresponding case studies about what leads to success.

Well-known examples of failures include Daimler & Chrysler and HP & Compaq. Examples of successes include Best Buy's acquisition of Geek Squad and Comcast's acquisition of AT&T Broadband.

Here are some consulting roles that fall within M&A:

1.1.1. M&A strategy and acquisition screening – M&A is typically a means to an end. The goal can be to increase market share, diversify, find cost sharing synergies, buy access to new customers, etc. Strategy consultants are hired to determine if M&A is appropriate given the business context and to create these M&A strategies. Sometimes consultants will search for the right acquisition target to achieve the strategic goal (i.e., assist in acquisition screening).

1.1.2. Due Diligence – After a firm has decided on a merger or acquisition target, due diligence is performed to determine the terms of the merger or price of the acquisition. Consulting firms are hired for their expertise and understanding of a target company's market. Common project deliverables for a due diligence analysis include revenue/EBITDA projections and a market analysis.

1.1.3. Post Merger Integration (PMI) – PMI is the process of integrating firms after an acquisition or merger. This can involve company reorganizations, streamlining back office functions, or locating unidentified capability synergies. Consulting firms are hired for their understanding of common PMI issues and resolutions in addition to their ability to think creatively about how to maximize the potential of the newly combined business.

1.2. Start a joint venture with another company – Sometimes a company may identify a need in the marketplace but lacks the core competencies needed to meet the need. One possible solution is to form a joint venture. A joint venture is where both companies retain full control of their respective operations. The companies are merely working together to bring an offering to the market that neither can provide individually.

For example, in one case, a global rubber manufacturer occupied a premium price point. A Chinese competitor cropped up that offered lower quality rubber for a lower price. Consequently, the Chinese competitor began seizing market share. The manufacturer turned to a consulting firm to determine what to do.

There were many facets to consider, but a great solution was a joint venture between the client manufacturer and the Chinese company. The client had the global market access (client contacts, distribution channels, etc.), and the Chinese company had the rubber that a certain segment wanted. As a result, the Chinese company received access to the client's network, which was extremely valuable. In the raw materials market, building a distribution network took a very long time. In turn, the client was able to set the price and essentially control the cannibalization. The margin was the same to the client, whether they sold their own product or the Chinese product, so it effectively negated the competitive threat.

2. Organic Growth – Organic growth refers to growth using purely internal capabilities and does not involve acquisition. If the client is interested in growing, but does not want to merge or acquire, the consulting firm can explore different ways to grow organically. Organic growth results from capitalizing on existing capabilities to improve current business offerings or to find new products/services/customers.

2.1. Core market growth (steal market share) – Many firms are interested in "beating market growth," meaning they want to grow their revenue faster than the market is growing. The only way to surpass market growth in a given market is to steal market share from a competitor. Consultants are hired to develop strategies that target core market growth. For example, in recent years, Netflix's revenue has grown substantially faster than the video rental market because it was able to successfully steal share from Blockbuster.

2.2. New Customers – A common expansion strategy is simply to offer existing (or slightly modified) capabilities to new customers. At times this can be "low hanging fruit" or "a close adjacency," because very little needs to change in terms of products or services offered. Other times this can be extremely challenging, because finding new customers for an existing capability can mean stealing a customer from a competitor. Brand loyalty can also be a difficult challenge to overcome. Consider your local burger restaurant; a growth strategy could incorporate determining effective ways to attract more customers or opening another store to attract customers in a nearby city.

2.2.1. Geographic/International expansion – As globalization continues, so does the consulting market. Most top tier consulting firms have offices worldwide. They capture growth in international markets by helping local companies with strategy development or by helping American companies expand their capabilities to international customers. International growth strategies have an extra layer (or two) of complexity due to differences in business, culture, ethics, etc. Consulting firms with a global presence are typically better at advising on international expansion due to their understanding of the local markets.

2.3. New products/services – Companies can use core competencies to capture more of a target market. For example, Pepsi was already good at making sodas, so they introduced Mountain Dew to target an audience that didn't overlap with Pepsi's consumer base. Alternatively, a company might need to increase market share in order to match a competitor. Coke introduced Cherry Coke in 1985, so Pepsi introduced Wild Cherry Pepsi in 1988. This introduction was not necessarily to boost profits. Instead, Wild Cherry Pepsi stopped the market effusion from Pepsi to Coke, which was present only because Pepsi did not offer a cherry version.

2.4. Go-to-Market strategy & Market entry strategy – These strategies remain the bread and butter of many strategy consulting firms due to the difficulties typically associated with entering a market.

Consider an East Coast transportation company that wants to expand its operations to encompass all of North America. The CEO of the transportation company knows very little about the customer and competitive landscape of the West Coast and even less about Mexico and Canada. The CEO gets in touch with a partner at Consulting Firm X who is in charge of the Transportation and Logistics business.

To inform the development of an effective go-to-market strategy, consulting firms routinely research concepts such as competitors, customers, barriers to entry, and the macro environment. As expected, the partner at Consulting Firm X tasks his team to do this market research. The team can then use this research as the foundation for the development of a market entry strategy. Does the transportation company need to hire more drivers? Who will do sales in Mexico? How does cross-country transportation affect costs? What's the best way to disrupt monopolized regions? These are the types of questions that the consulting team will answer as part of a holistic entry strategy.

Market Entry in Case Interviews

Market entry is a very common question in case interviews because it is a common topic addressed by management consulting firms. The basic formula for these case studies is that a client wants to know whether to enter a market, and the interviewee needs to determine whether entering the market is a good idea. The interviewee must also propose a way to implement the entrance.

2.5. Company Image & Marketing – Sales, marketing, branding, and image are vital components of any organization. Strategists are hired to use market research and experience to capitalize on the status quo and creatively think through options for improvement.

2.5.1. Customer research and competitive benchmarking - Often, analyzing these components are an integral part of larger strategic projects. For example, consider the development of a growth strategy for a telecommunications company. As part of this case, a consulting team will research the competition to find out what the key success factors are in this industry and what their margins are. A team may also survey customers to find out what unmet needs they have, how much they value certain services, and other customer data. Who is the target audience? What does the customer actually want? What is the competition doing differently? This research can then be used to rethink sales and marketing strategies.

2.5.2. Branding - When things don't work, try something different. Rebranding or brand expansion can make sense when the company has grown beyond its original purpose and wants to offer a different value proposition to the market.

Alternatively, a company may purchase another company, but maintain both entities under a single brand. As such, the purchasing company needs to phase out one of the brands. One example is JP Morgan's purchase of Wamu Bank in 2008, and the subsequent transition of Wamu accounts to JP Morgan.

It is not always clear whether to use an organic or inorganic approach. For example, the CEO of a consumer products firm meets a strategy consultant at a conference in Vegas and asks, "I have set as a primary corporate initiative to grow our top-line by 30% in the next 5 years. Can you help me put together an actionable strategy to achieve this growth?" The consultant responds with, "Of course we can help; help me understand the steps you have taken so far…" The conversation goes on for some time.

At some point in the back and forth, the consultant will almost certainly ask, "What is your appetite for M&A?" In other words, the consultant is trying to gauge whether or not the client is willing to merge or acquire another firm to meet the CEO's growth objectives.

There is a good chance that the CEO will respond with, "We are open to all expansion strategies including acquisitions; however, I would like to exhaust organic growth options first." Now it is up to the strategist to do the research, weigh the options, and make a recommendation about the optimal growth strategy.

Bottom Line Focus

1. Cost Analysis – Sometimes companies want to focus on cutting their costs. A management consulting firm looks at a company's costs and analyzes which ones can be reduced to produce an overall net benefit to the client. Think of "the Bobs" from the movie Office Space.

    Consider this example: A firm has a profit margin of 15%, but its primary competitor has a profit margin of 20%. The head of operations wants to cut costs to improve profitability in an attempt to impress the board of directors and increase the firm's competitiveness.

    The head of operations calls in a consulting firm to do an eight-week internal analysis to determine major cost contributors. The head of operations is also prepared to extend the contract with the consulting firm by 6 months to implement necessary changes to cut costs and achieve 20% profit margins.

2. Operational Consulting – Operations can be thought of as the "day-to-day" of the business. All businesses provide a service, product, or both, and operations determine how that is provided to the customer.

    For example, if you are the COO of a widget company that manufacturers widgets and sells to distributors, you could be concerned with at least a few of the simple issues below:

    2.1 Development – What does our pipeline of new widgets look like? According to our sales team, are we efficiently developing the products that customers most want?

2.2 Supply Chain – How efficient is our supply chain? Do we have the right number of reliable and cost effective suppliers? Do we have the right balance of a shorter lead time vs. cost?

2.3 Manufacturing – How effective are our manufacturing operations? At each plant, is our cycle time to produce each widget as low as possible? Is the amount of re-work we incur minimized? How is the workload most effectively balanced between all of our plants?

2.4 Customer Satisfaction – How well are we meeting our customers' quality requirements? Is our lead time to our distributors minimized? Is our cost to deliver minimized? How effectively do we support customers after we deliver?

3. Organizational Consulting – Organizational consulting, sometimes called "HR consulting," is a branch of management consulting focused on an organization's people.

3.1 Organizational Structure – How could the organization be better designed today to reduce redundancy, align incentives with maximizing profit, and more effectively serve the customer? For example, suppose a company today believes they are too slow in responding to customer requests in design modifications. How could they modify their organizational structure to better streamline the process from customer request to rolled out product?

Another application of organizational structure consulting is to bring out the crystal ball and look into the future, asking, "How should the organization change to effectively support growth?" Consider a company that expects to increase revenues roughly 3-fold in the next 3 years. How should their central office be organized? What positions need to be added to support each stage of growth? How can job descriptions be modified to support desired growth?

3.2 Talent Incentives – What is the right combination of incentives to ensure maximum performance from executives to employees? Clearly, salary is one component, but what makes up a competitive benefits package? What actions deserve financial (or other) compensation, and how much compensation? What other sort of intangible rewards can people receive to incentivize performance (e.g., awards, informal acknowledgements, etc.)?

4. Portfolio Analysis & Resource Allocation

4.1 Resource Allocation – A firm has a finite amount of resources available at a given time. The question here is, how do companies allocate those resources to maximize shareholder value? There are two parts: Where should resources be added, and where should they be removed? For example, in the dialysis industry, there are manufacturers of dialysis machines, and there are operators of dialysis clinics. The clinics buy devices from the manufacturers. There used to be two companies that provided both services: Fresenius and Gambro. Fresenius is still vertically integrated, but Gambro got out of the clinic operations business.

At some point, it is likely that Gambro performed a resource allocation assessment and determined that it would more effectively enhance their long-term shareholder value to funnel resources toward machine manufacturing and development as opposed to operating clinics. Consequently, they got out of the clinic business and put more resources toward developing new and improved machines.

4.2 Downsize or leave a market – A CEO may ask, "To address our current problem or corporate objective, should our company contract?" One book that discusses when to leave a market is *Where Value Hides* by Stuart Jackson. Jackson recounts numerous case studies in which companies have a presence in too many markets and consequently spread themselves too thin.

He argues that companies deliver a much higher stockholder value when they concentrate on markets where they can have a strong presence instead of spreading themselves too thin. This is true even when a company is large. The principles espoused in Jackson's book can also apply to any scenario where the client wants to achieve growth.

Options for downsizing or leaving a market

Discontinuing products – If a product is not profitable, consider discontinuing it. Be careful though – sometimes a product may be a "loss leader," meaning that it is unprofitable, but brings in customers who also buy more profitable items. For example, think of grocery store ads – they probably don't make much money on the advertised items, but the advertisement gets you in the door to buy higher-margin items.

Leaving Industry – To build upon the example of discontinuing products, sometimes a market is no longer favorable. Too many competitors have entered, or outside events have acted on the market, making the market unfavorable for certain products. In another instance, leaving the market might allow a company to focus their capital on the remaining segments of the business.

For example, Sega, a manufacturer of video game consoles, announced they were leaving the video game console industry in 2001 after several years of declining profitability. Instead, they focused on becoming a platform-neutral software developer and became profitable again just a few years later.

Leaving Geographical Markets – In 2009, Health Net, a large health insurance company, sold off their Northeast operations to UnitedHealth, the largest commercial health insurer in the United States. The CEO said the deal would enable the company to concentrate its efforts on health plans in the Western U.S.

Divesting acquisitions or divisions – Selling off a division can free up capital for more profitable ventures. For example, Jack Welch at GE divested any businesses that couldn't attain number one or number two in their markets. A division can spin off from the rest of company and become its own company. Booz & Co did this in 2008. The spin-off allowed Booz Allen Hamilton to focus in one direction (government consulting), and Booz & Co to focus in another (commercial consulting).

Consulting requires creativity. Solutions are rarely clear-cut. Consider this example: A CEO calls her contact at a consulting firm and says, "Our share price has taken a beating due to recent competitive pressures. I'm looking to beat analysts' earnings projections by a cent per share. I only have budget for a quick turn assignment; what can you do?" The consultant now has some options. Should he target revenue, cost, or both? The answer will be complex. That's why strategy consultants are paid so well.

It is important to note that strategy consulting firms typically specialize in multiple strategy categories. The type of work you will be doing as an entry-level consultant will vary depending on the firm's specialization. It is important to gain a perspective during the recruitment process on the types of strategy consulting that most interest you.

Peruse consulting firms' websites to determine how they characterize their strategic capabilities. Every firm characterizes their capabilities differently, so it's worth taking the time at information sessions and career fairs to identify the subtle differences. Additionally, asking intelligent questions about the core competencies of a consulting firm from recruiters at information sessions and career fairs will provide you a firm foundation for your upcoming interviews.

4

Why Do Companies Hire Management Consultants?

When companies hire management consulting firms, they are essentially renting brains. Companies want to hire consulting firms as a way to get smart people to answer important questions that they cannot answer themselves due to lack of expertise, capability, or available staff. Or perhaps they have already answered the important question, but they want verification from a third-party. As such, the array of questions tackled by consulting firms has always been very broad. Likewise, the reasons why consultants are hired are also broad.

Reason 1: Lack of Internal Resources

Consultants are hired because their clients do not have the internal resources sufficient to solve their problems. Many companies do not have dedicated strategy groups. In order to execute a strategic project, a company might have to pull employees from their day jobs and train these employees with consulting skills. This is impractical most of the time.

For example, suppose a company is looking to develop an optimal pricing strategy. They currently have some models/forecasts, but they want to make it even more robust. They've already maxed out their internal knowledge (otherwise, they would be using those tools), so they may turn to a consulting firm to help them develop such a strategy.

A time constraint is another reason why a company might hire consultants. For example, a board meeting is coming up, and the C-suite is expected to have their strategy ironed out. To do so, they need help from personnel in various departments. But the sales representatives still have to sell, the people in marketing still have to market, the people in production still have to produce. If the C-suite pulls employees from these functions to help out with a strategy project, there may be delays in shipping, decreased customer service, and other consequences of short staffing. Consequently, they turn to the consulting firms for help.

Reason 2: Expertise in Gathering Information

Consulting firms have the ability to develop comprehensive fact bases quickly. A key skill consultants develop is the ability to quickly figure out what's important in driving an industry – they have to in order to meet their expected deadlines and quickly convey to the client they are "experts." While the client may have some good intuitions on how to proceed, they may turn to a consulting firm to quickly develop a fact base to confirm those intuitions.

Reason 3: Industry Knowledge Gained From Previous Engagements

Management consulting firms are a storehouse of information on industries and companies within those industries. Consultants are familiar with key trends and success strategies. While any reputable firm won't share specific details of clients with other clients, they are free to share key insights on both industry and participants. For example, on the industry level, if the consulting firm has collectively executed hundreds of projects within the construction industry, they likely know the current key drivers of the market. That's valuable knowledge to a client within the construction industry (or one looking to enter the construction industry), particularly if that client holds contrary beliefs about the key drivers.

On the individual company level, suppose a consulting firm worked with one client that had an average lead-time of 4 days versus the industry average of 12 days, because this company effectively offloads its bottlenecks. This consulting firm, having learned how that client successfully offloaded their bottlenecks, could investigate this as a possible improvement for their next client in another industry.

Reason 4: Credibility and Shift of Blame

A fourth reason that consultants are hired is that they are an objective, third party "expert." If there are two or more parties in a company that disagree about the best way to move forward, a consulting engagement may provide a definite way to settle the disagreement. Furthermore, in the event that a recommendation turns out to be erroneous, the people in the company are somewhat protected because they obtained independent verification that the strategy was likely to succeed.

5

Why Management Consulting? I have a Million Career Choices!

Now that we've examined what management consulting is, let's look at some benefits that commonly attract people to management consulting over other careers.

Management Consulting vs. Investment Banking – The classic debate! Many individuals who are considering consulting also consider investment banking. Both professions attract intelligent individuals who enjoy working in fast-paced environments. Both involve delivering strategic advice. An "i-banker" makes more money, but a consultant works fewer hours, gets paid to travel, and has more "work-life-balance." There is no balance in investment banking. It is very common for 1st-year i-bankers to find only one free night per month to go out and socialize. And when they do make a monthly social appearance, their favorite topic of conversation is, "Who has gone the longest without sleep?" Their answers to this question are always impressive and quite concerning...

"I've already worked 75 hours this week since Sunday, and it's only Wednesday"

– Investment Banking Analyst

Management Consulting vs. Other Consulting – There are many different types of consulting: management, technology, design, healthcare, etc. Where you should go depends on your interests, but keep this in mind: It's easier to go from management consulting to any of the other consulting types than vice versa. Unless you are positive that you want to specialize in a single branch of consulting, give management consulting a serious look.

A story to illustrate this point: One woman graduated from college with a human resources degree, and she felt she could enter any industry she wanted. Her first job was at a major food canning company, but after she left, the only interviews she could get were for other food-related companies. It is scary how fast you get pigeon-holed.

Likewise, say you go into technology consulting. If you decide that you don't like it, you will probably have difficulty finding a position outside of technology consulting. In order to get the attention of management consulting firms after having specialized in a field, an MBA might be necessary. It's much easier to transition from management consulting to a more specific field than the opposite. From a career standpoint, management consulting sets you up for a broader set of options further down the road.

Management Consulting vs. Corporate Job – One major difference between consulting and a corporate job is the pace of the environment. You work longer hours in management consulting, 50-70 hours per week, while corporate jobs typically require only 40 hour per week (and that's without the time you spend traveling as a consultant). Consultants also experience spikes in which they work 80 hours or more. However, all of the extra hours translate into more learning. There's a reason why it generally takes five or six years for corporate folks to go to business school, versus two to four for management consultants.

Another advantage of management consulting over a corporate position is the breadth of experience. While a corporate rotational program can expose an individual to different functions within the company, a consultant is exposed to different companies and industries. A consultant gains a broader breadth of experience in less time.

Management Consulting vs. Other Jobs – Management consulting attracts smart people who are qualified to do most entry-level jobs. Academia, engineering, government, and NGO are all great career options. Consider what makes sense for your long-term goals and your short-term happiness. The problem solving abilities, communication skills and business acumen that you will develop as a management consultant can translate to any industry. In a nutshell, consulting gives you options that other starting jobs do not.

6
What Are Management Consulting Firms Looking For?

Management consulting firms seek candidates with specific attributes, but there are no clear-cut requirements. For example, firms want people interested in business; however, they would rather hire someone who pursued their love of theater rather than the person who gave up theater because "firms want to see a business major." Here are some common traits shared by people who receive offers. These are important to understand, because you will need to demonstrate these traits throughout consulting recruitment.

1. *Analytical Thinking* – An analytical thinker can easily see the logical progression of things – What do I need to research first, and then what do I need to research second? In consulting, it's very important to be able to quickly create a logical path to the solution. A consultant usually charges clients by the hour, so he cannot aimlessly flit around on a client's dime. In the case where a consultant is not working by the hour, he needs to be efficient so he's not in the office until 2AM every night! Some possible examples of analytical thinking include:

   - Using a spreadsheet to create a data model
   - Performing experiments that require formulation of a hypothesis, collection of data, and working to a solution
   - Identifying a root cause from an array of symptoms and developing a solution

2. *Business Background* – Consulting firms are looking for an interest in business issues. People who are interested in business would logically major in business or economics. This is why it may appear that a business degree is required. But engineering, communication, organizational change and art history majors can pursue management consulting as well. They just have to take the extra step to reveal their interest in business through another medium.

The best way to reveal an interest in business is to gain actual consulting experience. As with seeking any job, previous experience in the field helps. If you have done management consulting before and you are applying again, then there are several positive inferences a recruiter could draw about you:

2.1 The firm will not need to train you as much because you have consulting experience. Every firm has its own unique methodology, but you've already begun to develop the pertinent skills (e.g. using Excel/PowerPoint, researching, analyzing data, managing expectations, working on teams, etc.).

2.2 You enjoy consulting. Otherwise, you wouldn't be applying to a consulting firm. By hiring you, it is less likely that you will jump ship compared to someone who has never worked in consulting before. You know what you are getting into.

2.3 Depending on where you worked previously, it may enhance the company's reputation to hire you. For example, if a person jumps from a top-ranked firm to a lower-ranked firm, then that lower-ranked firm gets to tout their acquisition in recruitment presentations, client promotions and the like.

However, if you have no prior consulting experience, don't sweat it! You can find ways to showcase your past experience in a consulting frameset. Methods to do this are covered in Chapter 11.

3. *Business Judgment* – To have good business judgment, you must have a grasp of some basic concepts and how to apply them.

3.1 Basic Concepts – Knowledge of basic economic concepts is crucial during the interview process. Such basic concepts include supply and demand, elasticity, commodities and profitability.

3.2 Common Sense – Common sense is the basic understanding that most people possess in healthy quantities. However, sometimes intelligent people over-think their answer, or they let other factors cloud their judgment. As a result, they make decisions that don't make sense. To have good business judgment, you must always throw rocks at your answers before you deliver them – do they stand up?

For example, let's say you're asked to increase profits for a retail client, and you calculate a supply/demand curve to see what price you should recommend charging for a popular product. Your model shows that the client should be charging twice as much as the current price. This could be very exciting news for the client, potentially doubling their profit.

However, common sense calls for you to double check the data, to make sure that you have considered all of the pertinent factors. Suppose your competition provides this product as well. How does this affect the elasticity of your demand? Are you sure that your demand is inelastic enough to sit still as the price is doubled? Will your customer simply go across the street to WalMart? It depends! Always use common sense before making recommendations.

This is called "top-down quality check," and is a critical skill to learn. Before you pass your work onto your co-worker, your manager, your partner, and ultimately your client, take a moment to check your recommendation against everything you know about the client and their industry.

4. *High GPA* – Some (but not all) firms place a great emphasis on GPA. These firms have a GPA cutoff, which means they will only consider you for an interview if you have a GPA above a certain cutoff. Depending on the firm and the number of applicants, unofficial GPA cutoffs can range from 3.0 to 3.85. This merely serves as a gatekeeper function: once you get the interview, then

the interviewers' collective opinion will far outweigh your GPA in the hiring decision.

5. *Leadership* – Consulting firms don't hire analysts – they hire future partners. Firms want you to become a partner, because partners drive revenue for the firm. Of course, you would be very ineffective as a partner right out of college. Instead, as a new hire, you help current partners as you gradually adopt more responsibility. They want you to display leadership in the firm during your first year, and you may even lead client teams. Naturally, your interviewer will be interested to hear about any time in which you managed people, facilitated meetings, led a team in solving a problem or led an organization and made an impact.

    Don't make up a false example of leadership experience, because your interviewer will notice. You have surely demonstrated leadership in one way or another. You can draw examples of leadership experience through various activities, including student clubs, classroom teams, and fraternities/sororities.

6. *Passion* – Consulting firms love passionate people. Passionate people breathe life into an organization, bringing energy to teams even when burning the midnight oil. There is something inspiring about someone who has found something that makes them passionate, as long as it's not inappropriate. So leave your 3-story beer bong out of the interview.

    What makes you excited and happy every time you talk about it? Your passions are what cause your face to light up when sharing your story with others. Identify your passion and work it into your recruitment conversations and interviews.

    Your passion doesn't have to be business-related. One job seeker had a passion for scotch, and it took him as far as Scotland to tour scotch manufacturing facilities. This person brought it up in an interview with Diamond Management & Technology Consultants and got the job!

7. *Pedigree* – There are some schools at which all of the major firms recruit. Some schools receive only a handful of firms. Most schools will experience no recruitment from consulting firms.

If firms don't recruit at your school, it is more difficult to break into consulting, but not impossible. How do you stand a chance at a non-targeted college? Persistence is the key. A great place to start is to apply online via each firm's website. Responses will inevitably be limited, so play the numbers game. Apply to fifty, even sixty firms. Send follow up e-mails. No one uses the telephone anymore, so follow up via phone to stand out (unless the posting specifically says no phone calls). Nothing to lose, right? A networking connection can also help land an interview. Some call it nepotism; others call it working hard to know the right people.

So if you're at a non-targeted school, tell everyone you know that you want to break into the consulting industry. You might strike gold with someone who knows someone who works for a strategy firm, and then you're on your way.

Also, utilize your school's alumni database. Even if alumni at your school rarely enter consulting directly after undergraduate, some may have entered the field after getting an MBA. Search the database for alumni who work for firms you're interested in, and ask for 15 minutes of their time for an informational interview. While you are at that meeting, ask for another contact. Repeat that process until you have a good grasp on the firm, and then ask for advice on securing an interview.

8. *Professionalism* – Firms want to make sure that they can put you in front of a client. Can you handle yourself professionally in front of the CEO, or will you say something that will embarrass the firm? Will you commit the firm to something the partner doesn't want to commit to? If you don't have a good feel on how to behave professionally, pay attention to the customer service next time you visit a store. How do they interact with you? Are they concise? Friendly? Confident? Confidence, short of cockiness, is a crucial component of professionalism. This can be developed through mock interviewing.

Since these are essentially universal hiring considerations, it is of utmost importance that you convey these traits during an interview. Consider how you convey your interest in business though schoolwork, projects, and student groups. Take the time to consider examples that illustrate your leadership ability so that you can comfortably discuss it at length in an interview or at a networking event. When preparing for the interview process, pay special attention to these elements.

Don't Procrastinate!

The consulting industry is getting more and more competitive every year, so even if you exhibit all of the traits mentioned in this chapter, it doesn't guarantee you a job offer.

Most students who receive an offer put a lot of effort into practicing cases and reading business books. You will need to go to firm events, practice cases, and develop relationships with people at a variety of different firms.

Any position to which you apply will be very competitive. A number of consultants at different firms indicated that 1-9% of their candidates on average will receive an offer, depending on their hiring needs and the number of candidates that apply.

One in ten may not sound terrible, but keep in mind that the majority of those candidates are top students from a select handful of top universities. These students have little work experience to differentiate themselves, and so they must piece together a projection of accomplishment from grades, brief internships and extracurricular activities.

It can be a daunting process, but you can do it if you take the process seriously. The earlier you begin engaging in the process, the better. In college, most of students push things off until the last minute. Don't let recruitment be one of those last-minute things.

If your recruitment preparation has become "one of those last-minute things," flip to chapter 15!

PART 2:
THE RECRUITMENT
PROCESS

The typical recruitment process is highly competitive and somewhat daunting. These chapters offer strategies for putting your best foot forward at all phases. Pre-recruitment includes learning about the firms, building your resume, writing cover letters, and networking. Pre-recruitment can span the summer and school year before you plan to apply. After the recruitment season begins, management consulting firms try to convince you to apply through information sessions and career fairs. Then, carefully selected candidates undergo first-round interviews, consisting of case interviews and fit interviews. Among these candidates, some will be invited to the second round of interviews. Finally, offers are extended to the most elite candidates selected by each firm.

While there is certainly an element of luck in the process, those that prepare the most extensively are generally the ones who end up with multiple offers. This section will clarify the process and provide you a leg-up on preparation.

7

Learn About Consulting and the Firms

The first step in the pre-recruitment process is to do your research. Recruiters often question your understanding of the consulting industry and your motivation to join it. You need to learn what it's like to be a consultant and determine the real reasons why the work appeals to you. Are you attracted to the quick pace of life and the diversity of assignments? Is consulting just a stepping-stone to a different career, or could you see yourself advising CEOs for the next 20 years? Researching and answering questions like these will help to focus your energy before recruitment starts.

One particularly helpful resource is the *Vault Guide to the Top 50 Management and Strategy Consulting Firms*. While guides like this are a little generalized and full of cliché tips, they serve their purpose well by providing an overview of the industry. The *Vault Guide to the Top 50 Management and Strategy Consulting Firms* is particularly helpful in giving you a comprehensive overview of the major consulting firms.

Vault ranks the majority of management consulting firms every year. The following excerpt from Vault.com describes their information-gathering process:

> *"In spring 2008, Vault surveyed more than 4,000 consultants to generate our 2009 consulting firm rankings."*

"Survey respondents were asked to rate each consulting firm on the survey on a scale of 1 to 10 based on prestige, with 10 being the most prestigious. Consultants were unable to rate their own firm, and they were asked to rate only those firms with which they were familiar. Vault collected the survey results and averaged the score for each firm. The firms were then ranked, with the highest score being No. 1 down to No. 50."

The Vault Guide will you give you a general overview and feel of each firm, using quotes from employees working at those firms.

Look at Vault's Top 50 firms, and then look in your online career center database to see which firms recruit at your school. If a firm does not recruit at your school, be prepared to apply online and reach out to your network.

Next, look at the firms' websites. Read through their recruitment site, along with other sections. How do they appeal to students? To clients? What kind of articles are they writing? Are they more focused in one function or industry compared to other firms? Most importantly, are the articles interesting to you? While you may be unfamiliar with, for example, the cement industry, the business problem and solution should be interesting to read if management consulting is a good fit with your interests. All articles and case studies involve the same basic business principles at work, whether it's in the cement or the music industry.

Looking through 50 websites is an ambitious project that you should weave into your schedule over a period of time. Make sure the websites don't blur together. Start an Excel sheet in which you copy-paste Vault's top 50 firms, and fill in information about each firm. When the recruiting season begins, you can revisit this Excel sheet before meeting with recruiters to jog your memory of each firm. See *College2Consulting.com* for helpful templates.

Finally, google each company to see where it has been cited in recent news articles. In your Excel sheet, take note of articles that interested you and why they were interesting. You may find opportunities in the recruiting process to have intelligent conversations with recruiters about these articles.

For example, a search of L.E.K. Consulting provided a Reuters article on the second page of results. This article reviewed five new media usage myths that L.E.K Consulting had busted. Most notably, L.E.K. Consulting's research indicated that active internet users 50 years and older spend more time on the internet per week than 18-24 year olds. Of course, this finding gives rise to several questions:

- How did they define "active"?

- How much more time do older folks spend than younger folks do?

- What are the older folks doing on the internet? What types of sites are they visiting? How much variety is there in this basket of sites?

- And the most relevant question for a management consultant: How could a new media site (e.g., online newspaper) utilize this counter-intuitive finding?

Asking these sorts of questions is crucial to being able to hold your own in a discussion with an interviewer. When consulting firms hire you, they expect you to start contributing from day one. The sooner you can draw meaningful conclusions about how to best serve the client, the sooner you will receive more responsibility.

What Qualities Do I Find Important In a Firm?

To select firms that are right for you, establish criteria. Ask yourself which attributes are most important to you in your selection of a consulting firm. You should have an idea what kind of firm you want to join prior to your first information session, career fair or interview.

Identify why these factors are important to you. In your interview, you can ask questions to determine how closely the firm satisfies the criteria you have established in order to choose a future employer.

Company Image/Quality of Experience: The importance of working for one consulting firm or another is exaggerated by the typical undergraduate during the job interview process. It is a little like being drafted by an NFL football team – it is a good thing no matter what, because you are now in the big leagues. What you do with this opportunity is what counts.

The "brand name" of a consulting firm can help position you for future opportunities, but your experience and what you accomplish is much more important. In fact, simply working at a consulting firm, top ten or not, is enough to catch the attention corporate professionals who are on the lookout for experienced talent. You do NOT need to work at a well-known firm to secure admission to a great business school or to land an excellent corporate position later in your career.

As an intern, it is of paramount importance to gain meaningful experiences to add to your resume. Once a recruiter reads a top firm's name on your resume, he is likely to wonder "What exactly did this candidate do?" If the experience is mundane, it may have been better to work for a smaller, less prestigious firm and take an important role on interesting projects.

Working for a top tier firm can helpful to a career if you get the right experience. It is not a mystery why a well known firm can set you apart. A top firm naturally has access to top candidates. McKinsey, for example, has an advantage when recruiting because top candidates are generally interested in working at this prestigious firm. Future employers may assume that you are in the "first-choice" category if you worked for a top-ranked consulting firm. Keep in mind, however, that if you don't work for a name brand firm you can prove yourself to be top-talent in myriad other ways.

Firm Culture / Overall Work Atmosphere/People – You're going to be working 50, 60, 70, or maybe 80 hours a week with "the people," so it's important to make sure that you get along with them. When you attend company events, what is your gut feeling about the people? Could you see yourself spending time with them socializing after work? How much time is typically spent in a team setting vs. individualized work? How does the company typically like to approach their cases? Does the company's culture appeal to you?

See chapter 14 for specific questions to probe into a firm's culture.

Level of Responsibility – Some firms expect you to contribute your opinions from Day One, while others expect you to "listen & learn" more in the beginning. Which type of style fits you the best? Ultimately, the distinction among firms is slight when it comes to level of responsibility. Most firms will give you as much responsibility as you can handle. After all, the firm can charge more for your time as you get promoted!

Lifestyle/Number of Hours Worked – First of all, if you want to work 40 hours a week, you're going to be a poor fit for any firm. That said, if there's a firm that works its consultants particularly hard, and you enjoyed long hours as an investment banker last summer, that could be a good fit.

Office Locations – Where are the offices located? Besides obviously affecting your day-to-day life, the location can affect your work as well. Office size varies, giving a different feel to each office. Additionally, certain offices may specialize in different projects, based on the clients in that area. Midwest locations may have more manufacturing projects, while New York may have more retail/finance projects, and Los Angeles may have more entertainment and media projects.

Normally you are recruited for the office closest to your school. This will be made clear to you, but there may be opportunities to switch the city you work in before you start, and some firms offer these opportunities as well. Depending on staffing needs, sometimes consulting firms will offer you a position at an international office. This usually happens if you have previously spent a significant amount of time where that office is hosted, or if you are especially familiar with a culture or language.

Opportunity for Industry Specialization – Most people want to be generalists. Why not explore all the world has to offer? However, some people know what they want to do. For example, one student wanted to work with airline companies, so Oliver Wyman was a great fit for him. Since Oliver Wyman does a lot of work with airlines, they provided ample opportunity for him to specialize in this industry.

If you're passionate about "going green" and if you hope to pursue these projects long-term, then find a consulting firm that includes a green practice. Most likely, they would let you specialize in implementing green initiatives.

Likewise, consider the methods that different firms use to assign their consultants to projects. Some large firms essentially require you to "network" for your projects. Partners/managers choose their teams, so you need to get to know these people. Such a firm may excite you because it enables you to completely "customize" your path, because you can find the exact types of projects you want to be on. And then follow up with why that matters to you. The prospect of networking for projects excites some people, while it makes others uncomfortable.

I liked companies where they "assign" you to projects. I wanted to get a general business background and to explore different industries to find out which ones I enjoyed the most. I trusted in the firm's ability to keep me a "generalist" because they had a broader view of possible assignments than I did. Also, they knew which projects to select to ensure their consultants received a diverse set of projects.

Opportunity to Travel/Work Overseas – Are you in love with Paris and dying to make it back? Point this out in your interview to demonstrate your willingness to travel to overseas locations. If the firm places a high value upon overseas opportunities, this will demonstrate a good fit.

More commonly, management consulting firms send their consultants on domestic business trips. How frequently does the firm travel domestically? Do they travel every week for 4 days per week? Do they travel only some weeks during the project? Or do they hardly travel for any of their projects?

Salary / Compensation / Benefits – It's important to note that some factors, like salary, are not factors you bring up before you receive an offer. Rather, they're factors that play into the process after an offer is made. You can assume all major firms have competitive salaries, so you should be focused on finding out whether you would like to work at the company.

Size of Company – Do you prefer a broader range of opportunities, typically found at larger firms? Or do you like the more intimate, personal feel of a smaller firm? Either way, articulate what you want and why. Be careful of cliché answers like, "Your firm is really large with offices worldwide, I'd love to be able to travel to one." Instead, indicate that you seek international business experience in Country X because *<insert how it will help you achieve your acareer goals here>*. Really think through what it would be like to work at a large firm verses a small firm.

In addition, consider the size of the individual office. A large firm could have both large and small offices available.

Training / Professional Development Opportunities – What kind of training does the firm offer? What training does the firm offer after you start a project? In all honesty, most of the skills have to be learned on the job, so training can only take you so far.

Perhaps you can find a good fit between your personal goals and the type of professional development opportunities a firm offers. For example, L.E.K. Consulting has an "internal MBA" program, where, after four to five years, you're promoted to consultant – the level for incoming MBAs. Most firms will require a MBA to move up – L.E.K. is one firm that does not.

Additionally, what is the quality (and quantity) of feedback? Generally you are reviewed after each case, but how are long cases handled? What goes into a company's reviews? How in-depth are these reviews?

Variety and Content of Work – Type of work is one attribute that varies widely between firms. For example, Deloitte works a lot with consumer products, whereas Bain & Company works a lot with private equity. At the same time, Deloitte also has projects with private equity, and Bain & Company works with consumer products. It's just a question of which areas companies focus in on, because no consulting firm is perfectly balanced across all of their industries and functions.

Variety of work can vary along with industry and functional
dimensions. How broad are the industries with which the firm
works? How broad are the functions that the firm has (e.g., strategy,
operations, etc.)? How much exposure will you get to each function?

In general, entry-level responsibilities are similar between firms.
Common tasks include: building PowerPoint decks, conducting
research, making models, and interacting with lower-level client side
employees.

Lastly, how does the length of each project vary? This is generally
driven by the firm's functional specialties (e.g., strategy projects
tend to be shorter than operational projects). Strategy projects tend
to be anywhere from 3 weeks to 10 weeks long, while operational/
implantation projects can be from a few months to multiple years long.

8
Pre-Recruitment Networking

The term "pre-recruitment" refers to anything before the official "start" of the consulting recruitment season. This includes your preparation, along with any events, contacts, or meetings before a company formally comes to campus to actively recruit students. Here are a few examples of events, contacts, or meetings that can take place before "formal" recruitment:

- A firm sponsors a "get to know us" event at a local bar, maybe in the spring.

- You reach out to alumni, friends of friends, or official contacts in a firm.

- A firm sponsors a case competition.

It is important that you attend as many of these pre-recruitment functions as possible. Talking to firm representatives, collecting business cards, and sending follow-up emails provides recruiters with a face to match with your name. It is a great way to improve the chances that your resume ends up in the "yes" pile later on in the recruitment process.

Networking – An Easy and Effective Method

You may have just felt a chill go down your spine at the word "networking." It's one of those "corporate speak" words that has a bad reputation in American culture. But here's the bottom line: 48% of people get their jobs through a referral, according to the U.S. Dept. of Labor in 2001.

Your main networking objectives are two-fold: First, gather information on the firm. You will leverage this information in the application process and use it to assess your fit with that firm. Second, build a reputation among those who decide which students get first-round interviews.

Networking allows you to find promoters who will stand up for you in the screening process. For example, imagine a candidate with a low GPA. Since GPA serves as a gatekeeper, this candidate's application will automatically get weeded out. The only hope of surviving the GPA screening is if someone at the firm says, "Wait a minute, we should take a closer look at this candidate."

Tip For Success

Make sure you always read up on the company before you contact any alumni working at that company. Study the company's website and search for recent news articles about their company and projects.

Informational Interviews

After identifying companies that interest you through resources such as the *Vault Guide to the Top 50 Management and Strategy Consulting Firms,* use your school's alumni database to find alumni at those companies. Contact the alumnus, introduce yourself, and ask to meet him or her for lunch, breakfast or coffee. If that's impractical, try to at least talk over the phone. Here are some good questions to ask:

- Why did you join this particular company?

- What projects have you worked on?

- How does your firm approach a project? For example, some firms will have just one presentation at the end of a project, while others will have a "pre-presentation" to get feedback.

- What types of cases are most common in your firm? No firm is perfectly balanced, so the firm will inevitably have more cases of one function or one industry over another.

- For an entry-level analyst, what types of topics might they research? What types of analysis might they conduct? It depends on the case (and the day!), but there are certainly some common tasks you will repeat again and again, only with different flavors.

- How do feedback and review cycles work?

- How do you get along with the people at your firm? What would you say the corporate culture is like?

Company Culture

The company's culture is one of the hardest things to determine about a potential company, but culture is a critical driver of your satisfaction on the job. Company culture defines how people at that company interact with each other.

While it is difficult to get an accurate feel for a company's culture before working there, it's not impossible. The questions below will help you to get a feel for a company's culture:

Values – What is valued at the firm? Once you identify their values, you can compare them to your values and see how well the company matches up. This question is tough to answer when asked directly, but you can get a sense of it through "or" questions. Feel free to think of your own, but here are a few to get you started:

- Does the firm tend to ask entry-level employees to wear many hats, or are tasks segmented between entry-level employees, support staff, and outside support?

- Do people at your firm tend to prefer working a late night or working during the weekend?

- Do people at your firm tend to prefer eating lunch/dinner together, or eating at their desk and then leaving work a little earlier?

- Do people prefer to arrive and leave earlier or later on a typical day?

- Do managers at your firm tend to have entry-level employees "listen & learn" more at first, or do they throw them into the deep end with lots of responsibilities (and pressure)?

Career Development – How much opportunity is there for "listen and learning" from managers and partners on how they think about strategic issues? What sort of structured opportunities are there like this? While all firms are busy, some firms take more of an active role in helping you to develop than others do.

Work-life balance – How does the company officially (and unofficially) strive for a work-life balance? It's easy to maintain a work-life balance when the workload is light, but what about when the firm is busy, or a project is really hard? Do they generally give you a day or two off after such a case, or do they generally immediately staff you to a different project?

As you further familiarize yourself with the industry, you will think of more specific and thoughtful questions to ask your contacts.

Who do I contact?

Strive to build up a network within your favorite companies. Ideally, this network would include key interview decision makers. If you like these people, and if they like you, you are more likely to get an interview. One challenge is that you don't know who actually has influence. A business analyst may have more influence than a manager, depending on the degree of involvement with recruitment and the business unit.

If you have multiple alumni working at your targeted firm, there are tricks for determining whom to contact. First, estimate each person's seniority by looking at their graduation date. Someone who graduated in the '80s or '90s is likely a partner at this point, while someone who graduated in 2009 is more entry-level. Second, determine whether or not it would benefit you more to contact a senior-level employee this early in your recruitment.

At this point, do you want input from someone who has just experienced recruitment or someone who has a depth of experience in management consulting? Are you looking for someone with a lot of experience who could mentor you in making a sound decision? Younger employees are more likely to be on recruitment teams, while partners sometimes have more power to influence hiring decisions. There are benefits to both perspectives.

In addition to reaching out to consultants in industry, you can network laterally. Reach out to more accessible networks like business student clubs, Greek organizations, academic departments, etc. Tell everyone you know that you're looking for a job in consulting. Even if your initial contact in that group doesn't know anything about consulting, they might know someone who does. Sooner or later you will get passed on to someone who can help you.

Below is a sample email for contacting current consultants. Feel free to modify the email to reflect your preferred style of speaking, but do keep it professional and concise.

Dear Mr. Consultant,

My name is Charles, and I am a pre-senior Industrial engineer at Northwestern University. I found your name in the Northwestern Alumni database, as an alumnus who works at Firm X and who might be interested in helping students with their career search. I am looking to go through consulting recruitment in the fall, and I would like to learn more about Firm X and your experiences there.

Since I'm currently working downtown for my internship, I wondered if you might be available for lunch. My work hours are flexible, so I can meet you at your convenience. If possible, I'm hoping to meet sometime in the next few weeks: what does your schedule look like? Please let me know.

Best regards,

Charles

Approach these meetings as informational interviews. These informational interviews will not directly lead to a job. However, if you are relaxed and interested in the person and their company, they will probably like you. This is how a good relationship begins.

First Impressions

Every time you meet a person from a given firm, they are forming an impression of you. Always be professional, while letting your personality shine through; there's a balance to be struck. If you're not sure of how to strike this balance, try this. Every time you get served by someone (i.e. waiter, bar tender, grocery store clerk, etc.), make a note afterwards of how much you liked the person. If you liked them, why? And if you didn't like them, why not? This method is a great way to identify how to quickly form a positive impression.

In addition, pay particular attention to anything the waiter does that lets his or her personality through. Is it how they respond to your questions? Do they crack a joke? Do they attempt to relate to your problem? Do they answer you in a straightforward manner? How do they interact with the other employees?

Likewise, a recruiter has an equivalent length of time to form an impression of you. As such, it is beneficial to raise your awareness of how these impressions are formed.

To take this a step further, if you happen to have a part time job in a service role (particularly one where you can get tips), try out some of the techniques that you observed. This is because tips are a general quantitative measure of people's impression of you. Try to leave a great impression, and continue observing which techniques lead to friendlier interactions (and larger tips). You're trying to dial in on the balance between trying to make a good impression, while not trying too hard.

You can also pick up a copy of Dale Carnegie's famous book, *How To Win Friends and Influence People*, or other books about business etiquette or sales, for more tips on making a good impression.

Networking Tips for Success

Tip 1 – After meeting your contact, always ask for someone else you can contact in the organization. I met three great people in one firm from just one initial lunch. The first person with whom I met was a consultant. I asked if I could meet an associate, and he put me in touch with one. Then, when I met with her over lunch, I asked to meet with another associate. All three were very helpful in giving me a feel for the firm. One helped me to practice cases, and another gave me perspective on fit interviews.

Tip 2 – Do NOT ask multiple people in a firm, at the same time, to meet for lunch separately from each other. I once asked three separate people in one firm to practice a case with me: two of my interviewers from winter recruitment and one person on the recruiting team. Two meetings went fine, but then the third said he was too busy, and referred me to one of the people I had already met for lunch. To avoid mildly awkward situations like this one, stick with asking just one person unless they're unresponsive. Let the network grow from there.

Tip 3 – Ask your contacts to practice a case with you (Case studies will be discussed further in Part 3). It's important to get feedback from someone in the industry, even if it's the consultant's first year. If you excel in the case, they might want to pass you on to someone on the recruiting team.

Tip 4 – Rapport building may help you to secure an interview, but it certainly doesn't guarantee one. For example, there was one firm where I met with a couple of employees for lunch, and I didn't get an interview with the firm. My GPA was probably too low for consideration, and my acquaintances were not on the recruiting team. In addition, my acquaintances had worked at the firm for a year or less. As one confirmed, "I'm afraid you're talking to too low of a guy on the totem pole. Not much I can do."

Also, many companies will place a premium on your interest in the firm. They may limit their interview invitations to people who actively networked at most, if not all, of their events. In contrast, some companies routinely give interviews to people they haven't met, simply because they're impressed with the candidate's resume. This is particularly true of top-tier firms.

Thank you Letters

Always follow up with a thank you letter or email. Keeping the letter succinct is key. Consultants are genuinely busy people who often work 60+ hours a week. They always appreciate something they can quickly process. Here's a sample:

Dear Mrs. Consultant,

Thank you very much for meeting with me today. Your recruitment tips were very helpful, especially your comments on filler words. I now realize just how many I was using. I know you're very busy, and I appreciate your taking the time to speak with me.

Sincerely,

Joe Wanna Job Schmo

Many job seekers ask questions in their thank you email for the purpose of continuing the dialogue. This can be risky, because consultants are too busy to spend time answering trivial questions. Only ask a question if you have a genuine question. Your contact is smart, and they will know if your question is genuine or game-playing. Keep the message short and genuine.

In addition to writing an immediate thank you note, make sure to reach out to your contact to let them know how recruitment ended up for you. People are helping you "out of the goodness of their hearts," and derive intrinsic satisfaction from knowing "My efforts helped Joe land a job at X firm."

You should reach out to your contacts and thank them this final time, regardless of whether you got an offer with their firm or not, and even if you didn't get any offers. It brings closure to them, and is the polite thing to do. Just because you may not be working with them today, doesn't mean you won't be working with them in a few years or even decades. Building your network starts now, and you can keep in touch with some of these folks the rest of your career.

Stay in Touch

A professor of mine recommended that I stay in touch with contacts once every three months. He also suggested that it's never too late to re-establish contact if it's been longer than three months. Just mention the event that triggered your email or phone call. Maybe you found their business card, or maybe they came up in conversation the other day.

It is often stated that, "in life, the harder you work, the luckier you get." A friend of mine networked with about 100 people, between informational sessions, informational interviews, and mixers. He struck gold with one person. At the only firm where he received an interview, he had spoken to exactly one person at that firm. And now he works there. This all happened because of one conversation.

In conclusion, more time invested in networking leads to better chances of landing an interview (but don't neglect excelling in school, and all of the other steps in preparing for the interview process!).

9

Build Up Your Business Acumen

Business acumen is your ability to make good business judgments. Case interviews evaluate a candidate's business acumen though observations of the candidate's decision process. A person with good business acumen has an intuitive understanding of relevant business systems in their entirety, and he uses this understanding to help make decisions. However, business intuition takes a long time to develop through experiential learning, trial and error.

There's a reason why it takes really smart people 10+ years to become partners at consulting firms–business acumen takes time to develop through years of experiential learning. By the time a person is promoted to partner, they must be able to quickly understand the most important drivers of the business at hand and help the client focus on these drivers. While it takes time to develop this skill, there are a few things that you can do now to further your business acumen.

First, you should read articles on current business problems and think through how you would approach them. This exercise helps you develop the ability to think through and identify the key issues. This will ultimately help you in your case interviews.

For example, you are reading an article about the music industry. It reports that U.S. music sales are up for the first half of the year after experiencing declining music sales for the past 7 years. Now imagine that someone from the music industry has just hired you to find out how they should continue to accelerate growth. What key issues would you look at?

The beauty of this exercise is that while the number of available case studies is finite, news articles on business are virtually unlimited. There are a ton of businesses out there, and they all have challenges. So where do you find such stories? Great articles can be found in sources like *The Wall Street Journal*, *The New York Times*, *The Economist* and *Forbes*.

A second activity you can do to increase your business acumen is reading the consulting firms' websites. Here, you'll find articles written by partners, and you can see how they approached various business problems. How do their thought processes line up with your own? On what key issues did they focus? Did they consider the same key issues that you considered? Additionally, this exercise has a key side benefit: if you get lucky, you may even be interviewed by the author of an article that you have already read!

Finally, public filings are resources that are very underused, but extremely valuable. Every public company in the U.S. must file an annual report each year with the SEC, otherwise known as a "10-K." "10-K" is the government's name for the SEC filing form. These annual reports provide investors with a comprehensive look at the business.

The 10-K contains a lot of information, but there are several sections (item numbers) that are particularly relevant to developing business acumen:

> *Item 1: Business* – This section always describes the business. It typically describes the industry, the products & services offered by the company, the type of customer (individual customers are usually not named except for extremely significant customers), the competitors, and how the supply chain & distribution networks operate. This is a fantastic (and very easy) way to see how some of the world's leading companies think about their business, industries, competitors, customers, and operations.

Item 7: Management's Discussion and Analysis of Financial Condition and Results of Operations – This section contains management's explanation of the company's performance and how that compares to previous periods. This segment provides you with easy access to information on current business trends in the industry that are materially affecting the business.

Item 8: Financial Statements & Supplementary Data – This section contains the income statement, balance sheet, and cash flow statements for the business. The financial statements can provide a keen insight into the kind of company you are researching. While the general components of these statements are similar for all businesses, there can be significant variance in presentation depending on the industry. For example, some businesses may report interest on investments separately from their core product revenue lines. A financial company would report interest as an integral part of their costs and expenses. A company that sells commercial products would not report interest as an integral part of their costs and expenses.

Public filings are available through http://sec.gov/edgar/searchedgar/companysearch.html (see www.college2consulting.com for a quick link). Search for any company name that you know is public. If the company is not public, then no results will show, unless the company was required to file SEC filings for another reason. Read through information for a variety of industries; here is a list of a few companies in a variety of industries to get you started:

- Accenture (Consulting)
- D.R. Horton (Home building)
- United Continental Holdings (Airlines)
- Xcel Energy (Energy generation, distribution, and sales)
- Wal-Mart (Retail)

By reading through these annual reports, you will also get a sense of how interesting consulting may be for you. Consultants need to be excited about the industry pertaining to their case, as well as focused on the challenge of the strategic issue at hand. If you read through these 10-Ks, and you are bored to tears, you may wish to re-evaluate whether management consulting is best aligned with your interests.

10
GPA Cutoffs

Grade Point Average (GPA) is the first thing a recruiter observes on a resume. Many times, they will circle it if you hand them your resume at a career fair. Obviously, higher is better. Some firms will have explicit GPA cutoffs. This means they will only take a fixed number of candidates for interviews, and they will make that decision primarily based on GPA.

Suppose a firm wants to take 50 candidates each year for first-round interviews. In the first year, the 50th student may have a 3.65 GPA, while in the second year the 50th student may have a 3.70 GPA. The GPA "cut-off" varies from the first year to the second year, based on the composition of the pool of available applicants.

This fluctuation in GPA cutoffs explains why firms do not always specify an explicit GPA cutoff. They also want to leave the door open for that dark horse candidate who has a 3.0 GPA but found the cure for cancer in her spare time.

To help you determine whether you have a "low" GPA, the following table displays a snapshot of minimum GPAs witnessed by candidates at different firms. While the exact cutoff points may vary from year to year and from school to school, these cutoffs provide a ballpark reference. Please note that for McKinsey, BCG, and Bain, the GPAs listed are NOT official firm-designated "cut-offs," but they are based on empirical evidence. For example, BCG posts a cut-off of 3.0 at Northwestern, but over the past 3 years, candidates report that they have not witnessed anyone interviewing with BCG who had a GPA lower than 3.6.

If your GPA is below 3.6, keep in mind that BCG posts a low cut-off for a reason; there are always anomalies, and you could be one of those dark horse candidates.

	GPA Cut-Off					
	2.5	3.0	3.4	3.5	3.6	3.7
Consulting Firm (*Select Sample*)	Booz & Company	Accenture A.T. Kearney Diamond (now PwC)	L.E.K. Consulting	Bain & Company Cambridge Group Deloitte	BCG	McKinsey & Company

What if My GPA is "Low"?

There are two strategies for overcoming a "low" GPA. The first strategy is to create your own baseline for comparison instead of relying on a reviewer's internal comparisons. A second strategy is to demonstrate traits associated with a high GPA in alternative ways.

Strategy 1: Create alternative comparisons.

- Determine the average cumulative GPA for your academic major. If your GPA is strong relative to your major, point it out on a resume or cover letter.

- What if your major GPA is higher than your cumulative GPA? List both on a resume. If your freshmen year GPA is poor relative to your sophomore, junior and senior year GPA, point that out to recruiters. Chapter 13 provides details about how to convey this in a cover letter.

- If you have excellent SAT and/or ACT scores, include those on your resume to compensate for a lower GPA. Include your percentile ranking as well, if this is impressive.

Strategy 2: Demonstrate that you have traits shared by 4.0 students

Here is a list of traits that a high GPA can imply about you. In what ways can you demonstrate these traits outside of grades? It is important to convey these traits on your resume and cover letter if you have a low GPA.

- Academically curious – You're likely to do better in course work that you're curious about.

  Sample counter-point: What academic research have you done, and what were the results?

- Works well independently – You take tests and write papers independently, and at least do some parts of homework assignments independently.

  Sample counter-point: Have you worked independently in previous jobs? Consider the following scenario: Your boss gave you a deliverable. After clarifying the objective, you worked on it for a couple days and independently surpassed roadblocks as they came up. You then turned it in, and he acknowledged you because your work went beyond what he was expecting.

- Intelligent – People with a higher GPA are assumed to be more intelligent.

  Sample counter-point: How have you scored on standardized tests? Is your major likely to be perceived as more rigorous? How have you done relative to other people in that major?

- Achieving – A high GPA, especially at a tougher school and/or major, is an achievement in itself. It may catch a recruiter's eye with other achievements.

Sample counter-point: What achievements do you have outside of class? Performance on case competitions, or examples of quantifiable results achieved by a team or organization under your leadership.

In sum, GPA is key during consulting recruitment. If you have a high GPA (3.9 or above), you're almost guaranteed to get an interview at a few firms. If you have a GPA lower than 3.3, it's crucial to use the aforementioned techniques and to network your way into interviews.

11

Resume Experience

Building up your resume and repertoire of experience is one of the best ways to competitively differentiate yourself from the plethora of other candidates. A strong resume opens doors. A weak resume closes doors. Even if you have the right mind for consulting, you are unlikely to ace an interview without showing achievement and development of relevant skills in your experiences.

Consulting firms want battle-tested candidates who have first-hand experience in real-life situations. A candidate without the right experience is considered "high risk," because they haven't proved themselves yet. This is why developing the right experience is vital to both securing and excelling in the interview.

Outside of academic credentials, getting an internship, starting an organization, campus involvement, being an entrepreneur, and volunteering are the best ways to demonstrate your achievements and skills sets from the recruiters' perspective. If you plan on getting a job in consulting, you must have these achievements and skills on your mind.

The best experience that you could possibly add to your resume is an internship in management consulting. Interning with a management consulting firm significantly increases your chances of receiving a full-time offer and provides excellent leverage in fall recruitment.

Students with one or more management consultant internships under their belts frequently receive at least one offer in addition to the one from the firm where they interned.

Supercharge Your Internship – Conduct Informational Interviews With Your Co-Workers

One student who received an offer at a management consulting firm had this great bit to share:

"I worked at a small consulting firm during the summer between my junior and senior years. One of the most helpful things I did was drop by the offices of consultants [in the firm] and talk to them about their projects. I learned how they thought about different issues, and they always gave me good advice. Since they knew I was interested in consulting, I was able to turn my internship into a metaphorical summer consulting course - something that would later help me in interviews. Obviously, you don't want to just barge in, but identify people who you could learn a thing or two from, and ask if they'd like to talk. Most are pretty open to it."

Management consulting experience can be a golden ticket to getting interviews for full-time positions, but most students will not secure a management consulting internship. There are at least three reasons why:

1. Just as many students apply for internships as full-time positions, so the competition is intense.

2. Not all companies offer internships.

3. Companies hire less interns than full time positions each year.

But what if I didn't get an offer for an internship at a management consulting firm?!?!?

Keep your chin up and find a different internship outside of consulting! The majority of people who get offers during full-time recruitment didn't have a management consulting internship. However, it's crucial that you find an internship of some kind.

Internship Experience

What should you do at your internship to position yourself for full-time employment at a consulting firm? To answer this, let's think about the end goal: a job in management consulting. Your summer internship is going to help you achieve that goal by providing work experience. Therefore, it will benefit you to look for opportunities to make an impact on the projects that you have been assigned. By the end of the summer, you'll want at least a couple of "hooks" from your internship. These metaphorical hooks should catch the attention of recruiters. Recruiters are looking for impact. The easiest way to demonstrate impact is through *quantitative results.*

It's a big plus if you had an impact on your company that can be measured quantitatively, not only because the result is clear, but also because the results are (theoretically) verifiable. For example, perhaps you're assisting with a company's marketing campaign, and you found a marketing channel that delivered similar levels of sales but cost 10% less. Not only is your impact clear (your actions led to a 10% reduction in marketing costs), but they are verifiable (the interviewer could call up the company where you interned and ask if you really saved them 10% in marketing costs).

Ideally, every bullet point on your resume will have a quantitative result.

Skill Sets to Develop in an Internship

Let's think about what kind of skills you would want to develop at a consulting internship. That way, if you get this kind of experience at a non-consulting internship, you can still prove that you have what it takes to be a consultant. It is important to be able to illustrate these skills in a resume and during an interview regardless of where you worked in the past.

1. Collect and analyze data – The entry-level people in a consulting firm collect data, analyze the data, draw conclusions from the analysis, and then discuss their insights with their team. Therefore, the ability to analyze data is a crucial skill for consulting. If you have little or no analytical experience, you definitely need to look for how to work it into your internship or other experience. For example, a dance major once asked me how she could develop her analytical ability as an intern for a company that developed an Internet review site.

    I suggested that she look for opportunities such as preparing a user survey, evaluating site usage statistics, or conducting experiments on which ad layout generated the most click-throughs. It's hard for anyone to tell you what specific opportunities to look for, since every internship is different. In general though, you're on the right track if you're collecting data, and then analyzing it to generate recommendations on what to do next.

    Look for opportunities to analyze both qualitative and quantitative data. The latter is especially important if you're not in a math-heavy discipline such as engineering or economics: you can't be afraid of numbers as a consultant!

2. Research and pull out client relevance – Consultants spend large portions of their day doing research in order to solve a client's business problem. It is important to demonstrate your ability to research any given topic, sift through mounds of information, and pull out the insights that are relevant to solving the client's problem. Look for opportunities in your internship to research, write reports based on research, or solve a problem through research.

3. Present your findings – If you get to make a presentation to an outside client, A+ here. Odds are that you probably won't have this opportunity, so look for other opportunities to present

during your internship. You may have the opportunity to prepare materials for a client presentation or present your ideas to your team and superiors. You might want to let your boss know about your desire to practice presenting.

4. Find a leadership role – Leadership is critical to becoming a good manager, and consulting firms recruit top talent in anticipation of grooming future partners. Obviously, you aren't a manager yet, but there are ways to take on leadership during an internship.

Leadership Experience

The reason recruiters like leadership is because past behavior is an indicator of future behavior. This means if you're organizing things in past companies, you are likely to add value in a similar manner to the firm considering your application. To demonstrate leadership, you could:

Plan a social event – Dinner, basketball tournament, whatever you think people would enjoy. You don't even have to organize the whole thing yourself (as there may be a social committee), but it's important to take the lead on it, pushing the idea to fruition. This is the easiest and most common opportunity for leadership in an internship, so take advantage of it.

Make life easier – Is the kitchen a mess? Volunteer to label and organize it in your spare time. In short, if something bugs you, look for a proactive way to deal with it. Taking initiative is a form of leadership.

Manage a project – In the event that an internship offers such an opportunity, seize the opportunity and lead a project team!

Lead your peers – Put together a group of interns, find a problem, and solve it! Is the intern training confusing or boring? Offer to form a team of employees (interns and full-time) to review and improve it.

If you can prove that you have collected and analyzed data, researched a topic and derived client relevance, presented findings, and assumed a leadership role, then you have the right experience to set you up for management consulting.

If you receive multiple offers when applying for a summer internship, you should strongly weigh how receptive the company is to working with you on providing these opportunities. It's a sad truth that many companies hire interns and don't use them to their full ability. They're either not interested or do not have the time to develop you professionally. When discussing the internship opportunity with recruiters, discuss what sort of opportunities there may be for analyzing, researching, presenting, and taking on a leadership role, etc. Then, judge if they seem genuinely interested in helping you find those opportunities. Even if you only satisfy a few of these criteria with a summer internship, you will have made progress.

Non-Internship Experience

In addition to gaining relevant experience through an internship, you can develop marketable skill sets through non-internship activities. Great resume builders include starting an organization, being involved on your college campus, volunteering, or even starting an entrepreneurial venture.

1. Start an Organization – Another way to stand out as a candidate is to start an organization. Founding an organization takes ambition, vision, hard work, leadership, and dedication. The words "founder" and "president" stand out on a resume. Your organization could be a campus club, a volunteer group or even a company. However, it won't help to start a club that does not accomplish anything.

    I started a campus consulting club called CASE. This experience set me apart from other candidates, and helped immensely during the recruitment season. The club offered something uniquely impressive on my resume, and I accompanied this resume entry with quantifiable results: growing the organization from 2 to

12 people in fewer than six months, and helping other student organizations fundraise thousands of dollars.

During interviews, CASE was my "passion story." My eyes lit up, I spoke in a more excited manner when talking about CASE. It is important to find something to put on your resume that you can talk about with heightened enthusiasm in your interviews. What interests you? Genuine passion matters. Take the initiative create something new that is fueled by your passion. It will make you stand out, and it will give you something to brag about during interviews – not to mention, it is a great life experience.

2. Campus Involvement – People don't get into Harvard by being book worms anymore. Get involved. Consulting firms want people who do more than just study. They want fun people, with a diversity of experiences, and that have time management skills. Campus involvement is an easy way to demonstrate this. The words "member" or "participant" look good but not great on a resume.

    Leadership roles are very highly valued. "Co-president," "head of recruitment," or "manager" stand out a lot more than "member," but don't make the mistake of thinking the title will be enough to win the interview. Many students do not achieve anything in their on-campus leadership roles, and recruiters are good at revealing this in interviews. Be honest and don't exaggerate your roles and responsibilities for the sake of bulking up your resume.

3. Volunteer – Another great way to gain experience and enhance your resume is volunteering. I don't recommend volunteering just for the sake of your resume. You should genuinely care about the cause; it will be almost impossible to convince the interviewer that you enjoy volunteering if you do not actually care. Scattered, non-committal, one-time volunteering events don't count. Recruiters know when resumes are exaggerated, so be honest.

    Volunteering is an area where duration and commitment really matter. If you volunteered at a hospital every week for the last eight years, you should definitely put that on your resume.

Note that a short duration of volunteering is better than no volunteering (though obviously not as good as long duration).

This is your opportunity to showcase your talents and prove that you have what it takes to be a rock star consultant. Remember, there are a few key points that consulting firms want to see:

- Quantitative results
- Experience with analyzing data, research, presentations, and leadership
- A well rounded candidate

Finally, a recruiter at a small strategy shop had this great tip to share:

> *"After circling a candidate's major and GPA, the next thing I look for on a resume is experience. If they have only one relevant internship, I put their resume in the 'no' pile. Do they do anything fun or interesting on campus? If not, the resume goes in the 'no' pile. For remaining candidates, I briefly read the details of their experience. The best candidates prove to me that they made some impact. Honestly, the brand name of previous employers makes a big difference as well."*

Every recruiter has a different philosophy, but the statement above should illustrate the typical recruiter's thought process. People tend to have binary criteria – in other words, if you don't have criteria "X," then your resume will be put in the "no" pile.

To avoid the "no" pile, highlight any experiences you have had over the long term, and seek out new experiences as time allows.

12
Writing a Resume

The resume is a *one-page* document listing what you bring to the firm. If you don't have a resume, you shouldn't create one from scratch. Look at a few friends' resumes to find a template you like, or pay a visit to the career center for resume examples. You can also ask business professors for sample resumes. A well-organized resume is key to encourage the reader to read the actual content on your resume.

Overall, your resume should be lean and focused. Pick the most powerful experiences for your resume, and leave everything else out. You're far better off with quality over quantity. For example, you should include one amazing internship rather than three mediocre ones, or two powerful bullet points rather than six mediocre ones.

When writing the resume, students need to be careful about how many bullet points they choose to assign to each experience. Is it better to have many work experiences with a few bullet points, or a few work experiences with lots of bullet points? The answer is "it depends." Decide which scenario fits your experience better.

Depth of experience made more sense in my case because I had one internship that lasted for 1.25 years. It wouldn't make sense for me to cut this experience off in favor of other work experiences.

That said, a common solution is to include a lot of detail on the most relevant experience, and then only have a couple of bullet points for the remaining experiences. Don't be afraid of writing different resumes for different companies, which uniquely cater to a specific firm's job requirements.

As discussed in the previous chapter, make sure your resume presents a well-rounded candidate. If one internship isn't very impressive from an overall perspective, but demonstrates a key ability aligned with management consulting (like your breadth of business experience) then leave it on your resume.

Once you've written a lean resume that demonstrates that you are well-rounded, take one final look at your resume for the "big picture." What do your experiences imply about you and your interests? For example, I once had an interviewer tell me my background experience appeared to be primarily focused on improving an organization internally. Consulting firms are primarily externally focused, and my resume presented someone more interested in an internal strategy position rather than a normal management consulting position. This feedback demonstrated that I needed to show my interest in helping firms to help their clients.

The comment took me by surprise; I had never linked my experiences together like that before. The solution was to add more client-focused experiences to my resume. I needed to re-tool my work experience to show how it was like working for an external client. Look for what your experiences collectively suggest about your interests. The answer may surprise you.

Sample Student
111 1st St · College Town, X 55555 · (555) 555-5555 · sstudent@university.edu

EDUCATION

9/2004 – Present	**SAMPLE UNIVERSITY**	College Town, X

Bachelor of Science in Industrial Engineering, Minor in Business
- GPA: 3.57/4.00 (major); 3.43/4.00 (cumulative).
- ACT: 34/36 (99th percentile; Scores: 36 Reading, 36 Science, 34 Math, 31 English).
- Select Business Courses: Macroeconomics, Microeconomics, Engineering Entrepreneurship, Organizational Behavior, Financial Entrepreneurship, Marketing Management, Advertising.

CONSULTING

4/2008 – 5/2008   STRATEGY COMPETITIONS
- Company A – National Winner; Developed Company A's go-green strategy over two weeks; team of four made recommendations based on bottom line impact, environmental impact, and ease of implementation.
- Company B – Sample University Final Round Qualifier; Company C – Sample University Participant.

4/2008 – Present   CO-FOUNDER, STUDENT GROUP
Student-run strategy group helping other student groups grow
- Spearheaded initial recruitment campaign and hire of ten consultants out of 22 applicants.
- Planned and facilitated creation of membership agreement; collaborative process resulted in 100% of consultants committing to their case teams and clients.
- Helped two students raise $3000 in one week for a charity by defining their fundraising strategy.
- Collaborated to help Company A attract 180 resumes, a 100% increase over last year.
- Oversaw summer effort to find new clients; resulted in winning two key Sample University business groups representing over 900 students.
- Currently overseeing targeted marketing campaign aimed at boosting campus presence.

EXPERIENCE

1/2007 – 9/2008   COMPANY D (*Print Advertiser for Fortune 50 Retail*)   Sometown, X
Continuous Improvement Intern
- Alternated quarters of classes and working for Company D through SU's cooperative educational program.
- Saved $15,000 by researching and developing alternative to purchasing new backup server.
- Freed 40 production hours per month by collecting and analyzing data on failing image transfer process.
- Initiated project to shorten new employee learning curves; researched and proposed idea, wrote presentation script, and handed-off to team at end of internship.
- Led team of four in analyzing ad-based costing process, resulted in 25% reduction in process time.
- Created Excel tool that reduced production time by eight hours per month; tool automatically generates weekly production schedules.
- Increased employee utilization by leading team of six to standardize image naming conventions.
- Facilitated process documentation meetings, and created flowcharts to visually depict processes.

Summer 2006   COMPANY E (*Global Service Truck Manufacturer*)   Sometown, X
Manufacturing Engineer Intern
- Conducted time studies for two crane welding operations by collaborating with shift supervisors, and summarizing findings for plant supervisors; Company E continues to use findings as reference material.
- Measured all fixed objects in plant to within six inches, and quickly learned AutoCAD 2002 to use measurements in updating map for plant manager.
- Composed standard work for line workers involving photographs and written instructions.

LEADERSHIP

8/2006 – 6/2007   RESIDENTIAL ASSISTANT, SAMPLE UNIVERSITY RESIDENTIAL LIFE
- Managed residential hall of 225 residents with five other Residential Assistants.
- Organized program receiving largest resident attendance of year.
- Achieved highest overall performance rating in annual Residential Assistant Evaluation.

9/2005 – 3/2006   HOUSE MANAGER, FRATERNITY
- Led 20 residents in preparing for annual College Town housing inspection; achieved top marks relative to other SU Greek Houses.
- Established "floor RA" system, reducing average time for locked-out students to get into their room.

SKILLS / INTERESTS
- Proficient with Microsoft Excel, PowerPoint, Visio, Word, and Access.
- Dog rescue organization volunteer, All-State swimmer in high school, avid drummer, website entrepreneur.

Recruiters consistently look for the following key elements in a resume:

1. Work Experience – Clearly, a management consulting internship is ideal, but most students don't have one. In general, recruiters are looking for a few key traits within each bullet point on a resume:

    Results/Impact – What difference did you personally make? As mentioned previously, make sure you quantify your impact. Consultants are in the business of providing results, so naturally they want to find people who are already results-oriented. Being able to say, "Reduced widget manufacturing process time by 20%" is much better than "Reduced widget manufacturing process time," as long as it's true and you can explain how you reached that number. You may not be able to quantify every bullet point, in which case you may want to consider removing it. Here are some specific suggestions that are very quantifiable:

    *   Brought new customers and revenue into the company.

    *   Created efficiencies by saving money or time.

    *   Implemented an innovative idea. How was it innovative, and what results did it achieve?

    *   Improved service or responsiveness to customers.

    *   Set a challenging goal and achieved it (Note: This is weaker than the others because it's less quantifiable, but achieving challenging goals is always noteworthy).

    Analytics – What kind of work have you done?

    *   Did the job involve analyzing data?

    *   Did you take a large amount of information and arrive at conclusions? To whom did you present the conclusions?

    *   Did you identify a root cause from an array of symptoms and develop a business or technical solution?

- Did you perform experiments that required a formulation of a hypothesis, collect data, and work towards a solution?

- Did you identify a problem and take a proactive approach to solving it?

- Did you use an unexpected method to further progress toward a solution?

Presentation – Did you ever make a presentation to senior management? To clients? Were you able to persuade them?

Leadership – Did you manage a team? Did your mentorship lead to someone else achieving something significant? Did you take initiative in some way?

If you find your work experience lacks one or more of the four categories above (results, analytics, presentation, leadership), check your student group experience to see if it's covered there. If it's not, ask yourself how you can create that experience. For example, friend of mine started a consulting business while in college.

Alternatively, if you have an internship, discuss with your supervisor how you could create these kinds of experiences. Obviously what they're paying you to do is driven by what they need you to do, but there should be room to fit in a few key experiences that will help you out in recruitment.

Quick Tip

What if you were on a team that accomplished something great? For example, you may have worked on a successful class project for an external company. Include a bullet point describing the team's achievement. Then, include whatever accomplishments you personally made. Recruiters are not interviewing your team – they are interviewing you. For example, if you led the customer survey portion of the process, mention this in your resume.

2. Student Group/Leadership/Other Experience – You may have other experiences on your resume that are of interest to a recruiter:

- Case Competitions

- Student groups in which you've taken leadership roles or groups you've founded

- Volunteer work

All that experience is good. Just remember to quantify your results, and list your most important points first.

3. "Other Data" – One day, a professor of mine was going to lecture on how to write resumes. He walked into the room with a huge stack of papers. He said it was dozens of resumes from Kellogg (Northwestern University's business school). He waved them in front of us, and every resume looked the same. While that's an interesting point on its own, all of them had a section called "Other Data." This is where you put the fun facts about you that may catch an interviewer's eye.

Since this is your chance to differentiate yourself further, add an adjective to each activity in order to describe yourself better. For example, instead of writing "skier, guitarist, and scuba instructor," write "Double black-diamond skier, blues guitarist, and deep-sea scuba instructor." Notice how much more vivid and interesting the second sentence reads? It's ok to embellish as long as it doesn't misrepresent you.

Recruiters consistently ask questions about the "Other Data" section on your resume during an interview. Recruiters are trying to make a connection with you, and they want to hear about your passions. This can be a great opportunity to let your personality shine through!

The next step is to share your resume and get feedback from your friends, parents, and advisors. The following suggestion comes from a friend of mine who received an offer at a top management consulting firm:

"I like to ask a friend to read my resume and then mention the three things that he/she remembered about it. Did I have analytical skills? Was my leadership experience clear? Did one experience stand out more than others?

"Then I evaluate whether that is what I'd like a recruiter to remember when he/she finishes with my resume. Having a friend read your resume tests how well your big picture is coming across."

Guest Author – Former Consultant, BCG

Here are a few tips for your resume.

- Wherever possible, try and quantify your impact. Let's say you have a line that reads, "Saved Excel production time. " How much? Can you somehow estimate time savings or what value that time savings translates to? Make an estimate and be able to backup your logic.

- When you are comfortable with the content, edit the resume to make each bullet as concise as possible. For example, if you built an Excel model for the client "that summarizes page counts," you could just have built an Excel model for the client "summarizing page counts."

- When you have your resume to a point where you feel comfortable with it, review the resume with others (e.g., students, family, career center, etc.). In business school, we had our resumes looked over by tons of people, and everyone added their own tips.

- However, when you get edits from people, make your own determination on how to exactly word things given the general feedback. It's important for your resume to have a consistent "voice" – yours!

Results, results, results!

One of the biggest mistakes in resumes is focusing on what you do rather than what you have done. Resumes should showcase what you accomplish as evidenced by results. For instance, a standard resume might say, "Developed a marketing strategy for a CPG manufacturer," whereas a stronger resume would say, "Developed a marketing strategy for a CPG manufacturer, which resulted in a 20% increase in sales."

Sometimes, the issue is not that candidates don't know how to include numbers or results in their resume, but that they don't know how to access or support those numbers. Here are some ways to find the numbers you may be looking for:

- Metric already exists: Look at the performance of a project before you started and after you started. E.g.: "Managed the collection of survey responses, which resulted in an increase of 30% in response rate from the previous year"

- Project is currently in progress and there is no metric yet: State what the projected result is for the project. E.g.: "Creating a new revenue stream for a hair salon, which is projected to increase revenue by 20%"

- Project is only qualitative and there is no number: Outline the impact associated and state the number of things or people you worked with. E.g.: "Taught 10 school children to read in order to improve their long term academic performance"

Resume Formatting

Here are some general formatting guidelines for resumes:

- Include your GPA. Even if you have a "low" GPA, include it. Flags get raised if there is no GPA reported, and this effect can be much worse than reporting a low GPA.

- Break out a separate "Consulting" section of your resume if you have done some consulting work, case competitions or anything else related to consulting. It's an easy way to call special attention to these experiences.

- Shorter is better: try to keep only three bullets (maximum) per "experience" in your resume.

- Try to keep each bullet to one sentence. This will encourage the reader to read the entire line. Being succinct keeps a recruiter's attention.

13
Writing Cover Letters

One former engagement manager at McKinsey explained that when he reviews an application, he divides his time accordingly:

- 75% on resume
- 24% on transcript
- 1% on cover letter

When asked about the time he spends reading a cover letter, he said:

> *"Honestly, everyone's cover letters are the same, so I just make sure they used the right company name and didn't make any obvious grammatical errors that would demonstrate carelessness on their part."*

In general, cover letters appear to be what is called "table stakes." This buzzword comes from poker, where you must have a certain amount of money just to play in the hand (maybe $5). But the fact that you have $5 doesn't mean that you're going to win the table. Likewise, you need a polished cover letter that succinctly tells the firm why you're a great fit. If you do that, you will put yourself in the running. You cannot distinguish yourself through a cover letter alone, but if you don't write one, you won't be invited to the table to play.

Overall, people put too much effort into cover letters because they feel that they "have" to customize the letter as opposed to their resume. Get your resume up to snuff first, customize the resume for each firm as needed, and then worry about the cover letter after your resume is perfect.

Let's assume that your resume is great and tailored for the job at hand. What elements should go into a cover letter? Here is the standard format commonly found in successful cover letters.

- Name of person to whom the letter is addressed, and address of the office to which you are applying

- Salutation of recipient

- Statement as to why you are writing the letter (e.g., you're interested in the X position at Y company)

- Description of why you're interested in the firm

- Make sure to weave in any research you've done on the company – that shows interest

- Additionally, make sure to mention any persons and rank with whom you've met. This explains that you've interacted with their company, and it gives them a reference with whom they can confirm that you are a good candidate. This also stimulates examining the rest of your application. Here, suggest why it is in their best interest to interview you.

- Carefully incorporate prior work experience and student leadership experience. Explain how that translates to the job. Consider this example of a cover letter that landed an applicant a first-round interview at Monitor:

> "…*Last summer I worked at Bank X in the private wealth division. I worked on detail-oriented analyses of client portfolios to find weaknesses and then I incorporated research from other financial opportunities to recommend ideal allocations to our financial advisors. Furthermore, I prepared exhaustive performance reports that I presented to these advisors in a clear, concise manner so they could easily refer to this information in client meetings and effectively utilize the findings. These same skills are integral in the*

consulting process – analyzing a client's situation to find innovative, feasible solutions and being able to communicate that to a client successfully..."

Did you notice how he related his experience to the firm? He lays out the fact that the skills he developed are integral to the firm because of X & Y. This answers the question, "So-what?" Always make sure ANY experience you mention answers this question.

- Explain any shortcomings in your application

- Close by stating you are looking forward to an interview and by signing your name

Use the cover letter as a tool to explain any weaknesses in your application. It's your one chance to explain, in your own words, any shortcomings.

Explaining my shortcomings helped me to secure interviews. For two of my applications, I explained my low GPA in my cover letter, and for four applications I didn't. I secured an interview with both firms (and ultimately an offer) where I explained my GPA, and didn't get a single interview with firms for whom I didn't explain my GPA. One interviewer explicitly told me, "You know, you're the only person I'm interviewing today that has under a 3.5 GPA. They must've thought you were pretty special."

My low GPA created doubt in some recruiters' minds, and when I didn't explain that I was in a more difficult curriculum (engineering), that I had a high ACT score (to demonstrate intellect), and performed well in case competitions (one of which I had won), I looked weaker by comparison on a key attribute for which they were looking.

February 28, 2010

Ms. HR Manager
Human Resources Manager
Company A
111 N 1st St, 50th Floor
Sometown, X 55555

Dear Ms. Manager,

I am writing to express interest in interviewing for Company A's full-time Associate position.

Since last winter, I have tackled several small consulting problems. I co-founded Student Group last spring to answer the demand from students for more on-campus consulting experience, and achieved exceptional increases in our client base, membership, and campus presence by leading an aggressive growth strategy. Outside of Student Group, I led a team that helped a new College Town restaurant increase their campus presence, and assisted two students planning a consulting class for this upcoming Winter Quarter.

I am now looking to tackle larger-scale consulting problems at a business strategy-focused firm. Company A is very appealing to me for several reasons that became increasingly clear as I attended Company A's information session, spoke with Jane Associate and Jill Summer Intern, and stopped by Company A's career fair booth.

I believe the low-level of travel enables me to learn Company A's culture faster, which would aid me in positively contributing to the office sooner, through organizing social events or volunteering for recruiting. I also really like how Company A ensures their Associates are formally exposed to a wide variety of industries, instead of leaving an Associate's exposure to chance. Lastly, it is my experience that people at Company A like to have fun, from organized weekend trips to the office's annual ski trip.

I am aware my GPA is slightly lower than a 3.50, which is the stated minimum for this position on companya.com. I hope that my strong analytical course load at Sample University, my excellent ACT score, and my superior performance in case competitions are enough to address any concerns you may have regarding my 3.43 GPA.

Thank you for your time and consideration. I am looking forward toward an opportunity to interview with Company A.

Sincerely,

Sample Student

How do you explain that you're still a strong candidate, even when you don't look so strong on paper? Here's the exact wording that I used:

> *"I am aware my GPA is slightly lower than a 3.50, which is the stated minimum for this position. I hope that my strong analytical course work at Northwestern University, my excellent ACT score, and my superior performance in case competitions are enough to address any concerns you may have regarding my 3.43 GPA."*

Feel free to embellish, but never lie. It can be easily argued that engineering is heavily analytical, my ACT score was "excellent" (because it was in the 99th percentile), and my case competition performance was "superior" (because most people have never won a case competition). If I were in the 70th percentile for ACT scores and I simply participated but did not win the case competition, the statement would be misleading.

Guest Commentary on Cover Letters – Analyst, Top 10 Firm

Cover letters are risk-laden, if not considered altogether unimportant. Let's face it, after spending time on information sessions and crafting the perfect resume, writing letters to a bunch of firms is not an attractive endeavor. However, if you don't invest the time, it will definitely lessen the value of your application.

The reason that a great cover letter can only help you is a function of how much time is spent looking at your letter in the first place. Most consulting firms will do a brief skim of your cover letter only after looking at your resume. If your resume passes the sniff test, then your cover letter will be scrutinized. Otherwise, it is unlikely that the other interview selection committee members will read your cover letter.

During that quick skim, your effort can rapidly unravel if the cover letter is not up to par. Poor grammar or silly mistakes like having the wrong company name in your letter (the ultimate cover letter killer) can doom your candidacy in an instant. Committee members are looking for any mistakes like this to knock you out of the running. After all, they need to weed out dozens, if not hundreds, of candidates. Be on your guard!

So, how can the cover letter help you? Remember, you are applying for an elite position sought by many accomplished individuals with great resumes. Interview selection committee members sometimes face a situation where they have too many exceptional candidates and not enough spots. In situations like this, committee members will go back and look at the entire candidate's portfolio closely, including the cover letter. A well-crafted cover letter here can win you one of those coveted spots.

So what exactly do you have to do? When sitting down to write one, you face two major issues:

1. How much do I write?
2. What do I write?

Having solid answers to these questions create a cover letter that will get the job done.

First, how much to write? A cover letter needs to be 1-page, maximum. Some colleagues of mine even say no more than three-fourths of a page. Remember, interview selection committee members are going through hundreds of application packets. They don't have time to read a novel. Writing something long could easily turn them off. As such, don't do it.

Now within that one page (or 3/4ths of page), you want to break up the text. Imagine reading one long block of text. Would your eyes have a hard time following? Likely, yes. Breaking up your text into several paragraphs will allow your reader to easily follow your thoughts and stick with you longer.

Now, what do I write? A successful cover letter will state:

- Your intention (I want this position)
- Why this company (I like Company A for X,Y,Z reasons)
- What skills you bring to the table

It sounds simple but you would be surprised at how often applicants stumble; they forget that being concise is a mark of intelligence. Let's start with the intention. The first couple of sentences of your cover letter should focus on who you are and what position at what firm you are seeking (e.g., "I am a senior at University of XYZ applying to position A at Company B"). This allows for a natural transition into the next section, discussing why you want the position at Company B.

This part of the letter is a place for you to really shine. Include some deliberate research findings, of a favorable nature, on the position or company. Including some knowledge from an information session is an easy way to get this part done. In any case, you need to demonstrate that you have looked at the company and have accumulated some interesting factual data. Interview selection committee members will definitely be looking to see if you have taken the time to do your research.

After going through this process, the last section should, with a degree of modesty, emphasize the scope of your skills and your eagerness to work for the firm. In this connection, your cover letter should detail the relationship of your experience, skills, and knowledge to the position you are seeking and its requirements for qualification. Selectively choose experiences that illustrate how you meet the requirements while not regurgitating your resume too much. Introduce new experiences, if possible.

Finally, you should confidently assure the prospective employer that you are up the challenge of the job. At the end of the cover letter, be confident and respectful as you reiterate the fact that you would be an excellent fit.

14
Getting You To Apply

A new school year is starting. Freshmen are wandering around starry-eyed; people are chattering about their summers. Your calendar is already full. Welcome to fall recruitment.

Recruitment is a metaphorical dance: Firms pique your interest, you apply and interview, and then if they like you, they foster your interest in accepting their offer. There's something very rhythmical about the process.

In this section, we review info sessions and career fairs. Both are tools used by firms to generate interest in their firm.

Interview With a Rock Star: Questions for the Candidate Who Got Three Offers in Fall 2008, One of the Worst Recruiting Seasons of All Time

Q: Did you do anything extra because you knew this season was going to be extra tough?

A: You have 2 choices: you can focus on just consulting, or spread your focus over a bunch of industries. I went with the first choice, even though I knew the economy was going down the drain. When the job market is tough, sometimes people suggest spreading your focus over a bunch of industries.

My main concern was that firms might categorize me as strictly a finance person, given my PE and fund of funds experience [a mutual fund that invests in other mutual funds rather than stocks or other investments], so I did take a job at a retirement consultancy during recruitment season.

Q: Recruitment is stressful! How did you keep relaxed during recruitment season?

A: I went to the gym a lot. I also decided to run a marathon, figuring if I can run a marathon, I have what it takes to do a job in consulting.

What is an Info Session?

From a firm's perspective, the purpose of an info session (or information session) is to generate interest in their firm. Throughout recruitment season, firms come to the campuses of targeted schools, and they typically give an information session about their company. Their goal is to convince as many people as possible to apply, because this allows them to be more selective. They have a fixed number of interview slots. Therefore, if their applicant pool increases, their selectivity increases.

At these info sessions, firm representatives are there to answer questions. Most students, however, arrive at the info session with the sole purpose (or mission) of trying to impress recruiters and to be remembered. This is a mistake. Consultants can tell when someone is on a mission, and it generally turns them off. The info session is not the time to behave in an overly eager, unnatural manner, because the recruiters are not there specifically to recruit individuals at this phase.

In this phase, build rapport by asking thoughtful questions. This strategy is a win-win, because they get to erase any doubts in your mind about applying, and you start to build a relationship that may secure you a first-round interview. Just remember, while you are trying to be memorable, it shouldn't seem like your only purpose.

The info session is your chance to get a feel for your fit with the firm. Ask yourself – do I like these people? One time I went to an info session and tried to make small talk with the presenters before the presentation. Every attempt I made at conversation got sucked into a black hole of silence. After I sat down, it was clear to me they just wanted to talk to each other. The only thing that prevented me from walking out was my stubbornness to get a consulting job. Unsurprisingly, I didn't get an interview with them, nor did I particularly want an interview with them. If your experience interacting with a certain firm doesn't sit well with you, go with your gut and focus on other firms.

At an info session, get a feel for the company. Do they participate in many industries, or do they tend to focus on a few industries? Likewise, do they perform multiple types of projects, or do they tend to focus in a particular area, such as operations, due diligence, or implementations? How do the companies treat their employees – as people or as numbers? Carefully listen to the answers to help inform your perceived fit with the company. Asking a question for the purpose of asking a question will not get you far.

Do you believe the firm is a good fit for you? Given the number of info sessions that you will attend, you won't discover a great fit with all of the people at every firm. All consulting firms attract similar types of people, so pay attention to any differences that you perceive. These nuances are subtle, but a key element in determining your fit with a company.

What if you are already convinced that the firm is a good fit for you? Then, rationally, the firm has no incentive to talk to you. A recruiter's objective at a career fair or info session is to get you excited about the firm so that you apply. If you arrive at the event and excitedly announce that the firm is a perfect fit, then their job is already done. They will move on to the next person.

At info sessions, adopt the attitude that you're not sure if the firm is a good fit, and you're there to learn more. The mindset should be "Do I fit in here?" rather than "I know I'm applying, and I'm just here to rack up face time and/or get someone to remember me." Actively learning more will present you as a more genuine person. More importantly, the information you gather will help you write your cover letter and ace your interviews.

Format of an Info Session

The basic format of an info session is small talk in the beginning, and then firm representatives talk for 30-45 minutes. Afterwards, there's a chance to interact for about an hour. The goal for you is to establish a connection with at least one person, so that they will remember you as someone they would like to see again. If you make two or more connections like that, great!

Tips For Success

1. Arrive early to info sessions. This will offer a few quality minutes of one-on-one time before other students join the conversation, making it exponentially harder to establish a connection.

2. Don't touch the food or beverages. A bottle can distract attention from what you're saying as you're nervously unscrewing and re-screwing the lid, as I often did. Food not only ties up both hands, but it can get stuck in your teeth, or could land on the consultant's face. Food is a quick way to destroy a good conversation. However, if you really need the security of drinking a bottle of water, go for it.

3. What should you talk about? You should talk about two things: your questions and their experience, interests and background. Remember, you are trying to determine your fit and to establish connections. Do not talk about your experience up front. It's tempting to "stand out," but nothing is worse for a campus recruiter than an arrogant, blathering student who thinks they

are so awesome for being VP of something at a student group on campus. Rather, work in your experience naturally when it relates to the conversation, or if they ask directly for it.

4. People love talking about themselves. Ask questions to find out about that actual person with whom you're talking. Not only is it a more engaging conversation, you may even strike upon common ground from which a connection is born. Many students make the mistake of focusing too much on themselves in conversations with recruiters.

When the lights dim to start the session, ask for a business card from the person with whom you're speaking. Most likely, you will be talking with different people after the presentation. Carry paper and a pen, in case they forget to bring business cards. I was intrigued by how many consultants did not bring business cards going to an info session. Since the consultants are not there to recruit individuals (they are there to get students to apply), this happens more often than you'd think.

The presentation is followed by an especially frustrating period of time. Everyone is trying to engage the consultants in conversation. Commonly, 6-12 students are talking with one consultant. In the consulting world, they refer to these as "conversation circles." These are efficient ways for them to field student questions.

Feel free to join one, or feel free to leave – you're biding your time until the crowd dies down. Make sure you're back within 20-30 minutes, after the crowd has died down, but before the consultants pack up and leave. Alternatively, talk to other students who are eating and waiting to talk with firm representatives. This is a great way to meet other students with whom you can practice cases.

After many students have left, this is the time when you can finally engage in 1-on-1 conversations and ask your burning questions about the firm. You need to ask sincere questions and let your personality shine through. I had a friend who would stiffen up at info sessions, and not act like himself, much to his detriment. It's good to be professional, but be yourself at the same time.

If you're talking to someone and another student drops by, ask for the consultant's business card and scope out two consultants talking to each other, or the partner wandering around by himself, both of which happen frequently toward the end of open discussion time.

After you meet with someone, write down a summary of what you talked about on the back of the card you asked for. What did you learn about the firm? What did you learn about them? What did you find interesting?

You could take this a step further and enter all names and information into an Excel sheet, along with a column regarding whether you have followed up or not. Even later in your professional career, it is always helpful to maintain an electronic network-tracking database. NOTE: A spreadsheet for doing so can be found at *www.college2consulting.com*.

Follow up with your new contacts within 24 hours. Thank them for their time, remind them of something you talked about, and express your excitement about the position discussed. Ask a question if there's something you're unclear about. As mentioned previously, don't ask them a question just to ask a question, and don't ask questions that can be found on their website, Vault – or worse – their presentation you attended. Remember to keep it as brief as possible. Being brief demonstrates a key ability of a consultant: the ability to summarize succinctly.

If you didn't connect with anyone, reflect back on the info session. Did you engage anyone in conversation? At every info session, I saw many students who would join circles of conversation with a consultant, but they never asked a question. Then, when someone excuses themselves and asks for a business card, many other people in the circle will obligatorily ask for business cards as well. How do you think a consultant feels when they get a "thank you" email from someone with whom they never spoke?

The Purpose of Info Sessions

By Grant Anderson, Diamond Consulting

The main point of an info session is lost on most job-seekers. While many people sit through the initial "info" part of the session, the real point is the networking opportunities at the end. Sure, it is useful to learn more about the firm's values and their approach to consulting, but selling the firm on your fit is what will get you both an interview and (hopefully) a job. Demonstrating fit is acknowledged as the easiest way to get an initial interview. Demonstrating that you fit well with a firm is a vital step toward an eventual offer.

My approach to info sessions changed because of this fact, moving more from the "why consulting" type questions to natural conversation. Natural conversation is what truly "sells" fit. Many of the job seekers who actually stay to network, do so poorly.

Very often, they simply sit there listening to consultants talk and nod quietly, leaving absolutely no impression on any of the firm's employees present. If they do talk, the students will often rattle through a list of questions, such as:

- What is your educational background?
- Can you tell me about a recent project?
- Why did you consider consulting?
- How's the travel?

These questions can be useful, but not by themselves. They must fit into a real conversation. When talking to your friends, you don't usually come in with a list of questions, rattle them off until you're finished, and then leave. This is what most job seekers try to do, and generally receive canned answers.

Did you think asking "What is your background?" was original? Surprise! No one will think you're even a real person if you pester them with scripted questions. These questions are only a tool to help you get into a conversation, and the conversation is truly the goal. You want to talk about interests (both yours and the consultant's) and work, but not in a canned way.

In one info session, I asked a consultant a mundane background question, but then moved on to discuss one of the consultant's recent projects. The consultant talked about the airline industry, and we talked for a while about various strategic problems in the industry, the new pricing system, etc. The conversation flowed naturally to our common major, math, and we talked about the pros and cons of the field. It wasn't canned, and I left the impression of being knowledgeable, enjoyable to talk to, and intelligent. These are people with whom you could work everyday, in a close team environment. You should show them that you are fun, or at least pleasant to be around, and that you are "client-ready," (i.e. you can have the same conversations with a VP or CEO of a client company).

If you get the chance, try talking with partners at as many info sessions as you can. They are usually a great example of polished talkers and consultants. If you make a good impression on a partner at an info session, their word is gold.

Bottom line: Lame questions will get you lame responses. Use them only to open the conversation and briskly move to more interesting and original topics, resulting in more enjoyable and productive info sessions for both you and the consultants with whom you're speaking.

Career Fair

A career fair is an exhausting endeavor for all parties involved. In the old days, these were primarily a chance to discover companies you liked. That may still be the case to some extent, but most students show up already knowing which companies they want to target. These students zero-in on the relevant booths, looking to make another connection.

To prepare, go to your career services website, and review the list of employers that will be at the career fair. Do some basic research on all the companies that interest you, and figure out which employers you want to target. Prioritize, because you won't have time to visit every single employer.

When researching your targeted firms, find the names of open positions, the nature of the work, the size of the firm, office locations, and interesting pieces of information. One experienced Human Resources specialist said that she was always most impressed with candidates who knew a nugget of information that most people did not know. It demonstrated the candidate's interest in the firm, and provided a more credible understanding of the candidate's fit with the company.

When I say nugget of information, I'm not talking about something archaic, such as the company's explosive growth during the 1970s. Instead, you could mention the fact that a company such as Deloitte will develop the strategy and also implement the strategy, instead of strategizing and leaving the implementation to somebody else. Be careful not to take this to an extreme, but do try to find something you found interesting about the work they do.

How do you know when you have found such a nugget? Mention it to a friend who is interested in the same firm. If you get the surprised and intrigued reaction from them, you've hit gold, so to speak.

Career Fair Tips

- Print out your resume on regular paper, because the ink may smear with nicer paper. A friend of mine printed his resumes on nice paper, but the paper was so thick and soft that the ink could not dry. At the career fair, he put his resume into one company's pile, and went to talk to some people from the firm. When he walked by later, after some more students had put their resumes on top of his, he noticed a corner of his resume was jutting out, and saw the ink had completely smeared.

- Print two resumes per targeted company, and then a few extra. In this day and age, some firms won't ask you for your resume, and they will encourage you to submit your resume online. Most companies will accept your resume with the purpose of writing their impressions of you on the back. For example, a consultant told me that her firm writes a code on the resume to signal if that person is a definite interview, maybe, or no.

- Arrive early. It won't be long before the place is overwhelmed with students. You should receive some map of where the companies are all located. Quickly map out the locations of your target companies, and get hustling! I'd recommend going to the more popular firms first, before the waves of other students arrive. If a firm on your route has a ton of students standing in line, go to the next – you can always come back.

- When you speak with a firm, express interest in something unique about that particular firm (i.e. a nugget of information). I'm convinced that I got an interview at a smaller consulting firm only because I connected with the manager at the booth. How did I connect? I expressed excitement and interest in their specialty, not salary/benefits/travel/employee programs, or whatever else is "me-me-me."

Here's an amusing anecdote about trying to be remembered at a career fair: I was talking with a recruiter at a major consulting firm. Another student arrived, and patiently waited for our conversation to end. As a sharing, inclusive individual, I asked her, "Would you like to ask a question?" She said "Oh no, I'll wait until you're finished." And since I thought she was being polite, I insist that she asked her question, assuming we'd take turns.

Instead, she launched into a two-minute elevator pitch. Sparing the details, she basically talked about every activity she was ever involved with on campus. She then proceeded to thinly veil her motivation by asking at the end, "Do you think someone with my experience could apply to your firm?" The recruiter's reaction was simply to say, "Yes, you can apply." This reaction was not at all what the candidate was anticipating!

Moral of the story: At a career fair, long-winded elevator pitches may work on smaller firms, but recruiters at top firms don't care. They've heard this impressive song-and-dance from 200 other extremely qualified applicants.

The question, "Do you think someone with my experience could apply to your firm?" is vapid and unimpressive. Surely, this candidate visited each and every consulting booth at the career fair and regurgitated the same thing. Instead, arrive with a question that demonstrates an understanding of their company, specifically. If you show genuine interest in their company, and if you ask a thoughtful question specific to their company, you have a better chance of being remembered.

To determine a thoughtful question or two, visit company websites and gain an understanding between the nuances of each company. Also, read articles about the current events pertaining to these companies.

As mentioned earlier, your goal at a career fair is to ask questions, listen, and determine whether or not the 'fit' is good. If you are able, be sure to use a 'nugget' to stand out. This can improve your chances in securing an interview.

Stand Out with Memorable Questions

Time with recruiters is limited at career fairs. As such, it is extremely difficult to make a lasting impression. Put yourself in a recruiter's shoes. If you meet a hundred people, who stands out? Sometimes it can be trivial such as a unique shirt or a funny joke. Unfortunately, at a career fair, remaining professional is a must. Trying to stand out is a challenge because being too aggressive or too outgoing can be a negative in some recruiters' minds. Always be careful with jokes in a professional setting; what may be funny to you may not be funny to someone else. While remaining professional, let your personality shine and showcase your intellect.

One great way to do this is to ask memorable questions. Asking memorable questions is a way to show your personality through conversation with the recruiter while also illustrating how intelligent you are.

Here are some sample questions:

- I've heard that your M&A due diligence business has been doing quite well. This sounds like something I would be interested in. What role do new analysts typically have on a diligence team? (good)

- In what cities are your firm's offices located? (bad – find this out on the website)

- I'm interested in strategy consulting for the problem solving and client interaction aspects. I hear your firm gives analysts a lot of opportunities to contribute during client briefings, which is definitely important to me. Can you describe what a typical client briefing would entail in terms of how each of the team members contributes? (good)

- What are the hours like at your firm? (bad – ask after you get the offer)

- Last semester, I was captain of a club soccer team, was the president of the consulting club, got straight A's, and even volunteered every Saturday at a homeless shelter. What leadership roles are given to new analysts? (bad – the recruiter will see right through your thinly veiled elevator pitch)

- I try to seek out leadership roles in whatever I do. For example, I am the president of the consulting club and grew membership from 10 members to 40 members. I know as a new hire, I won't be managing projects, but what types of leadership opportunities are there for first and second year associates? (good)

- What type of consulting do you do? I mean like strategy or IT or operations? (bad – find this out on website)

- I've been doing some research on your transportation and logistics practice. This is an area that has always been interesting to me. I haven't been able to find many specifics on this practice area in particular. Can you help me understand a bit more about the types of work that you do for the transportation and logistics clients? (good)

- What don't you like about your job? (bad – no one currently employed will want to answer this)

- How long have you worked at your firm? What has been your most favorite client project so far? (good)

- I read that your firm entered the aviation industry in 1975. What led the management to make this decision? (bad – obscure subject matter that is irrelevant to recruitment)

- What's your minimum GPA requirement? (bad!)

Get the picture? A great question does not guarantee that the recruiter will remember you, but it will definitely help your chances.

Submitting Your Application

You've met every firm, shaken a lot of hands and learned a lot. Now it's time to apply, and the power will begin to lie entirely with the firms.

All firms want some combination of resume, cover letter and transcript, with some requiring all three. Every firm requires a resume, most firms require a transcript, and many (but not all) request a cover letter. Requests for writing samples or letters of recommendation are less common.

Quick Tip

You may need to apply to each firm in two places – through your university's career services and through the firm's website.

Punctuality and organization are key. When you're applying to dozens of firms, it can be easy to miss one while scrambling to meet everyone's deadlines. If you miss the deadline, there's nearly a zero percent chance you will get an interview. It creates more work for them to evaluate your application separate from the batch, and why would they want to interview someone who is irresponsible enough to miss an important deadline? Use a spreadsheet to track deadlines and submission due dates to ensure that you apply to these firms before their deadline.

A spreadsheet for tracking deadline and submission due dates can be found at *www.college2consulting.com*.

15
Preparing for Recruitment

For targeted schools, the internship process and full-time process are almost identical. There are two main differences. First of all, more firms recruit for full-time positions. Second, internship and full-time recruitment processes take place at different times during the year. Internship recruitment typically takes place in late January through late February. Recruitment for full-time positions typically starts during the first week of classes and continues for the next six weeks or so.

This chapter includes two recruitment preparation timelines: a "normal" plan if you have at least 3 months to prepare, and an "emergency" plan if recruitment is impending with fewer than 4 weeks to go. If your personal timeline is between these two plans, feel free to combine elements of the two.

If your school is not targeted, be sure to apply online during the active recruitment period. If you are unsure when a firm's particular recruitment timeline and due dates are, just call or e-mail that firm's HR department.

Recruitment timeframes for full-time and internships are as follows:

Full-Time – September to early November

Internship – January to late February

Why Start Now?

If you have time on your side, congrats for preparing early! As I tell my students in the *College2Consulting* classes, consulting recruitment is not like cramming for a test. It's much more like learning to play a sport or an instrument.

For example, I was a swimmer from the age of 8 up until I started college. The first thing you need to learn as a swimmer, no matter what age, is how to stay afloat in the water. If you read in a textbook, "Move your arms and kick your legs," do you think you'd immediately float when you jumped in the water? No, because depending on how exactly you move your arms and legs through the water directly impacts how well you float, and that is developed through practice. If you've ever seen a person who hasn't learned to swim, who accidentally ended up in the deep end of a pool, they move their arms and legs a lot, but still sink in the water.

Eventually, through practice, you learn how to stay afloat. Later on, it becomes habit: you don't even have to think about how to stay afloat. Then, you learn how to move forward through the water. Eventually when that becomes habit, you can move onto learning advanced techniques that help you move faster through the water.

In sum, advanced habits build on basic habits, and each level takes time to master. To differentiate yourself during consulting recruitment, you need to develop top-tier habits to drive your performance in every interaction with consulting firms. But habits arise only with practice: they aren't learned in a few days. Those who attempt to "cram" end up much like the drowning people I mentioned earlier. They have learned lots of facts on how to do well, but they haven't practiced enough to develop good habits. As a result, everything falls apart when a stressful situation arises.

Top Tier Habits

What are these "top-tier" habits? While this book covers all of the habits in-depth, here are a few examples:

- Structuring – Structuring is the art of categorizing things. Structuring is important because it makes it clear how the various elements are related to each other. For example, if you asked me what kind of computer you should buy, I could structure my answer by first looking at desktop computers, then laptops. All the discussion within desktop computers will be about desktops, and all the discussion within laptops will be about laptops. Wouldn't it confuse you if I started talking about the lower price of desktop computers while I'm talking about the portability of laptops? The more you can structure your communications and analysis during a case interview, the easier an interviewer can follow you.

- Labeling Everything – When I taught a class on how to get a job in consulting, one of the most common ways students shot themselves in the foot was not carefully labeling numbers provided in a case interview. For instance, let's say that fixed costs are $20,000/month for a business. Many times, particularly after some time has passed and they're referring back to their notes, they will assume that I said "$20,000/year."

- Not Trying To Impress – Lots of students will give "elevator pitches" at the info session or career fair, which honestly is the last thing a consultant wants to hear. They've been working crazy hours, they have a lot of work to do after the recruitment session, and they just want to have some interesting conversation and brag about their firm a little bit (please forgive them, they are human). The worst buzz kill for a recruiter is a student bragging about their "awesome" experience, because even if the student is unique, the student is still bragging about themselves.

In my experience, people (including consultants) are far more interested in bragging about themselves, so when in doubt, let the recruiter do the talking. However, there's no problem sharing interesting bits about yourself. Your experiences often make for great conversation if shared in moderation, so be sure to find a balance.

All of these are habits take practice to develop. You may do some of these naturally already, but if you don't, then I guarantee you won't do it perfectly the first time you try. You need to practice and integrate the habit.

Normal Recruitment Preparation Timeline

In order to develop these habits, you need to tackle all aspects of the consulting recruitment process. Read through this timeline to get a big picture sense of what you need to do, then read through the later chapters for the context on why these items are important.

3+ Months Out

1. Read through this book.

2. Send out emails to friends looking for people who are interested in practicing cases with you. Join student groups pertaining to consulting and meet peers interested in practicing cases.

3. Conduct research on firms to figure out which ones you like most.

4. Begin practicing cases – I would aim for 4 cases every week (2 sessions x 2 cases per session).

5. Every day, read two *Wall Street Journal* articles (*The New York Times*, *Forbes* magazine, and *The Economist* would be fine as well). For each article, identify the main business issue, and spend 15 minutes on each, developing an issue tree of how you'd approach the case if it were a case interview. Discuss both articles with your case buddy, and see what other areas they would have considered. You're striving to learn to structure things in a

MECE way (Mutually Exclusive, Collectively Exhaustive – See Chapter 17).

6. Answer behavioral questions found in Chapter 18. Focus on providing concrete examples that illustrate your accomplishments, your role on teams, your leadership ability and your analytical ability. Write out answers to those questions.

7. Reach out to one or two people in industry (see Chapter 8), and schedule a lunch with them. Not only can you ask them to look at your resume, but also they can offer feedback on your case interview performance.

8. Create space on your resume for your summer experience, and think through what sort of "results" you want to show.

2 Months Out

1. Continue practicing cases, reading *The Wall Street Journal* and/or other articles, practicing behavioral questions, researching various consulting firms, and meeting with professionals at firms in which you're most interested.

2. Update your resume.

Final Month

1. Continue practicing cases, reading *The Wall Street Journal* and/or other articles, practice behavioral questions, and research various consulting firms.

   By now, you should be very comfortable with cases, feel like you have a broad base of business stories to draw on, and have several key succinct stories you can fit to most behavioral questions.

2. Wrap up any informational interviews that you intend to fit in – have you spoken with at least one person from each of your favorite firms?

3. Write out your cover letters, based on all of the secondary research and informational interviews that you have had to-date.

4. Finalize your resume.

Help! I Only Have One Month Until Consulting Recruitment!

So far, this chapter targeted people who have time on their side. But what if you don't? What if you just found out about consulting, or have procrastinated? What are the most critical things to do?

Practicing cases is the most critical thing you can do. You need to achieve both depth of experience with cases (i.e., practice a lot), while also practicing from a variety of sources (e.g., *The Wall Street Journal*, along with stories and cases from Part 4). It is equally important to articulate and define your fit with firms, too. As a BCG associate pointed out, the interview includes multiple cases to "ensure that you have consistent performance; once they see that, it's all about fit." Aside from case interview preparation, make sure to spend time finalizing a rock star resume and getting to know the consulting firms.

The One-Month Emergency Action Plan

Week 1

1. Read through this book.

2. Send out emails to friends and/or consulting student groups looking for people who are interested in practicing cases with you.

3. Answer behavioral questions found in Chapter 18. Focus on providing concrete examples that illustrate your accomplishments, your role on teams, your leadership ability and your analytical ability. Write out answers to those questions.

4. If time allows, reach out to one or two people in industry (see

Chapter 8). Try to get at least one lunch scheduled for Week 3 or Week 4, after you've practiced cases. Not only can you ask them to look at your resume, but having that deadline will also help you stay motivated to rapidly improve your case analysis abilities.

Week 2

1. Practice two cases per day with friends. Practice at least three "market estimation" questions sometime during this week.

2. Every day, read two *Wall Street Journal* articles. For each article, identify the main business issue, and spend 15 minutes on each, developing an issue tree of how you'd approach the case if it were a case interview. Discuss both articles with your case buddy, and see what other areas they would have considered. You're striving to learn to structure things in a MECE way (Mutually Exclusive, Collectively Exhaustive).

3. Practice answering one different behavioral question per day, either in front of a mirror or have a friend ask you.

Week 3

1. Practice at least one case per day from Part 4. Once those cases are exhausted, take cases from other sources. Alternatively, have a friend make up one based on recent business news stories. For example, I made up a case based on Redbox entering the DVD rental market – what should Netflix do in response?

2. Keep up parts (2) and (3) from Week 2.

Week 4

1. Repeat parts (1) and (2) from Week 3.

2. Meet with someone from industry. Ask about the company, their experience, and whether they can give you a case or provide feedback on your resume. It's vitally important to have someone review your resume before things get too serious. It's also important to get a professional opinion on your current case-cracking ability.

If you follow this plan, you will have achieved the following milestones before recruitment:

- 42 cases (3 weeks x 2 a day)
- 42 *Wall Street Journal* articles (3 weeks x 2 a day)
- 21 behavioral interview questions (3 weeks x 1 a day)
- 1 meeting with someone in a management consulting firm
- 1 review of your resume

This should give you a solid base of business and case experience from which to draw upon during interviews. Continue practicing throughout the next few weeks during recruitment, but the big push is over. At this point, you should be comfortable with cases, you should be able to "invent" a framework to suit the case (rather than blindly applying a standard one), and you should have received professional feedback.

Interview With a Rock Star: Questions for the Candidate Who Got Three Offers in Fall 2008, One of the Worst Recruiting Seasons of All Time

Q: How/when did you decide to go into consulting?

A: After sophomore year, I did an internship at Target, working in an internal consulting department. That following fall, I worked at a PE firm in Paris in fall. I wanted to try working internationally and to see what finance was like.

In the winter, my mind was made up to enter consulting. When applying for internships with consulting firms, I didn't receive any interviews except with Monitor. So ultimately I accepted a job at a fund of funds* for the summer, because I wanted to show some kind of experience in fall. It looks strange if you don't do anything during the summer before full-time recruitment.

I then participated in AT Kearney and Accenture case competitions in the spring.

Over the summer, I kept busy by preparing myself for the fall. I spent much of the summer networking and meeting people from various consulting firms for lunch. I wasn't meeting the recruiters; I was meeting the people on the "front line," so to speak. I also went out with interns in these firms to get an even more realistic perspective on what the firm would be like for me, as the work they're doing would be very similar to the type of work I'd be doing.

I also began prepping for cases. I wanted to develop a good business mind to intelligently discuss issues without leaning on [canned] frameworks. I believe success in a case interview would not be memorizing frameworks, any frameworks. Instead, I felt success would come from being comfortable and knowing you're going to do well. I wanted to get to the point where I could be given a case and always be able to have an intellectual discussion.

To accomplish this, I:

- Read *Wall Street Journal* 4x a week online

- Read *Business Week* every other week

- Read business books, such as *Good to Great*

- Read articles on consulting firm websites. This was especially helpful, because sometimes I interviewed with the author of the article.

When I got back to campus in the fall, I spent a lot of time practicing cases with whomever was interested. I did one to two cases per night. I was able to practice so many because whenever anyone asked me to do a case, I made myself available.

In the end, all that reading paid off. When an interviewer asked me about one of my experiences, I didn't talk so much about "I did this and that." Rather, I looked back at my experience, and applied the ideas I had recently learned. I would begin talking about how Target might improve its supply chain, since that was the area I had studied. The interviewer would sense my interest, and would start to discuss bigger-picture issues with Target. And sometimes, the interviewer would skip the case all together!

*A *"fund of funds"* is a mutual fund that invests in other mutual funds rather than stocks or other investments.*

PART 3:
THE INTERVIEW
PROCESS

The field of management consulting has developed a unique and rigorous interview process. Part 3 reviews what to expect during the interview process and how to excel in both case and fit interviews. The case interview examines your analytical ability, professionalism and business sense. The fit interview determines how your background and capabilities fit with the firm. There are typically two rounds of interviews, and each consulting firm distributes the two types of interviews differently within each round. Fit interviews require almost as much preparation as case interviews, because you have to take the time to examine all of your experiences in the context of management consulting and what characteristics of a firm you value most.

After two rounds of interviews – that is, if you make it that far – you will hear back from the firms.

16

Introduction to Fit and Case Interviews

You've submitted all of your applications on time, and now you wait to see where you're invited to interview. This would be an excellent time to continue to practice your cases and behavioral questions.

If you are invited to a first-round interview, that means you look good on paper. Now is your chance to impress them in person. First-round interviews are mostly a weed-out round. They observe whether you are personable and whether you have the skill to handle a case. If you've been practicing cases without running and screaming into the closet, you should stand a strong chance here.

There are two types of management consulting interviews: fit and case interviews. Fit interviews determine how well you fit within the company. Fit interviews assess your past experience, your personality, your level of professionalism and other factors by engaging in small talk. The interviewer will ask behavioral questions, and at the end, let you ask questions in return.

Case interviews, on the other hand, are a chance for consulting firms to assess how you think and solve problems. In a case interview, recruiters attempt to simulate your future job; however, in a normal situation, a team of consultants would have many weeks or months to generate recommendations. Instead, you must produce recommendations of your own within 30 minutes. Sounds intense, right? But don't worry; recruiters are able to do this because they keep the discussion at a very high level. They also have data available should you ask for it.

The key thing recruiters look for is your ability to structure an approach to a task, dig into it, and then draw conclusions from your findings. Anyone can be trained to find data, but not everyone can structure an efficient approach to a task. Not everyone can draw meaningful and insightful conclusions from the data they find.

At an extremely high level, firms are attempting to evaluate a candidate's ability and potential to be a good consultant in the case interview. The thought process is as follows: *If I give this individual a task, can he develop an efficient approach to breaking it down? Can he chase after the data until he finds what he needs? Can he overcome the inevitable roadblocks encountered while chasing the data? Can he synthesize what he has learned into a concise and meaningful result?*

It's important to practice a lot of cases to develop familiarity with them. You must also develop a broad business acumen. However, it can be detrimental to practice too many cases, because you need to also prepare for the fit portion of the interviewing process. The fit interview is just as important as the case interview portion. Firms need smart problem solvers, but if the candidate is difficult to work with, they're not as valuable to a company.

Interview Scheduling

Once you find out where you've been invited to interview, then you will probably have a choice of when to interview. The most important consideration is when you can perform at your best. Here are a few ideas to think about to help you achieve that:

First in the morning – When people are asked to memorize lists of nonsensical words, the primacy effect dictates they'll remember items at the beginning of the list as opposed to the middle. As such, the primacy effect suggests that it is more likely for the interviewer to remember you. While the difference between nonsensical words and people is debatable, one clear disadvantage of this time is that the interviewer will be comparing you to an absolute standard rather than a relative standard. The interviewer may not know how hard the case is if he hasn't tested it out, or he may be unfamiliar with the case if someone else prepared it for him. So you're the guinea pig, at the possible expense of your performance, but you are likely to be remembered.

Middle of the morning – Here, the interviewer is awake, and starting to figure out how students are performing, so he can begin to make relative comparisons instead of absolute comparisons. While the recruiters usually have score sheets, humans are still much better at relative comparisons than absolute. For example, suppose a football team scores 50 points. That sounds pretty good, until you hear the other team scored 52 points!

If you're a "morning person," snagging a time slot in here may be good. For me, 10am was my favorite morning slot time: all the kinks have probably been worked out from the interview process, and the interviewers aren't ready for lunch yet.

Last before lunch – I believe this is the worst interview slot. You have a firm time for the interview to end (lunch), and if any interviews before yours ran over, then yours will start that much later. Given less time to interview, combined with the fact the interview is thinking about lunch, means you would have to do a fantastic job to make an impression here. That said, it may have the benefit of the recency effect, or people remembering the most recent item on the list, because interviewers have time to digest your interview while they digest their food.

First after lunch – This is widely believed to be a terrible time for an interview, as the interviewer is full from lunch and falling into a food coma. Conversely, it is also thought that you have some primacy effect working in your favor. Interviewers may decide over lunch whom they like from the morning session. Therefore, you're the first in the "afternoon list." Also, some people believe that the interviewer is energized from relaxing over lunch, and he is at full attention.

Middle of afternoon – Supposedly this is when people get their afternoon work done, and have recovered from a lunch food coma. Personally, I tend to be more lethargic in the afternoon than the morning. This wouldn't be a good time for me, but maybe it would be for you!

Last in the day – This was my preferred time slot for two reasons. One, it has the benefit of the recency effect, or people remembering the most recent item on the list. Second, and more importantly, this is the only interview slot where the interviewer doesn't have a firm time limit. If the interview is going well, then you two can keep chatting. My latter first-round L.E.K. interview, which was originally scheduled for a half hour, lasted a full hour, because we lost track of time talking about the interviewer's PhD research experience. However, there are some people who believe that, by this point, the interviewer has made up his mind about whom to pass on. This can be true in some cases. However, it depends on the interview.

When all is said and done, there is no optimal time for everyone because you have no control over your interviewers and how they're feeling or acting that day. More important than anything, identify the time when you can give your strongest performance.

17
The Case Interview

What is a Case Interview?

The case interview is a type of interview used by (almost) every management consulting firm. Essentially, they are giving you a test run working as a consultant. Consulting firms will tend to use real projects they worked on to create a case study. However, firms may use a standardized case across interviewers, or borrow a case from someone else in a pinch. Regardless of whether the interviewer uses a case they worked on or not, the case is a way to show candidates a representative project. The case is a more accurate judge of whether a candidate can actually do the work that will eventually be asked of them.

In the real-world, cases can take a few weeks up to many months. For a case interview, consulting firms distill a case into a format that can analyzed in 30 to 45 minutes.

Since the case has been condensed, the discussion is at a very high level, and a lot of the details are removed for simplicity. Case interviews do not allow for use of a spreadsheet or calculator. Instead, you will be asked to use mental math and pen and paper, and remember that time is critical. Pay attention to the time so that you can get through the case in the time allotted.

A Walkthrough of a Case Interview

The case interview will sometimes begin with a little small talk. Often times, the interviewer jumps right into the case by reading you the description. Here, you should be jotting down the facts of the case as your interviewer lists them.

Once the description has been read, paraphrase the facts back to the interviewer to illustrate your understanding of the case. However, don't parrot back every detail; it wastes time and fails to demonstrate your ability to summarize. Consider the following example:

> *Your client is a gum manufacturer and a market leader in sugar-free gum here in the U.S. But over the past year, with TV commercials aimed at young adults and teenagers, a less expensive gum manufactured in China has gained market share in several of your client's cities. The client wants to know how it should respond now to ensure its long-term market share is not significantly eroded by this new entrant.*

How would you paraphrase the case? Here's one possible example:

> *Great. So our client is a market leader in producing sugar free gum, but a Chinese competitor has begun to erode our client's market share. The client wants to know what they can do to protect their market share against further erosion, and I'm assuming that they want to know how they can grow their market share as well. Are there any other objectives I should know about?*

Notice the summary did not specifically mention that they are losing share in a key end market, nor did it mention the Chinese competitor is using TV commercials to win new business. These are important facts that you should note and they may play a crucial role during the case. However, they are not essential to understanding the overall objective, so you do not need to repeat these to verify your understanding.

Once you have verified the objective(s), write them down at the top of your paper. Throughout the case you must ensure that you're answering the objectives exactly. By putting the objective at the top of your note page, you may continually refer back to it.

If you don't understand any part of the case objective or description, ask any clarifying questions to help you understand the objective. For example, taking the example above, you may want to clarify if the client has any specific goal of increasing market share, such as a "5 percentage point improvement."

You can also ask questions around unfamiliar items. For example, if the case is about "a sputtering target manufacturer wanting to grow its business," you should definitely ask what a sputtering target is (it's a large metal disk that spins fast and "sputters" off small metal particles, forming a thin metal film on some other surface). Generally, cases given during case interviews involve industries or products that are familiar to the general population. That way, some candidates are not unfairly put at a disadvantage.

In addition to listening to the facts of the case, listen for anything the interviewer doesn't say. Use the omission of information to your advantage. For example, if a client wants to increase profits by entering a new market, they don't necessarily need to achieve a high market share in order to increase profits by a certain amount. If you state this assumption to the interviewer, your possible solution space increases. By making this assumption, you can also look at solutions that would increase profits without achieving a high market share. The singular assumption that high market share is the most profitable may not be correct. This is much harder than just focusing on the explicit objective(s) and it takes your solution a step further. Most students will not listen carefully enough to note information that was omitted.

Once you understand the objective, it's time to lay out your approach to solving the case. It's important to lay out your plan for tackling the case very early on, because this allows the interviewer to efficiently redirect you as required. If you don't lay out your plan until later, and just dive in, time will be wasted and there will be a higher time cost in redirecting you.

For example, suppose you work for a sandwich delivery shop, and you are making your first delivery. The delivery is far away, so the manager asks you to run your plan by him first. You say that you're going to take Street A for 2 miles, then Street B for another 2 miles.

He shakes his head and asks you to take Street C (a diagonal road) that will get you there much faster. You take Street C, and make the delivery in time.

Now, consider if the manager had not asked for your approach. You made the delivery, and the manager is angry because you took twice as long to deliver the sandwich as he expected. This now has delayed other deliveries and is causing delays. By that point, the damage is done, and it may be a while before he lets you take another long delivery.

Likewise, in an interview situation, a small difference in direction early on can destroy your chances as you deviate further and further from where the interviewer wanted you to go. An interviewer won't let you stray too far, but you will get dinged for needing to be redirected (because other interviewees got buy-in from the interviewer at the beginning).

Therefore in a case interview, you need to lay out a roadmap so you get the interviewer's buy-in as soon as possible: "I'm going to look at A, then B, then C to get to the answer. Is that the best way to structure such an approach?" In response to this question, the interviewer can provide useful, time-saving feedback.

As you practice case interviewing, you will hear about the importance of structuring ad nauseam, but what does that mean exactly? "Structuring" means organizing key components of the problem in an interrelated way. For example, suppose you are in the market for a dress shirt. You are deciding between shirts with 3 brands and 3 different colors. You could organize the data in the following way:

Red Brand A, Green Brand B, Yellow Brand C, Red Brand B, Yellow Brand A, Green Brand C, Green Brand A, Yellow Brand B

Now, have I listed all of the combinations? Which one(s) am I missing? How long did that take you to determine? Now consider the following list:

- Red
  - Brand A, Brand B, Brand C
- Yellow
  - Brand A, Brand C
- Green
  - Brand A, Brand B, Brand C

Now, have I listed all of the combinations? Which one(s) am I missing? How long did it take you to determine the answer? How much faster did you comprehend this list compared to the first list?

The reason that the second list took you less time to evaluate is because it was set up in a structured format. It was first organized by color, then by brand. By incorporating a similar approach in your interviews, it allows the interviewer to check your approach at each level (e.g., "Did he include all of the colors? Ok great. What about the brands for each one?")

You'll notice that this structure looks a little bit like a tree – each color is a branch, and each brand is a sub-branch. Draw out your tree on paper, so you can both remember it and show it to the interviewer.

Now, let's look at simple structuring example within the context of a case. Many interviewers will ask you to investigate declining profits. The basic issue tree for this type of problem is as follows:

In this simple example, the broad issue is profits. The two components that make up profits are revenues and costs. Two ways to increase revenues are by looking at price and volume, while two

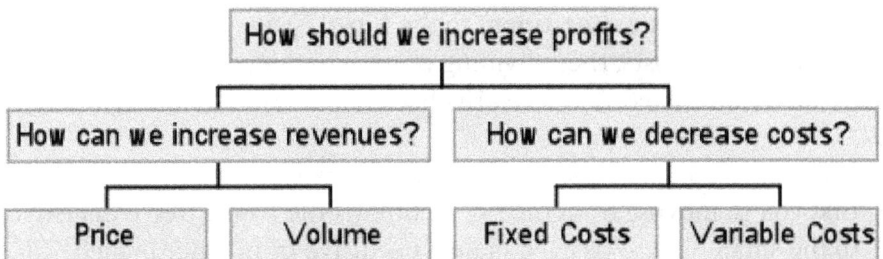

ways to decrease costs are to look at fixed and variable costs.

The interviewer can easily evaluate this approach:

Level 1 – Profits – Is the candidate answering the question? Yes

Level 2 – Revenue/Costs – Is the candidate examining all components of profits? Yes

Level 3 – Price/volume/fixed costs/variables costs – Is the candidate examining all components of revenue & costs? Yes

But it's not enough to simply structure your answer. You ultimately want to show you have a "MECE" structure. Consultants love this word; it stands for "Mutually Exclusive, Collectively Exhaustive." But what does that mean, exactly?

It simply means that you are considering all of the relevant areas (collectively exhaustive), and that no two areas overlap (mutually exclusive). The first check is important to make sure you sufficiently address the question at hand, and the second check is important to make sure you don't examine the same issue in two (or more) work streams.

Take the profit tree above: Is it MECE? Let's check:

Mutually Exclusive – Each branch of the tree should be completely exclusive of other branches. They should not overlap. Revenue is completely separate from costs, while price is separate from volume. Variable costs are separate from fixed costs. This tree is mutually exclusive.

Collectively Exhaustive – Together, the branches of the tree should examine all areas pertinent to the broad issue. Since profit = revenue – costs, then dividing profit into the components of revenue and costs is collectively exhaustive.

If it helps you remember, reverse the acronym to form CEME, so that you're moving from the big picture (is the whole tree exhaustive) to the small picture (is each branch exclusive from other branches?).

To me, it's easier to think about first determining that you've covered all areas first (collectively exhaustive), and then examine if there's an overlap in the way you've chosen to break it down (mutually exclusive).

In case interviews, the number one challenge that students encounter is a lack of structure. Structuring your questions allows you to zero in on the important points of the case and systematically eliminate unimportant areas. It also allows the interviewer to see how you approach a problem, and makes it easier for him to follow your logic throughout the case.

Let's now see what a structured roadmap looks like vs. a non-structured roadmap. The case question is: "Your client is Pepsi, and profitability is down 10% over the last year. Why and what can Pepsi do to improve profitability?"

Example A: Unstructured Ursula

> *Ursula:* "OK...well first I'd like to know about competition. Did Pepsi lose market share to Coke or other competitors?"

> *Interviewer:* "No"

> *Ursula:* "OK, that doesn't seem to be an issue, has Pepsi been losing customers?"

> *Interviewer:* "No"

> *Ursula:* "OK then, has the cost of materials increased?"

> *Interviewer:* "No, where are you going with this?"

Example B: Structured Sammy

> *Sammy:* "Can I take a minute?

Interviewer: "Yes"

Sammy: Spends 1 or 2 minutes developing a structure. "OK, I'd like to look at Pepsi's revenues and their costs. I've noticed they recently re-branded all their pops, so my hunch is that may have negatively affected their costs. However, I doubt it's the sole cause of such a large loss in profitability, and I don't believe I can adequately analyze costs until I look at revenues, so I'd like to start there, sound good?"

Interviewer: "Yes"

Which answer did you like better? The first answer is not terrible, but is very common for students who are not experienced with case interviews. Unstructured Ursula lacks an overall structure for questioning. She is raising good points and may have even identified the problem correctly as cost of materials rising. However, the questions are not tied together in a logical fashion. The interviewer cannot follow along, and very likely will ask a student where they are going (as they did in Example A).

Structured Sammy, on the other hand, develops a structure for questioning: revenues and costs. He set up the structure and communicated where he was going. As a result, the interviewer now knows that student is going to ask questions related to revenue.

You may also notice that in the second answer, Structured Sammy threw out his thoughts on where the problem may lie, even before digging in with questions. This is called hypothesizing, and is covered in Chapter 23. The student also turned the dialogue into an interaction by asking the interviewer if he thought the approach was good and demonstrated business acumen by weaving in a personal observation.

Additionally, he gut-checked those observations by thinking "Does it make sense that a re-branding would cause a 10% decline in profitability in a huge firm like Pepsi? No." Finally, he added a comment accordingly "I doubt it's the sole cause..." In short, this is an example of a solid opening to a case question.

So now you know to seek out all relevant areas to include in your structure, but how do you identify which areas to look at? You could memorize a bunch of frameworks from a book, but these help you only so much. There are just a few common sources of frameworks, and because most applicants memorize the same frameworks, they then cannot differentiate themselves.

True mastery is achieved when you invent your own frameworks. You do this by developing business acumen. Business acumen offers a base of experience to know what possibilities might matter (build a framework) and then to quickly determine what matters and what doesn't (trim it down to the most relevant areas). Chapter 9 overviews how to develop business acumen. Chapter 24 includes exercises for inventing unique frameworks.

So now that you are familiar with structuring, let's revisit the sugar-free gum manufacturer. You may say something like this:

> *So here is what I'm thinking of looking at. First, I'd like to examine whether there's some way to stop their importation. My gut feeling is that there is not, given the success of other Chinese imports, but I'd still like to briefly look into it. Second, I'd like to look at ways to gain market share by benchmarking our company versus theirs – What do our cost structures look like? How much do our product lines overlap? What customer segments are served by these product lines? How do we market? Finally, I'd like to look at other competitors and future customer trends to help inform a market share growth strategy – why did this competitor recently enter the marketplace? Are more Chinese competitors likely to enter? How many other significant competitors are there? What advantages or disadvantages do they have relative to us? Are there any that have recently gained share? How are consumers' tastes for sugar-free gum expected to evolve over the next few years?*
>
> *Is there anything else I should focus on?*

You'll notice that this answer includes many rhetorical questions. These help sell your approach, particularly if you use a more innovative framework, by giving the interviewer a sense of the questions you'll soon be asking.

For example:

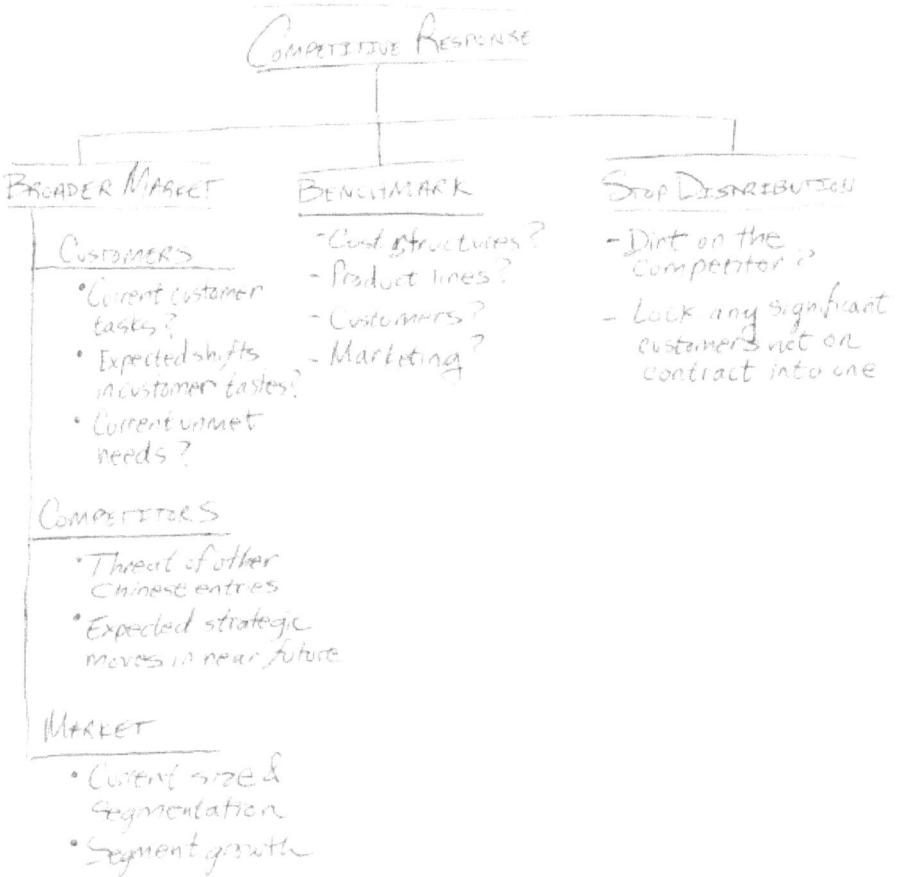

Take some time to show the logic of your framework. Draw out your approach on a piece of paper as a tree, then list each key question below in shorthand so you can remember.

Don't panic – you do not need to create that entire structure in 10 seconds. Rather, when you are ready to develop a structure, ask the interviewer for a minute or two. This is your chance to take a first crack at what to look at. If you do not have a structure in a minute (two at most), discuss with the interviewer what you have so far, and what else you're considering. They are usually very willing to help you with the occasional small roadblock. Contrary to popular belief, you do not need to be perfect (though perfection is always a bonus).

You could have outlined the case differently and asked different questions – this is just one possible structure. The important thing is that the framework represents everything that you think is important to look at, and your interviewer agrees that you are not missing any key issues. The fast track to rejection is to include only very obvious issues, while neglecting other issues. This is not to say that you need to think of 100 things to look at, but you don't want to only hit 1 of 3-4 key issues an interviewer is thinking about.

This is where practice comes in. Remember to read *The Wall Street Journal* and think about the key issues you'd look at. That is how you practice your structuring – looking at lots of different problems and identifying issues that will drive the answer.

When you practice, identify a key issue, make sure you ask yourself why it is a key issue. For example, in the sample structure, consider the expected shift in customer tastes. This could impact the answer because it may provide opportunities to capture share. If we assume that consumers of sugar-free gum are watching their sugar intake, do they also watch their preservative intake? A preservative and sugar-free gum may then be more attractive to these customers than regular sugar-free gum, and it may provide an opportunity if the current or future percentage of customers who watch both sugar and preservative intake is large enough. In addition, some consumers who don't care about sugar-free may be attracted by the preservative-free content.

At this point, you may be curious as to how many clarifying questions are you allowed to ask before the interviewer expects to see a structure or roadmap. Limit clarifying questions solely towards helping you understand the facts given to you and not additional facts, such as who the competitors and customers are, market sizes, etc. Consultants typically want to see a structure right away to get a sense of your overall plan and how your individual questions will help drive in that direction. So once you draw out your structure, you can swing your paper around to the interviewer and quickly walk them through the framework. Consultants are visual people – showing them your structure can increase their confidence in you to solve the case.

Now you proceed through your road map. Ask questions, and then draw conclusions from the answers. For example, suppose your client is growing slowly, at 1% per year. You ask what the industry growth rate is where the client participates, and the answer is "10%." You then may say "Ok, so we know that the client's slow growth rate is not an industry-wide problem."

Thinking aloud creates interaction with the interviewer and allows them to evaluate your thought process. One of the worst things you can do is be silent for long periods of time, unless you asked for a minute to think. The interviewer can help guide you if you're stuck, but only if you're thinking aloud and engaging. Otherwise, there is no way for the interviewer to tell if you're going down a good path or not.

You may get slides during the case, showing a graph or table. One consultant from Bain & Company, the firm most reliant on slides during cases, recommended that you describe what you see, and what key impact(s) the slide has on the objective.

For example, if your objective is to increase profits, and the slide shows the company is experiencing increasing costs, you might say that reining in these costs may increase profits. Another example: If the slide shows product volume over time, broken out by product, and volume from one product has decreased, you might ask about the gross margin on that product relative to other products. If it has a higher margin, you might state that product mix shift to products with lower gross margins have lowered overall profit. One way to increase profits in this case is to increase share of the higher gross margin products.

Sometimes, the data just might not be there for you to proceed with your case. If that's the case, don't be afraid to make assumptions to push forward, because the interviewer will tell you if you're going off track. For example, in the sugar-free gum case, suppose you asked for expected shifts in consumer tastes over the next 2-3 years, and the interviewer says they don't have that data. You can then say something like "Ok, then I'll assume that there are no significant shifts anticipated in customer tastes over the next 2-3 years."

Once you have determined the root cause(s) of the issue presented by the interviewer, it is time to think through a recommendation. This is where the joy of being a consulting comes in. Creating recommendations is what makes being a consultant so rewarding. Consultants have huge influence over the direction, and ultimately the success and failure, of the world's most successful businesses. As such, developing a thoughtful and creative recommendation during a case interview is vital. Use as much of the information provided in the case thus far and incorporate that into a comprehensive recommendation. It is okay if the recommendation is multi-faceted, but if a single solution can address multiple problems, even better.

Creating recommendations is another area where business acumen and all those *Wall Street Journal* articles will come in handy. Benchmarking a recommendation based on the experience of another company that you are familiar with really impresses recruiters.

For example, suppose your client is experiencing declining profits, and your recommendation is that they should focus on their core area. You might think of how Sega was losing profits in the early 2000's when they were making game consoles, but then focused on developing games for other platforms and returned to profitability in 2003. By weaving this story as an illustration of your recommendation, it will only serve to support your recommendations.

Finally, once you have reached an answer (or you've run out of time), you will need to summarize your case. Pretend your client's CEO just walked in, and wants the answer. Don't bore him or her with the details; rather you might touch on a few of the following areas:

- What was the objective?

- What areas did you look at?

- What was the root cause(s)? What insight(s) led to the discovery of the root cause(s)?

- What was your recommended solution(s) to fix that root cause(s)?

Ask for a moment to gather your thoughts on the summary if you need it. Like a GMAT score in the business school admissions process, a great summary won't guarantee you advancing, but a poor summary could sink your candidacy. Make it count!

What if You Run out of Time?

What if you run out of time during a case interview!?

If you only have 2-3 minutes left in the case interview, and you are not finished with the case, the interviewer will most certainly ask you to stop and summarize your findings. The summary is a vital component of the case study because it shows the interviewer that you can synthesize a business problem into a logical story. If you didn't have enough time to finish the case, don't panic. You can still impress the interviewer by presenting a logical story. Be sure to include a comment on 'next steps' though. You can say something like:

"Although we have yet to determine the root cause of X, my hypothesis is Y. To prove this hypothesis I would research Z."

or

"As a next step in a project such as this, I would be sure to follow up to learn more about X. This information could serve as a helpful input in solving problem Y because of Z."

If the interviewer does NOT stop you, make sure to proactively ask whether you should continue analyzing or stop and summarize. I had a friend whose interviewer lost track of time, and the interview lasted 45 minutes before the interviewer realized the time. He got angry that he was now late for the rest of the day, and blamed my friend for not keeping track of time. You do not want to find yourself in that situation, so always bring a watch and keep track of the time, regardless of whether the interviewer says they'll keep track of time or not.

What Interviewers Look for in Candidates During the Case Interview

Case interviewers tend to look for the same characteristics in candidates – either consciously or subconsciously. If you get the chance, ask a case interviewer what they look for during the case interview. Most likely, they will rattle off a list of traits almost exactly like the one below. The goal is to be 'excellent' at all of these traits, not just average.

"Through interviewing many students at different schools for our entry-level positions, I've noticed that there are certain major traits that consistently separate excellent candidates from average candidates."

-L.E.K. Consulting recruiter*

Excellent Candidates	Average Candidates
Clearly articulates thoughts, findings, and conclusions throughout the case interview	Thoughts are not communicated clearly to the interviewer
Structures insightful ideas to probe on and communicates these thoughts to the interviewer prior to jumping into case	Provides limited organization or structure to their thoughts; or, jumps right into solving the case
Listens to and responds to cues and hints from interviewer	Misses interviewer's cues or relies too heavily on interviewer for hints
Shows comfort with quantitative tasks and basic financials	Fumbles with numbers or does not have basic understanding of financials
Controls nerves	Allows nerves to affect their communication
Shows their personality during the interview	Case-solving robot; does not let their personality show

Take a minute to think about which boxes you identify with right now. For those in the "Average" category, how could you improve? Here are a few top case-cracking tips, to help you move from the "Average" to "Excellent" category:

- Thinking aloud – Be transparent in your thinking. By thinking aloud, you're giving the interviewer a chance to evaluate the logic of your thinking, which is a key consideration. It's also good to throw out your reactions to things you see. For example, if you see a graph where revenue is going down, don't just say "Hm, revenue is going down." Hypothesize why that may be. Say "Revenue appears to be going down – I'm thinking that could be because fewer people are buying widgets, or our price has been going down." It may sound painfully obvious sometimes, but it's important to say all of these logical conclusions out loud, so when you reach your final answer, the interviewer was able to follow your logic all the way through.

- Thinking aloud – Be willing to take a risk and take a position. Sometimes people are afraid to say what they believe, for fear that the interviewer will shoot them down. That can be an unneeded stressor in an already stressful environment. But by not taking a position, you're not giving the interviewer the chance to evaluate your ability to synthesize and draw conclusions.

  Basically, it's akin to if you were in a fit interview, to say "pass" to a question you didn't know the answer to. You wouldn't do that, because that's an obvious ding right? Same thing in case interviews – you need to hypothesize, draw conclusions, and in the end, come up with a recommendation for the client. But be sure to mention the considerations – no answer is ever 100% clear-cut!

- Leveraging a structure – Take your time when asked the question to formulate your response. The number one mistake that students make is diving right into the question, eager to provide an answer. It's far more beneficial to consider your approach, to think of all of the key possibilities you'll want to look at.

- Comfort with numbers – Keep numbers round and easy to manipulate. Often times candidates are tempted to maintain exactness in numbers, in order to get to a more "right" answer. But the interviewer honestly doesn't care whether the answer is 47 or 48 – they care more about a logical answer that you can defend.

The danger in using exact numbers is that it may cripple your ability to get to any answer because too much time is spend on multiplying 9 *113, when you could have chosen numbers such as 10*100. Think about it from a client's perspective. A client's ultimate decision probably won't sway if the market size is 1000 units vs. 1017, but they will care if the market size is 1000 units vs. 2000 units.

Estimating Market Sizes

Market estimation is a basic skill that you will definitely use during your case interviews. The basic idea is to estimate a market size in order to quickly test your ability to structure an approach. Here, it is necessary to make assumptions and calculate a result. Market estimation type questions are frequently asked in conjunction with a case interview to inform a client recommendation.

Sometimes market size questions are completely independent of case interviews and could be considered "mini-cases." The "mini-case" is used to determine certain traits about a candidate such as how comfortable is the candidate with numbers? How does the candidate logically think through problems? Does the candidate think in a structured manner?

Example Market Estimation Questions:

- How many ping pong balls can you fit on a 747 jet plane? (the most cliché question in the book)

- What is the annual size of the pet accessory market?

- How many fire hydrants are in New York City?

- How many nails (the ones on you, not in a wall) are painted today in Chicago?

- How many planes flew out of Los Angeles today?

- How many manholes are in San Francisco?

- How many donuts are consumed per day in the United States?

- How many rounds of golf are played each day on Pebble Beach?

- How many bottles of shampoo does the TSA confiscate every year?

The first tip is NOT to panic! There is no way you are expected to know any of these numbers off the top of your head. The interviewer is far more interested in how you get to the answers. These questions simulate the job – often times consulting firms estimate market sizes for markets where there is little (or no) data available on the market size. All you need to do is to break the problem down.

There are two basic approaches to solving these cases: a top-down approach or bottom-up approach. Think of a top-down approach like a funnel: you start with a population, and then you apply different criteria to filter more and more people out until you're left at your relevant market. This approach is most appropriate when your answer is readily tied to a population, such as the annual size of the pet accessory market, as more people presumably means more pets which means more accessories.

A bottom up approach, on the other hand, is more like building something out of Legos: you build the answer brick by brick to reach your answer. This is more appropriate when you have few players in the market, and could reasonably estimate every component of the market, or when the answer is not readily proportional to a population (for example, the fire hydrant question – it's tied more to city size).

For example, how many sandals are worn in Chicago on a given day? This is an appropriate question to solve with a top-down approach. Let's assume it's long-term average summer (considering weekdays and weekends – make sure you specify these types of assumptions during an interview):

- Start with: population of Chicago = 3,000,000 people

- Now, are all 3 million people equally likely to be wearing sandals today? No, so let's segment the population:

  - Based on what I've seen living in Chicago the past 2 years, I think females are somewhat more likely to be wearing sandals than males, and that younger generations are more likely to wear sandals than older generations. Even with higher proportions among younger generations, still plenty of people aren't outside, are dressed up for work, school uniforms, etc.

  - I assume population is evenly distributed among age groups and sexes.

- Prepare a table to illustrate your assumptions

Age / Sex Group	People in Group	Percentage Wearing Sandals	People Wearing Sandals	Sandals / Person	Number of Sandals
0-30 Women	500,000	40%	200,000	2	400,000
0-30 Men	500,000	20%	100,000	2	200,000
31-60 Women	500,000	20%	100,000	2	200,000
31-60 Men	500,000	10%	50,000	2	100,000
61+ Women	500,000	10%	50,000	2	100,000
61+ Men	500,000	5%	25,000	2	50,000
Total	3,000,000	N/A	525,000	N/A	1,050,000

- My answer is there are roughly 1,000,000 sandals on average being worn in Chicago on a summer day, or roughly 1/6th of the population wearing them

Let's try a bottom up estimation: What's the annual revenue of Ritz Carlton Hotels?

- Estimated number of Ritz Carlton hotels in the United States: 25 hotels based on the number of large American cities. (note that this number could be way off, and feel free to ask the interviewer if they have a number for you)

- Revenue Sources: Hotel room rates, conferences, miscellaneous (including bars, restaurants, gift shops, etc.).

- Assume conferences and miscellaneous revenue is rounding error compared the large amount of revenue generated from hotel room rates. (Ask the interviewer if this is a fair assumption)

- Estimated number of rooms per hotel on average: 100 (note that this number could be way off, and feel free to ask the interviewer if they have a number for you)

- Bucket rooms into three categories: Suites, high end, economy

- Estimate number of each type of room: 25 Suites, 25 high end, and 50 economy

- Estimate room rate per category:

    *Suites: $400/night,

    *High end: $300/night,

    *Economy: $200/night for Friday and Saturday night, but less Sunday through Thursday

- Assume a weekend utilization rate of 100% and a weekday utilization rate of 50% (acknowledge that the percentages are likely a bit off, but you want to keep the math easy)

- If you want to get complicated we could modify utilization rates based on seasonality, but to keep things simple let's assume a consistent utilization profile year round.

Hotel Room Categories	Penetration Rate	Number of Rooms	Nightly Rate (weekend)	Nightly Rate (weekday)	Utilization rate (weekend)	Utilization rate (weekday)	Weekly Revenue
Suites	25%	25	$400	$300	100%	50%	$38,750
High End	25%	25	$300	$200	100%	50%	$27,500
Economy	50%	50	$200	$100	100%	50%	$32,500
Total	100%	100	N/A	N/A	100%	50%	$98,750

- When determining the weekly revenue per hotel room category, remember to multiply through correctly. Use the Suite example: $38,750 per week revenue = ([25 rooms] x [$400] x [100% utilization] x [2 days a week]) + ([25 rooms] x [$300] x [50% utilization] x [5 days a week])

- The average weekly revenue for total is about $100,000. Assuming 50 weeks a year to make things easy and 25 Ritz Carlton hotels gives us an annual revenue of about $125 million.

Depending on how good you are at math, this example may have taken you too long to complete during an interview. If that is the case, make life easier for yourself. By taking out the weekend and weekday assumption, the problem becomes much easier. By removing the categories of rooms assumption, you could have made the question even easier.

- Assume 25 hotels with 100 rooms each. The average price per room is $300 and the average utilization rate is 75%. So [25 hotel rooms] x [100 rooms] x [$300/night] x [365 days/year] x [75% utilization] = ~$200M

Notice how different the final answers are; $125M vs. $200M! But there is no right answer. What matters is that you thought through the problem logically, applied a structure, acknowledged key assumptions, and followed through on your math.

Tip For Success

One math error could kill your candidacy.

Many recruiters will tell you that if you make a math error, don't worry about it, simply acknowledge your mistake, fix it, and recover. The truth is, if you make a math error, there are probably 5 other candidates who executed flawlessly. You might be able to recover from 1 small math error if you are lucky, but two mistakes is a show stopper.

It's better to take your time and get the right answer. Practicing mental math throughout the recruitment process is a great way to get more comfortable. It look you 16 paces to cross the street. At that rate, how many steps will it take to get to your economics class? You spent $22 on beer this week. How much will you spend on beer by the end of senior year? Doing math like this all day can really improve your mental math skills and prepare you for interviews.

18
The Fit Interview

Interview With a Rock Star: Questions for the Candidate Who Got Three Offers in Fall 2008, One of the Worst Recruiting Seasons of All Time

Q: What do you think about fit with a firm? How important do you think it is?

A: If you have an offer at McKinsey, BCG, and Bain, something is wrong, because they're very different, and you won't fit perfectly with all of them. Few people got offers at multiple firms, which is indicative that fit is important.

I believe I got multiple offers because my personality fits in at multiple places – a "chameleon" personality if you will.

By my second rounds, I knew which firms I wanted an offer from. I knew exactly what I liked about each of these firms, and I was able to convey that in my interviews.

Q: What thoughts do you have on the role of GPA in the recruiting process?

A: In my circle of friends, many people who got offers didn't have a GPA over 3.5. Many more people had a GPA over 3.5 and didn't get an offer. These people often got the first-round interview, but then did not advance to the next round.

I don't think there is a strong correlation between GPA and a candidate's fit with a consulting firm. Personally, I'd rather hire a person who took a broad range of classes in college and experienced lots of things compared to a person that focused exclusively on academic achievement.

Here, the Rock Star implies that a person's fit with a firm is more important than their GPA (among other numbers-based qualifications) once the person secures a first-round interview.

The fit interview is just as important as the case interview. However, your "fit" with a firm is much less straightforward than doing well in a case interview. A candidate has a good "fit" with a firm when he meshes well with the firm's consultants in a team environment, shares common perspectives towards business practices and interpersonal dynamics, and aligns well with the firm's priorities and company mission.

When a consultant interviews someone, it's easy for him or her to intuitively feel a fit or not, but it's difficult to explain why he feels one way or the other. Now, let's review ways to figure out your fit with a firm prior to the interview. This section also includes behavioral questions commonly found in fit interviews.

A common misconception among management consulting reference books is that case interviews will make or break your candidacy. This simply isn't true for consulting firms overall. Your fit with a firm is just as, if not more, important!

Much like a square peg will fit better in a square hole than a round hole, the purpose of the fit interview is to detect your fit with the company. A few broad areas they look at are listed below:

1. Would you fit into their culture?

2. Is your background relevant and useful to the work they do? Keep in mind firms generally like to have different perspectives, so just because you're not a business or econ major doesn't mean that you can't be a good fit.

   a. There's a tradeoff having a business major vs. having a different major. The upside of having a business major is your demonstrated interest in business, while the downside is that much of your competition has the same major, so you have to work harder to stand out. If you don't have a business major, you'll stand out easier, but then you'll have to be able to explain why you're interested in consulting or business.

      i. Why is the content of the career (the work, culture, etc.) appealing to you?

      ii. How is consulting going to help your long-term career objectives?

      iii. Perhaps most importantly, do you know what you're getting yourself into?

3. How much have you quantifiably achieved, inside the classroom and outside? How large of a role did you play in those achievements?

   a. How do these achievements compare to your classmates (i.e., other candidates the interviewer sees that day)?

Tips For Success

One useful thing I did during interviews was pretended everyone else interviewing had a management consultancy internship with a top-10 firm – ask myself, why am I a better candidate than a candidate with that experience? Adopting that mindset forces you to take a hard look at all you've done, and figure out what truly sets you apart. And, in case someone else interviewing did have a consulting internship, you're prepared to give it your best shot.

Make Personal Connections

In the fit interview, establish connections and find common ground
with your interviewer. If you both grew up in Canada, if you
both play hockey or if you both speak Spanish fluently, be sure to
emphasize this commonality. A seemingly trivial connection might
be what pushes you past an equivalent candidate with whom the
interviewer did not feel as connected. One student who received an
offer at a management consulting firm had this bit to share:

> *At my first round with Company X, my interviewer and I talked for 10
> minutes about a student group that I was involved in and about her
> own Middle East version of this program. Additionally, the first 5-10
> minutes of another interview with Company X, we talked about college
> football. Always be mindful of ways to make it a conversation, after all,
> you're going to be working with these people.*

Basically, the interviewer is looking for people who add talent to
the firm, who get along with the interviewers, and who have the
highest probability of being similarly liked by the partners. If the
interviewers give their stamp of approval to great candidates, it
makes them look good; likewise it could be embarrassing for them if
the candidates clearly don't meet the partners' expectations. This is
why they generally don't take chances on candidates who don't have
immaculate track records (i.e. high GPAs, successful involvement in
student groups, strong past work experience, etc.).

An Overview of a Typical Fit Interview

The fit interview usually begins with small talk and a question
along the lines of "Tell me about yourself." Then, it proceeds to the
resume. The interviewer will ask about whatever on your resume
interests them the most. They might hone in on your consulting-
related experience, if you have some. Sometimes they include a
behavioral question or two. At the end of the interview, there is time
for you to ask questions about the interviewer's experience working
at the firm or about the firm itself.

Small Talk

The purpose of "small talk" is to get a conversation "warmed up" and to put you at ease. For on-campus recruiting, this starts when the interviewer comes out to the lobby and calls your name. Acknowledge your name, and then walk over. No need to rush, but try to avoid bringing 50 things to gather up. Smile and greet him or her with a "hi!" and a firm handshake.

At this point, what should you talk about, exactly? Small talk, by definition, is banal. It's not meant to be anything deep or profound. Ask about their commute to the interviewing center that morning, or if they're currently traveling for a project. Basically, choose whatever topic that is on par with weather, that you are interested in, and that can engage the interviewer.

As you talk about things like the weather, match the interviewer's walking speed down the hall. It's easy to walk behind them a little since they're leading you to the interview room, but it's tough to carry on a conversation with someone behind you. Also, your body language suggests you're placing them up above you, which communicates fear and nervousness. When they stop, then you stop, but stick with them so they can easily talk to you. Body language is important to keep in mind from the very beginning of an interview.

The Elevator Pitch

Once you're settled into the room, out pops the statement, "So, tell me about yourself." This question overwhelmed me at first – what areas of my life should I talk about? What would be the most relevant to this interview? An associate at Boston Consulting Group (BCG) offered the following advice:

> *"Specifically on 'so tell me about yourself,' I wouldn't rehearse too much. I'd go with 1-2 bullet points of your life that you want to make sure to fit into the conversation regardless of what questions they ask during the interview, and just go with it. If you can, get some back-and-forth going." So speak naturally as you engage the interviewer to initiate back-and-forth dialogue during the "tell me about yourself" statement.*

Your one-or-two-bullet point answer to "tell me about yourself" is also known as an "elevator pitch." An elevator pitch is basically a sales pitch in which you sell yourself, except you only have a length of time equivalent to an elevator ride in order to convince your audience why you are great. Like a sales pitch, an elevator pitch is a rehearsed, concise summary of the most important information that you would like to convey to the interviewer. It should be about 30 seconds long and communicates, "this is who I am and what I am about." What are you the go-to person for? What is your life passion and primary ambition? What about you is unique and sets you apart from other candidates? Demonstrate why you are a great candidate in a short, concise "blurb."

Rehearse, and even write down your "elevator pitch" before going to your interview. By the same token, do not let it sound rehearsed. Sound genuine, enthusiastic and confident when giving your "pitch."

Your Resume

One of the most important parts of the fit interview is speaking about your resume. Here's a good exercise – prior to your interview, find someone to read over your resume and ask you about things that pop out to them. Ideally, you should find a contact in the consulting field to help you, but friends, parents, professors, and volunteers at your school's career center could help you with this as well.

Also, look through your resume on your own, and pretend that you have been assigned to find all the exaggerations in this person's resume. When you find something that might be an exaggeration, ask what data do I have to back it up?

For example, I claimed on my resume I saved a company $15,000 during my internship. When reviewing my resume, I asked myself, "Where did I get that figure from? Can anyone else at the company vouch for that number?" In this case, I was able to quantify the savings when I developed a way the company could avoid purchasing a new server and still meet the original request, and the IT Network Administrator stated that a new server would have cost $15,000.

Here are some common things that are likely to stick out to your interviewer:

Work/Student Group Experience – Any bullet point is fair game. You should be able to tell a story about each one. Follow the STAR format: describe the Situation, Task, Action, and Result.

If you're unfamiliar with STAR, here's the breakdown:

- Situation – What background information is needed to understand the problem? Should be 1-2 sentences. Aim to provide enough background so that the interviewer understands the context, but do not provide so much background that you spend a majority of your time here.

- Task – What was your task? 1-2 sentences. Ensure that the task that you relate to the interviewer is directly answering the interviewer's question. Consider using the exact wording in the interviewer's question.

- Action – Keep the focus on YOUR actions. Even when discussing a group project, keep the focus squarely on the actions that you took as an individual. A lot of students I've interviewed will tell me what their team did. Here's the deal: if I was interested in what the team did, I'd be interviewing your whole team! Just tell your interviewer what you did.

  For example, suppose you were asked to give an example of a good team experience. You were on a design team that worked together seamlessly, and the interviewer asks you about a time that you helped a team to work really well together. Instead of talking about how in general the team bonded, talk about specific examples of how you brought snacks to late night meetings, or how you broke out into singing Disney songs when the team was really frustrated to lighten up the mood. What did you do to help the team gel? That's what the interviewer wants to know!

- Result – Finally, because of your actions, what did you achieve? Talk about the impact of your actions. Further, tell the interviewer the lesson that can be learned from your story. Your result should match the result on your resume. 1-2 sentences.

Practice getting your stories to under 30 seconds. Conciseness is a valued skill in consulting, and they can always ask you for more information after you answer. Like an elevator pitch, all answers should convey the most important points in a short length of time.

Highlight experiences that would translate to skills used at a consulting firm. For example, I worked in a project-based environment at my non-consulting internship, and I developed a spreadsheet to keep track of the status of each project I was working on. That way, I wouldn't have to keep track of everything in my head. This would translate to a consulting firm where you may be working on several things simultaneously, so I made sure to work this experience into the interview somewhere.

Extracurricular Interests – These should lead to some passionate stories. Keep the STAR format, and let your enthusiasm shine through. It's alright if you have an achievement related to your passions, but a discussion of extracurricular interests is more for the interviewer to learn about you as a person and to determine your potential fit with the firm culture.

Things To Avoid

Avoid Trash Talking – If any of your experiences involve co-workers or other departments, speak of them positively. "I.T. wanted to increase their department efficiency, so they asked me to help them develop an order management system" sounds better than "I.T. was completely unorganized and kept losing work tickets, so they asked me to help them develop an order management system." You may think the latter paints you as a hero, but more likely it paints you as arrogant.

The notorious "Um" – Pay special attention to your use of filler words. Words such as "uh," "um," "like," "you know," etc. Each one of these words distracts from your message and conveys nervousness. With a little attention, you can quickly minimize the number of filler words you use until it is a habit. Additionally, have a friend give you a behavioral question, and then have them count the number of filler words you use. The result may surprise you!

Behavioral Questions

After asking questions about your resume, the interviewer may ask a few behavioral questions. Take the time to read through the following questions and create a unique answer for each one. To take it a step further, it is always a good idea to write down your answers to these questions in addition to rehearsing your answers. Writing them down will improve your chances of answering flawlessly (i.e. mentioning all elements outlined in the "STAR" technique).

Here are some popular behavioral questions asked by consulting firms:

Why do you want to go into consulting?

Talk with your network of friends, alumni and external sources to discover your answer to this question. With this question, the interviewer is trying to figure out "What sparks this candidate's interest in consulting, and what are they hoping to get out of it?"

Why do you want to work at this firm?

Ideally, you must demonstrate your ability to articulate your "story" and how it relates to this firm specifically. The best approach is to make your answer as "firm-oriented" as possible.

A former associate at Boston Consulting Group (BCG) suggested that you should mention "the 2 or 3 things that excite you the most" about the firm. For example, if the firm does a lot of media work and if that really excites you, point this out. You could say something similar to, "I've always been interested in working with media companies, because <insert your personal reason here>, and would like to run one some day. Your firm is really strong in the media industry, so I would be very excited to work here over other firms." It shows that you have done your homework and considered your fit with the firm. Note: Make sure what you say is true!

Furthermore, if you had the chance to network with individuals in these firms, you can mention that you "took initiative to meet people from your firm." Or you could combine both concepts in the following way. "When I met with Ms. Consultant, she mentioned that your firm sees many projects in the private equity industry, and that excites me because I'd like to be an investor someday, and it would be great to receive a lot of exposure to the funding side of a business."

Other Behavioral Questions

- What is your greatest strength?

- What is your greatest weakness?

- Give me an example of a time when you showed initiative and took the lead.

- Describe a situation in which you were able to use persuasion to successfully convince someone to see things your way.

- Give me an example of a time when you set a goal and were able to meet or achieve it.

- Tell me about a time when you had to use your presentation skills to influence someone's opinion.

- Tell me about a time when you had to go above and beyond the call of duty in order to get a job done.

- Tell me about a time when you had too many things to do and you were required to prioritize your tasks.

- What is your typical way of dealing with conflict? Give me an example.

- Tell me about a time when you were able to successfully deal with another person who did not personally like you (or vice versa).

- Tell me about a difficult decision you've made in the last year.

- Give me an example of a time when you tried to accomplish something and failed.

- Tell me about a situation in which you dealt with a very upset customer or co-worker.

- Tell me about a time when you missed an obvious solution to a problem.

- Describe a time when you anticipated potential problems and developed preventative measures.

- Tell me about a time you demonstrated leadership abilities.

- Tell me about a time you verbally disagreed with an authority figure.

- Tell me about a time when you worked in a group setting and a member wasn't participating. What did you do?

- Tell me about a time when you demonstrated creativity.

- Tell me about at time when you used assumptions to make a decision.

- Tell me about a time when you encountered a vague situation.

- Tell me about a time when you showed integrity.

- What does communication mean to you?

- How do you deal with pressure or too many tasks?

- Where do you see yourself in 5 years?

- What other industries are you looking at?

- If you could have any position on a team what would it be?

- Explain a time where you were extremely busy and then something unexpectedly came up. What did you do? Why? How?

- Explain a time you dealt with a difficult person. Do you deal with them often?

- Tell me about a time when you made a decision against popular vote.

Guest Authors

Here are a smattering of Do/Don'ts tips on answering fit interview questions from a McKinsey Business Analyst and a Boston Consulting Group Associate:

Do:

- Think through everything on your resume as well as other experiences so that you have quick ideas when a question is asked.

- Make sure to answer the question that was asked.

- Use STAR technique (Situation, Task, Action, Result) to structure your answers.

- Highlight what you learned from each experience.

- Think of "outside the box" experiences. (Ex: Leadership from organizing trips for groups of students in New Zealand.)

- If two interviewers ask the same question, tell the second one, "I just spoke to [Interviewer's name here] about a time I [...] and can tell you about that or if you would like, I can try to come up with a different example."

- Try to vary the activity, student group, etc. (Situation in STAR technique) to demonstrate a wide array of experiences.

- Read your interviewer's cues. Explain further if he seems confused or lost but know to conclude if you are rambling or he looks bored.

- Focus on what you did, NOT what others did.

- Be enthusiastic, personable and sincere.

Don't:

- Don't get too personal. No stories about relationships, family issues, etc.

- Don't throw others under the bus. No one wants to hear excuses; always shine a positive light on everyone, even someone you are describing as difficult to work with.

- Don't say you can't think of an example. ALWAYS tell a story.

- Don't forget to give credit to those who helped you; don't illustrate yourself as flawless.

- Don't lie. They can tell. Always.

Your Questions

At the end of the fit interview, you will have the opportunity to ask questions. Typically, it is good to ask one question about the firm and one about the interviewer. The first question demonstrates that you have researched the company and the specific job. This is a great opportunity to learn more about the company, the place where you might be spending 50 to 70 hours per week. Dig deep enough so that the a person could not answer the question by looking on website or by visiting info session. Don't dig so deep that the interviewer won't know the answer.

The second question is directed to the interviewer personally. This question gives the interviewer a break from asking questions. It could be about where they are from, the project that was behind the case you just cracked, what they like to do when not working, etc. Don't be afraid to write your questions down on your notepad before arriving.

Guest Author – Business Analyst, Top Consulting Firm

What people commonly forget is that the fit interview isn't only an evaluation of their compatibility within the employer's organization. The fit interview is also a chance for the interviewee to decide if this is the type of work environment and role that they themselves may thrive in.

- What are the personalities of potential co-workers?

- How do current employees interact?

- How have others starting off in your potential role fared and progressed through the company? What is the company's short term and long- term strategy?

These are only a few types of questions that you should be asking your interviewers and contacts at the company. At the end of the day, you want to obtain enough information to understand the company and role such that you can confidently envision your day-to-day tasks and interactions and how those translate into your long-term career ambitions.

Characterizing career goals during an interview

Most top-tier consulting firms expect that undergraduate students will go to graduate school at some point. It is perfectly acceptable to tell a recruiter that you are planning on going back to business school in the next 2-4 years. Recruiters don't want to hear that you want to go to school in less than two years – this implies a lack of commitment. Be cautious if you want to get a masters or Ph.D. instead of a Masters of Business Administration (MBA). Most recruiters want candidates passionate about business, entrepreneurship, and finance. An MBA implies continued interest in these fields. During a fit interview, be prepared to answer questions like these:

- Are you planning on going back to school after you complete your undergraduate? When?

- What do you want to study?

If you say MBA, then you are probably off the hook. If you say something other than MBA, be prepared for more questions:

- If you are interested in studying (non-business related random topic x), how does consulting fit into your longer-term career goals?

- Are you planning on getting back into consulting after (random topic x)? If so, how does (random topic x) expand your capabilities as a consultant?

- Why should we hire you when you are clearly more interested in (random topic x)?

If you don't know what you want to do, that's fine, but stress a passion for business. *"I am considering getting an MBA, but I am still weighing other options. I believe a job in consulting will be fantastic training for my longer-term goals in business entrepreneurship. I could also see myself working up the ranks at a consulting firm."*

If a recruiter asks about your 10-year or 20-year career goals, almost anything is fair game. The goal here is to demonstrate ambition and to articulate how consulting fits into those longer-term goals.

19

First and Second Round Interviews

Round 1

Most first-round consulting interviews involve two 30 minute interviews with varying degrees of focusing on fit or cases. Some firms, such as Bain & Company and L.E.K. Consulting, employ two full-blown cases in the first-round interview with the assumption that they can detect a candidate's fit from the candidate's answers to the cases. Some companies, such as Booz & Company and A.T. Kearney, employ one case portion and one fit portion. Keep in mind that firms constantly tweak their interviewing process, so you may experience a different format with a particular company. These examples illustrate the range of possibilities that you may encounter.

Interview With a Rock Star: Questions for the Candidate Who Got Three Offers in Fall 2008, One of the Worst Recruiting Seasons of All Time

Q: During second-round interview, what type of tone were you trying to convey? What traits were you trying to showcase?

A: During first-round interviews, these were people [i.e. the recruiters] you've met at info sessions, so I felt I could be more laid back. But you shouldn't be unprofessional. Saying "cool" or "go team" or whatever can insert doubt in their mind, as I did on at least one occasion.

During second-round interviews, I wanted to be excited, yet professional. I showed this through my intensity: I would debate with partners. I really wasn't afraid to disagree with partners, if we were having an intellectual conversation about [my internship experience at] Target or some article they wrote.

There are more interview sessions in the second round than in the first round. Different firms place different emphases on fit vs. case-solving ability. In my individual experience, L.E.K. Consulting had three interviews in the second round, all of which emphasized a case. Booz & Company, on the other hand, had two interviews in second round, both of which emphasized fit (i.e., the case portion was easy and short in duration compared to first-round case). Some firms have all day marathon interview sessions with what seems to be an entire office. Cases in this setting tend to be more impromptu (i.e. testing business judgment without the use of a formal case study) and up to the discretion of the interviewer.

Typically, 20-30% of students that had first-round interviews are passed on to the second round. While statistically the cut for a second-round interview is not as steep as getting a first-round interview, it's still a significant jump to make it to the second rounds. Initially, you were competing against others who looked good on paper. Now you know they like you in person as well, so that's the good news. The bad news is that everyone whom they brought in for second rounds was good both on paper and in person, so you've got your work cut out for you.

You stand a good chance of making the second cut if the interviewers like you, if you display good potential in the case interview, and if there's nothing that could expose the interviewers to disapproval from the partners (e.g., a border-line GPA).

Round 2

Compared to first-round interviews, the format of second-round interviews is a bit more of a wildcard. There is no rule about whether firms are more likely to give cases or fit interviews in the second round. Most firms use a combination of fit and case interviews, but every firm is different in their approach. Some will wine and dine you with a full day of interviewing, info sessions, and lunch, while others will bring you in for a few interviews and send you on your way.

In addition, some firms use other interview types to evaluate you. When I interviewed with Marakon, I encountered a role-playing scenario in which I pretended to interview an industry expert. Then I was required to report my recommendations to a pretend manager. Other firms may employ a case exercise where you're on a team.

Expect the second-round interviews to be more intense, but don't panic. Confidence is key. Relax, smile, and let your enthusiasm for consulting shine through.

Be aware that firms will sometimes adjust their second-round interviews based on notes from the first-round interviews. For example, let's say you aced the case in first rounds, but your background looks a little weak. They may give you an easy case just to confirm, and then focus on your background.

After all, most firms make a decision after second-round interviews, so they want to make sure they have adequately probed for your strengths and weaknesses. For example, a first-round interviewer at another firm suggested that I work on making my language a little bit more professional, because the second-round interviewers would be watching for that to see if they could trust me in front of a client (in case you're curious, I was using the word "cool" too often, so watch that word in your interviews).

After the second-round interview, it's time for the verdict. The moment of truth. Did all that hard work pay off? Will you get the offer? Usually the firm will call you with their decision, but there's no telling who makes the call or when they will call.

Unfortunately, not all firms call. Instead, they send an unsatisfying generic e-mail from HR. Since you might be a future client someday, it's in a firm's best interest to give you a courtesy call. This way, they remain professional and maintain the best image possible.

When you see that strange number on your cell phone, find a quiet place and wait with baited breath. Make sure you pick it up, even if you're in class. If they leave a voicemail, it may be next to impossible to ask for feedback on how you did during your interview, because you would have to catch them at a separate time.

Quick Tip

I have a second-round interview – What can I expect when I arrive? What happens after the interview?"

Firms will normally reimburse you for travel expenses associated with getting to the interview. Sometimes in second rounds, they'll also give you gifts as a thank you (e.g., a USB key). There may be time for idle chit-chat with lower level consultants assigned to entertain you, or they may sweep you out of the door as soon as you're done.

Interview With a Rock Star: Questions for the Candidate Who Got Three Offers in Fall 2008, One of the Worst Recruiting Seasons of All Time

Q: Based on your recruitment experience, what do you think is important at each phase of recruitment?

A: I think you need to determine who's important at each firm for each stage. For example, a partner may be able to swing for you to get a first-round interview, but ultimately the analysts/ consultants are making those decisions. It'd be better to get to know several of them. At this stage, they're looking for fit with the company.

For first-round interviews, it's a weed out round – Are you smart enough to work here? They may also continue to determine fit. Your two interviewers are the decision makers.

Finally, for second-round interviews, the partners/managers are looking at whether they can put you in front of a client. [Editor's note: They've worked hard to foster their relationships, and they don't want to risk a hit to it.]

In order to prepare for second rounds, I'd look on their website for articles. Which areas are they writing the most about? How are they thinking about those problems? What are the benefits of that approach, and what may be some drawbacks?

20
Thank You Letters

Email a thank you letter no later than the evening following your interview. Consulting firms move so fast that they may review your candidacy that night. A thank you is always appreciated, and it may swing a vote during their decision process. Keep it short, and mention one interesting point that occurred during your interview. The interviewer has met with as many as 20 candidates, so help jog his or her memory a little bit. Also, if you have a logistical questions about the recruiting process and next steps, include them in your thank you letter.

On the other hand, if you have continued questions about the firm, wait until you receive an invitation to the next round of interviews or a final offer, then you can send another follow up e-mail. First-round interviewers rarely respond to extra questions via email. More often, they wait until they invite you to second rounds, at which point they will answer all of your questions. Same thing goes after the final round of interviews. Always follow up with a thank you note, but don't expect to hear a response to questions relating to the firm until after you hear back about getting that offer.

Example of a successful thank you letter after interviewing:

Hi [Recruiter's name],

I just wanted to thank you for the opportunity to interview today. I really enjoyed breaking down the RadioCom case and getting a feel for the kind of work Avascent does. The opportunity for analysis and idea generation in the defense industry is why I was originally drawn to Avascent, and the interview today amplified that interest. Thank you again for the opportunity, and please let me know if there is anything else I can do.

Best,

[your name]

Components of a successful thank you letter:

Hello [Recruiter's Name],

Thank you for the opportunity to interview today. [Comment on enjoyment of the interview itself and getting to know company x better]. [Comment on what excites you about company x]. [Optional comment on personal connection with interviewer]. Thank you again, and please let me know if you need anything else.

Best,

[your name]

21
Dealing with Rejection

Interview With a Rock Star: Questions for the Candidate Who Got Three Offers in Fall 2008, One of the Worst Recruiting Seasons of All Time

Q: What advice would you have for someone who ends up not receiving any management consulting offers?

A: In my understanding, it's better to get some kind of job, and then re-apply after MBA School. Many firms simply won't accept applications from people not currently in school. As they say, when one door closes another opens, so keep your eyes peeled for opportunities.

Rejection is sadly a large part of the recruitment process. No one is a good fit for every firm they apply to. And frankly, even when you're a good fit, you may be turned down. There are too many qualified candidates, so the firm is inevitably forced to split hairs to make offer decisions about who to offer a job.

One example of "hair splitting" is demonstrated by an email a partner wrote me, when I asked him for feedback on my interview with him:

"I am sorry we were not able to extend you an offer. I thought you handled the interview with me just fine – you were personable and articulate, and came across as capable of doing the job. That said, we are dealing with a situation this year where we need to make very hard choices, and that means being highly selective amongst what is already a talented group. In some cases that decision is just not as clear cut as we would all like, but we still need to make it.

I wish you the best in your continued job search efforts. I am sure you will land something you can get very excited about."

While it's still disappointing to not get an offer, you must not take rejection personally. Sure – it is possible that you said or did something to lose favor with the interviewer, but agonizing over what may have gone wrong and feeling bad about yourself is unproductive. Unless you can extract feedback from the experience, it is necessary to assume that the result was luck of the draw. Firms need to make tough decisions, and it's not always your fault. Beyond any feedback given, you must always assume that it was not your fault and the next opportunity is right around the corner. Pick yourself up, and move on!

A Note on the Economy's Impact on Recruitment

When I went through the recruitment process in fall 2008, one principal at a top 10 firm told me, "This is the worst year I've seen since I entered consulting in 1991, which also was a terrible year." Barack Obama at the time said this was the worst crisis in a century, though I'm sure he took some artistic liberty with that statement. The president of my university told a group of students over lunch that this economy is the worst in the last 30 or 40 years. Everyone's opinion was different on the magnitude, but there was no denying the fact there was a hiring freeze across the board, including consulting.

Consulting firms will tout that they have business in good and bad times. While it's true to an extent, the amount of business in bad times is far less. Most companies consider hiring consultants to be discretionary spending. In bad times, companies cut discretionary spending first. In response, some firms did not recruit in 2008. More than one top 10 firm laid off consultants, something firms try very hard to avoid.

Most firms thankfully did recruit, if anything, for the purpose of propping up the pretense of being okay. We naive interviewees were thus surprised when we found these firms sharply reduced their hiring numbers from previous years. Firms that normally gave 6 or 7 offers in previous years gave out 1 to 3 offers in fall 2008, depending on how well they were doing. One firm even interviewed at my school, but didn't give out a single offer to anyone. Even the largest firms, which had other divisions outside of consulting, curtailed their hiring: no firm was immune.

So I went into this season knowing that half of the consulting jobs were cut. To make matters worse, the major financial jobs also froze hiring, either because they collapsed or turned into bank holding companies. Many interns were even turned loose from these banks. In sum, fall 2008 offered twice the applicants for half the jobs.

Even in this economy, "rock stars," a term used to describe outstanding candidates, still got offers. For example, Bain & Company hired two people from my school, and Booz & Company hired three people from my school. What was the difference between them and you? After reading this guide and practicing cases, the answer is hopefully "nothing… I am a rock star" (go ahead; chant that in your mirror three times – just make sure your web cam isn't on).

But the reality is, in tough times, you may be a rock star. You may rock the cases, and maybe blow your interviewer away with your awesome volunteering experiences, and still not get an offer from a top firm. Someone may have connected a little better with a particular interviewer because they both love surfing, or the other candidate has a higher GPA or a management consulting internship – none of which you have any control over when you enter recruiting.

As my university president told us, "while others are damning the dark, light a candle." Not everything is in your control, so focus on what you can control and let go of the rest. You may not get the job at the firm your heart was set on. You may not even get an interview with that firm. But instead of cursing that firm, the economy, or your peers, focus on what you have control over, and minimize stress over the factors you have no control over

Short-Term Rejection

Rejection will happen. It's a part of life, and even though it sucks, it affords an opportunity to learn. Rejection confirms that you're reaching outside of your comfort zone. If you never fail, then you aren't trying new things!

In order to learn from rejection, it is critical to ask for feedback. You have nothing to lose and everything to gain. Some firms will politely turn you down with non-specific excuses, but some interviewers can give you great advice.

Take the feedback and decide what you believe and what you don't believe. Next, develop a plan for improving upon the relevant areas. Some areas might be easy to change mid-season. For example, someone might tell you that you say "Um" too much. With a concerted effort, that's pretty easy to fix. But some things you might take longer to remedy, such as lack of relevant experience.

After you ask for feedback, that firm should be a dead dinosaur in your mind. If you find yourself fixating on why you were rejected, reframe your mindset. Look forward and begin fixating on alternative opportunities at other firms – "I didn't get an offer at Company X, but Company Y has got some great things going on too. Maybe they're a better fit for me. And even if I don't love them, at least I can build my experience base there and jump to Company X after getting my MBA."

There is one exception to the rule that you must pick yourself up and move on: When you are not invited for a first-round interview. Resume judgments are fairly superficial, and firms routinely miss out on great candidates that had interest in their firm. If you really like the firm, call up the lead recruiter and plead your case. Do not get angry, and do not sound desperate.

Better yet, go down to their office (if you live in the same city) and ask for the recruiter. That's audacious, and it just might work. Ask if you can interview with them, and be extremely flexible. Can you interview then? Can you do a phone interview? Could you show up extra early to your career center? Could you come back down to the office another day, no reimbursement needed? As a friend of mine is fond of saying, *everything in life is negotiable.* Rules are enforced by people, who are not robots. You have nothing to lose, but a whole lot to gain.

Long-Term Rejection (Or No Consulting Offers)

The Long View of Things

So you didn't get a management consulting job offer at all. Unfortunately, your next opportunity to be a management consultant is after you get your MBA. If you are interested in consulting, an MBA is encouraged. Graduates of other master's degrees typically have a more difficult time getting hired by consulting firms. Those non-MBA graduate students who are hired, tend to be hired at a more junior level. For instance, L.E.K. Consulting hires PhD graduates for its life science program, but these PhDs come in a lower level than MBAs. Intuitively it makes sense – in management consulting, the best preparation would be a master's in business administration. With an MBA, you'll have to wait a few years, but you will have more opportunity to distinguish yourself during this time.

There are plenty of examples of successful consultants that took the MBA-route. I know two consultants at BCG who didn't start off in a top firm out of undergraduate. One consultant worked at the headquarters of a large retailer for six years before business school. Another worked at a small consulting firm before business school. The key, for them, was getting into the top business school, and for that there is no "right" profile. Don't despair: you just may have to wait a little longer to get into your "dream job." Remember, you're not blocked out forever!

> " ... *There's always an element of luck in recruitment, so you may be a great candidate and not get an offer. One thing to keep in mind is that many partners didn't start off as analysts – they came in after business school or later. Furthermore, you don't need a consulting firm to get into a top business school; you can come from industry because the cream will always rise to the top ...*"

> – Former BCG Associate

Delay Graduation?

Some students choose to delay graduation to recruit again, because alumni do not have the same access to the career service center as undergraduates. This may or may not be a wise tactic depending on your situation. Firms will recognize that you applied last year. They may be flattered that you have continued interest in their firm. Alternatively, they may question why you didn't receive any offers and reject your application. Generally, I recommend saving your tuition money and getting a job in a field that will set you up for a great business school.

22
Please Accept Our Offer!

First, pat yourself on the back! Getting an offer to work in management consulting is a rare thing.

How to Compare Offers

When comparing offers, first consider your career goals. Identify how a given position will help you achieve your goals faster than the other offers.

For me, my career goal is to start my own business. Not just a small business, but one that would require VC funding.

In my case, I was choosing between one consulting offer and various engineering positions. Clearly, consulting would better enable me to learn how to run a business, research potential markets and manage teams – all good skills for an entrepreneur to have.

After some soul-searching, you should select an offer that sets you up for the rest for your career. In addition to considering your career goals, consider factors like career development opportunities, the people at the firm and the lifestyle.

Career Development

Promotion – Is the firm up-or-out? What's the time frame for promotion? A "sink-or-swim" feel has strong appeal for some folks, while turning off others. Ask whether promotion criteria involves comparison to peers or to an absolute standard. It is rare for a firm to solely judge you based on how you compare to your peers, but some firms will take the comparison into account. Obviously, this leads to less job security, but if you are a rock star it's easier to stand out.

If promotion criteria involves comparison to peers, it inevitably leads to more competition. The most extreme example of this was Enron, where the bottom 10% of the employees were let go every year, and traders were downright cut-throat.

Project Variety – Does the firm take more responsibility for selecting your projects (e.g., Bain or LEK), or do you take more responsibility (e.g., Booz & Company, Accenture Strategy)? If the firm takes responsibility for staffing, you won't get pigeonholed into one industry. However, you may have to delay gratification if you find an industry or function you really enjoy.

Training – What kind of training does the firm offer? There's lots of training in every firm, so it's a matter of which programs you like the best. In my case, I liked how L.E.K. brings in instructors from business schools to teach MBA topics, so that after a certain number of years you've learned many of the most important topics that you would learn while pursuing an MBA. They'll even promote you to consultant after ~4 years: no MBA required to move up.

The People

Different firms have different cultures. As a result, they all attract different types of people. While some firms may attract a more diverse set of people, they will still select the candidates that best fit their mold.

When deciding between two offers, put in the effort to get a feel for the people. Arrange an office tour on a day when most people will be in the office. Go to their sell dinner, where firms will wine and dine you in an attempt to convince you to accept their offer. Are you comfortable? Do you enjoy yourself around them? You will be working 50, 60, maybe 70 hours a week with these people, so it is important to enjoy their company.

The Lifestyle

Travel – Most firms travel. Some firms travel only as needed, while most travel consistently 4 days per week for the entire project. It's sexy to think about getting paid to travel, but are you OK with working in Bentonville, Arkansas for 6 months? At each firm you're considering, how often will you be travelling and for how long? Ask current employees, or, better yet, ex-employees.

Hours – Some firms try to mitigate the number of hours that their consultants work, while other firms may work you around the clock. Are you OK with that? While there is no set number of hours in consulting, you can ask people how many over-stretched weeks and weekends they have worked in the past year. Some firms have compensation policies that reward you for long hours worked. Some firms, for example, give you a day off the following week if you are required to work more than 80 hours in a week.

Social Events – Some firms hold regular formal events. For example, Accenture Strategy holds a monthly meeting for all of its strategy consultants. Others may only have one formal event a year, and the rest is ad-hoc.

Benefits

Benefits should never be deal breakers, but can enhance a company's candidacy for your acceptance.

401K – Does the firm offer a 401K? Do they match your contributed funds? Matching contributions is essentially free money, and allows you to grow your "nest egg" much quicker. What's the vesting period? This is not important if you plan to be there a while, but it is if you plan to only be there for a handful of years.

Health/Dental/Life – The firm will offer coverage (most likely), but what's the extent of the coverage? What's the cost (deductible, monthly fees, etc.)?

Bonus – If bonuses are primarily based on firm performance, ask what it has historically been in the past, and what's the lowest bonus that has been given recently? If the bonus is primarily based on your individual performance, that means your compensation will be more your responsibility. If you like a higher-pressure environment, a performance-based bonus is a good thing. If you like relaxed environments more, a performance-based bonus may be undesirable.

The Name

Did you skip right to this section? I understand that the name is a badge of achievement, to be worn for both peers and future employers and business schools alike. All of the factors listed previously are more important for your job satisfaction, long-term career goals, and happiness. Also, a smaller-name firm can offer you a more unique experience in the eyes of a business school. Each year, a large percentage of consultants from major firms apply to top business schools; however, how many Joe Schmo & Associates consultants apply? Working for a small firm might set you apart.

Another benefit offered by a smaller firm is that leadership opportunities may come your way much earlier. For example, one consultant took a job with a smaller consulting firm. He ended up being one of the fastest-promoted people in the company's history, left to go to business school and now is working at BCG.

That said, big-name firms do offer numerous benefits as well. At the end of the day, you need to decide what factors are most important to you. Just don't weigh name so heavily that it overrides everything else.

Quick Tip

"But it's Not My Dream Job!"

If you know what your dream job is, congrats! Generally, most young professionals don't have a clue, given the boundless opportunities we have.

Do not immediately turn down an offer just because it's not your "dream job." Keep in mind that it may be your only offer. Second, consider how well it will set you up for your dream job down the road.

Guest Author: Jeff Bartow - Booz and Company

Introduction – Congratulations! The most challenging part of your Consulting job search journey is over – you have an offer. This will be an exciting time for you because from this point forward, the power shifts back to you, but using that power wisely can be challenging. This section is designed to guide you through the offer decision process with two important goals – making the right decision for you and putting you on the path toward success with your new employer.

Offer Decision Process

Step 1: Decision Framework ➤ Step 2: Data Gathering ➤ Step 3: Evaluation ➤ Step 4: Decide & Communicate

Step 1 – Decision Framework: While it is an exhilarating part of the job search process, deciding between offers can be tricky to navigate. In Consulting, the key to managing difficult problems is to break the issue into smaller, more manageable pieces; the same process works well for the offer decision process.

In order to better frame the decision, I recommend that you create a "Decision Framework" which helps prioritize what is important to you about your new career and will guide the decision process. The Decision Framework will be completely unique for very individual because we are all looking for different things. However, the thought process for creating your Decision Framework is something that can be used across the board, and I have created a sample one to guide this discussion.

The key question entering any new endeavor is "what do I want to get out of this?." It may seem strange to think about the end when starting a new career, but this is the best way to set yourself up for success. Hopefully you've already thought long and hard about this question, otherwise, how would you know you want to go into Consulting!

Once you've answered the high-level question about what you are looking to get out of Consulting, it's time to convert that high-level answer into tangible aspects, or "buckets" in Consulting lingo. Each of these aspects is a part of the answer to "what do I want to get out of this?"

I've created a sample framework that I believe will be very relevant for most new Consultants. It describes each aspect with bullets and provides space to evaluate offers against that aspect. This is an example for our discussion, but you will need to work to create one that best fits your needs.

Decision Framework

	Valuable Core Business Skills	Position for future Career / Education moves	Long-lasting relationships	Intellectual Intrigue	Compensation
Examples	• Analytical thought process • Leadership experience • Managing yourself	• Firm prestige • MBA Acceptance rates • Connection to future industries of interest	• Cultural fit • Mentoring	• Pure "Strategy" work • International travel • Intellectual Capital	• Salary + Bonus • Other Benefits (Health Care, etc.)
Offer 1	◕	●	◕	◔	◑
Offer 2	◑	◔	◑	●	◕
Offer 3	◕	◑	◔	◔	◑

Step 2 – Data Gathering: Once the Decision Framework has been created, the challenge of deciding between offers begins. In order to evaluate each offer against the aspects, you are going to need some data to help make your decision. Gathering the necessary information can come from several sources.

• Your personal experience with the company through the interview process – the same people who were interviewing you work at the company, so you can learn quite a bit from the time you spent with them

• Publications and articles – these are great sources of preliminary information, but they approach the company from a very high level and may not reflect the precise opportunity that you are investigating

• Advice from people within your network – I think the best person to talk to is someone who knows the Consulting industry well. They will give you the "inside scoop" on things that you have learned from other sources

• The company itself – the "selling process"

Each source is valuable, and it is up to you to weigh the importance of where to find the necessary information. However, the last bullet deserves special attention because there is an entire process devoted to having you learn about the company that just gave you an offer – the "selling" process.

For reasons that can occupy a second book, Consulting firms have a process dedicating to converting offers into offer acceptances. This process works to your advantage for two reasons – it be very fun for you and it will provide you with the opportunity to get almost any information you want about the offering company. These opportunities will likely consist of dinners, outings, phone calls etc. There aren't any "rules" about the process, but by following a few simple guidelines you will be able to both enjoy it and get the information you need.

- This is the one time when the company is "selling" you – take advantage of every opportunity to meet people and find out what you want to know. Don't be afraid to ask some tough questions; the company is used to it and will be happy to answer it.

- Be respectful and courteous always! – you are looking to work for one of the companies "selling" you, so never forget that the people you are interacting with will be your future colleagues, managers, mentors etc.

- Learn to "read between the lines" and investigate anything that is unclear to you. The companies you are deciding between will be similar in many ways since they are in the same industry and want the same person – you! The difficult part is teasing out the subtle differences between companies that is going to make the difference between a good experience and a great experience.

The Decision Framework can be a very helpful tool, but only if we can find the data needed to support a thorough decision. If you approach the Data Gathering step with the same effort as the actual interviews, then you will be in great shape to make your decision.

Step 3 – Evaluation: The Evaluation process is the most stressful but straightforward step when deciding between offers. You now have all the information you need, but it is time to put all of it together into a single choice. If you have followed the Decision Framework well and gathered all the information you wanted, then the decision will be as easy as it can be. Don't be afraid to take your time to make a decision. I find that discussing your decision with people close to you is the best final step before deciding; they will be honest and ask the tough questions you may not want to answer!

Step 4 – Decide and Communicate: Now that you have decided on which offer to accept, there is still one step left in the process – communicating your decision. This step is often forgotten because after the effort of deciding, many new Consultants simply want to step back from the process and relax.

The key thing to remember about communicating your decision is that you are going to work for the company whose offer you just accepted. This sounds obvious, but it's easy to forget. The person who interviewed you may be your first manager and the person who took you out to coffee may be your first team member. The best way to ensure a smooth transition from offer to first-day-on-the-job is to accept with enthusiasm.

There are many ways to show that you are excited to be a part of the company. They can range from delivering the signed offer letter in person, calling and thanking the people you interacted with or even helping with the company's future recruiting efforts. There is not a best way to do this, but by thinking about how the company will perceive your acceptance, you are halfway there.

The last part of this step is to politely turn down the offers you won't be accepting. Many people forget this is an important part of the process – the professional world is smaller than you think and it's likely you'll come across some of the people from the other companies at some point. The good news is that turning down an offer gracefully is pretty simple. Call your main point-of-contact and politely turn down the offer while expressing your gratitude for being considered. You want to ensure they received the message, so if you don't get them in person and don't hear back, then send an email. Once you've received confirmation that your decision has been received, then you are finished.

Closing: Once again, congratulations for Getting a Job in Consulting. You are now ready to relax for a little while and then get excited to begin your new job. I hope the entire process has been a rewarding experience and that it has met all of your expectations. Best of luck with the beginning of your career!

Should I Negotiate?

Starting Salary

Given our materialistic culture, your friends may be encouraging you to negotiate your starting salary, especially if those friends received higher salaries.

If you have multiple offers, it is acceptable to ask one company to match the salary of another. If you don't have the leverage of multiple offers, negotiation becomes a little dicey.

Whether you negotiate depends on many factors. First off, is the economy good or bad? If the job market is good, you will likely find more leeway than when the market is bad. Second, consider the implications of a successful negotiation – let's say you're making $5000 more than any of the other analysts in your company. One of Northwestern professor, who was a CEO at a large Chicago company for many years, noted that a higher salary could potentially lead to a bad situation. If your performance is average, you will look terrible, because you're making more money than your peers. Compound this in a consulting environment, where they only hire exceptional students, and it becomes a risky proposition.

Tread carefully if you plan to negotiate your salary, as it's very easy to come across as an egotistical college student with an inflated sense of entitlement. Instead, be grateful for the amount you were offered. Channel that confidence and energy toward proving you deserve more money between your start date and your first annual review.

Start Date and Office

Start date and office location are a lot easier to negotiate than starting salary.

Most firms ask for your office preferences up front, so hopefully they will consider your preferences in your offer. If you're truly stuck in an office you don't want (e.g., Hong Kong instead of New York), you can ask for reconsideration, but don't hold your breath. Instead, work for 2 years and then look to transfer. Once you have experience under your belt, your request to transfer will hold more weight.

Note that being located in Hong Kong instead of New York is an unlikely scenario, given that you are most often recruited for the office closest to your school. Such an extreme relocation would be more likely for students fluent in multiple languages.

Many firms also are adopting programs to facilitate inner-company office transfers and visits. Bain and L.E.K. have established programs, while firms like AT Kearney are just beginning to adopt them.

Accepting an Offer

The recruiter announces he would like to give you an offer. It's a fantastic feeling! I remember I was at the dinner table in our fraternity house when I received an offer. After I hung up, I tossed the phone on the table, leaned back in my chair, and yelled out loud! I had worked so hard over the last year, and had earned that offer!

After the offer, the company begins their effort to get you to accept. They took a risk in giving you an offer, because in giving you one, they had to turn down quite a few people. Consulting firms will usually give out a larger number of offers than open positions. They expect some students to turn down their offers. Consulting firms do not maintain a waitlist -- They reject candidates during the same time frame that they extend offers.

Most firms will have a sell event, to which they invite all the people who were extended offers. This event gives you an opportunity to meet people in the firm on a more casual level. Sell events can range in complexity, from simple dinners to full days and nights planned out with activities. In my case, there was a presentation in the afternoon, followed by dinner, followed by bottle service at a bar, staying over night downtown, and ending with breakfast the next morning.

It's at these sell events that you will also meet your peer group: the summer interns, other students from your school and students from other schools. While you will not frequently work directly with these individuals, this peer group will form the backbone of your social life during your time at the firm. It's important to talk with them to get a feel for your fit with these students.

The sell event is the time to ask any questions that you have been hesitant about asking previously. You already have an offer, and now it's the firm's turn to hit home in selling themselves. They are not going to rescind your offer unless you do something really inappropriate (but if you were apt to do that, they probably would have found out long ago).

What Not to Do

Here's an anecdote about what NOT to do: One candidate who received an offer, let's call him Bob to protect the innocent, really had his heart set on investment banking. However, fall of 2008 was a really bad time to try to get into finance – no one was hiring. Even some summer interns weren't receiving offers. So, like many finance hopefuls, Bob tried his hand at consulting to maybe get into finance later. He received an offer from a management consulting firm, and seemed like a normal person up to that point.

Then, Bob began asking questions, openly stating that he wasn't sure if consulting was what he wanted to do. At first, everyone was very willing to help Bob. But every time he talked to someone, it was as if he wasn't satisfied, so he contacted a new person and started asking them questions. After Bob had exhausted the recruiting team, he logged into our school's alumni database, and contacted nearly every alumnus who worked at this firm downtown, even people in different divisions (i.e., not strategy). It was almost as if he were looking for some "dirt" on this company, which is silly to ask people still employed by the company. Understandably, people were starting to get annoyed by his "questionable" behavior. Finally, a partner ended it when he directly emailed the student, and said something to the tune of "Look, if you are this undecided about whether to join our company, just don't accept, it's OK." Bob accepted.

How Soon Should I Accept?

After thinking long and hard about whether the firm is the best fit for you and your career goals, accept the offer. It would be highly unlikely for a firm to offer a reward for accepting an offer immediately. In fact, it may be foolhardy to do so.

At the same time, waiting until the offer deadline isn't exactly a vote of confidence in your interest in the firm, unless you have a legitimate reason, such as waiting to hear back from another firm. As soon as you have heard back from your favorite firms, take the time to make a decision, and move on to enjoying your senior year (or the rest of your junior year if you are applying to internships).

How to Accept an Offer

First, fill out the paperwork provided by the company whose offer you would like to accept, and submit. Next, call the HR manager, and let them know you're accepting. Re-iterate that you're excited to begin working there.

Normally, the HR manager will let the rest of the hiring team know that you accepted, but if there are a few people you were particularly connected with, feel free to give them a call as well.

That's it. The final steps are quite anticlimactic. For the most part, you say yes and that's it!

Some firms throw a special event or dole out presents for those who accept. One of my friends received Tiffany cufflinks from his firm. Another friend got a huge box of food and branded stuff (water bottle, bag, etc).

You may also receive your entire bonus, half of it, or none of it at the time of signing. Whatever they don't provide at signing will be provided when you start. Be prepared for your bonus check to be much smaller than you thought it would be -- Uncle Sam wants his cut too.

Turning Down Offers without Burning Bridges

When you decide to accept an offer, make sure that you are sold on that firm. Let's say you decide you like Firm A, because Firm B has crazy work hours. But Firm B fits your career goals better. Instead of making the decision in a vacuum, talk with Firm B about your concern(s).

Whether you are unable to work out your concerns, or you're just not interested in a firm, there comes a time to turn down the offer. First, always give them the courtesy of letting them know. It's hard to do, but if you were in their shoes, you would like to know too, right?

When it comes time to reject an offer, contact your HR contact by phone. Email is slightly cowardly, because it essentially cuts off dialogue – "Here's my decision, deal with it." Be brave and contact the person who extended you the offer.

Stick to the facts of why you're not accepting the offer. Keep it brief, and then thank them for their offer again. If you liked the firm, be sure to keep in touch with them. Maybe someday it will fit better with your career goals.

How to not burn bridges:

Hi [Recruiter's name],

I am contacting you to inform you that I have taken an offer at a different firm. I would have loved the opportunity to meet more employees on March 14th, but I do not want to take an interview spot from another potential candidate and take up more of your resources. Thank you again for all the help you have given me, and I hope we can stay in touch through the summer and after graduation.

Thank you,

[your name]

Components of a successful letter:

Hi [Recruiter's Name],

I am contacting you to inform you that I have taken a full-time offer at a different firm. I would have loved the opportunity to [generic comment on working with talented/fun people], but [comment on wanting a different industry, type of consulting, or other non-fit reason for taking another job]. Thank you again for all the help you have given me, and I hope we can stay in touch after graduation.

Thank you,

[your name]

PART 4:
Case Studies

Case interviews require skill development and disciplined practice. You could memorize a bunch of frameworks from a book, but these only push you to the level of your competition. To rise above the competition, you must learn how to invent your own frameworks. Most applicants memorize the same frameworks, and therefore, they cannot differentiate themselves.

Part 4 is targeted towards helping you to develop the important skill of cracking cases during an interview. Case studies require good communication, logical thought processes and creativity. By practicing cases included in this book with your friends and mentors, you can set yourself up for success.

23

How Do I Master Case Interviews?

For most consulting candidates, the case interview is the most stressful component of the entire recruitment process. In preparation for fall recruitment, I dabbled in case interviews in the spring, did quite a few cases over the summer, and then was practicing cases almost nightly during fall recruitment. Hard work, preparation, and persistence are key.

How Do I Practice a Case?

What to bring: The practice case, scratch paper, a pencil and a mock-interviewer

1. Ask your friend, classmate, professor or family-member to read the case in its entirety

2. Ask them to read the beginning of the case out loud, without giving away "extra information." Sometimes case study interviewers will provide extra information, graphs or charts, but only if the student requests the information.

3. Concisely summarize the case in a way that demonstrates that you understand the key business ideas at hand.

4. Take a minute to ponder the case question as you jot down notes

on your scratch paper. Ask any further questions in a thoughtful and formal manner. Pretend that the person you are talking to is a management consulting recruiter at your favorite firm.

5. Note some insights and allow your mock-interviewer to let you know if you are on the right track.

6. Complete your notes, calculations and diagrams. Explain your thought process to your mock-interviewer.

7. After finishing the case, review what you missed or should have asked by reading the case yourself.

Note: Do not read the case through before practicing it with a person, unless you are really crunched for time. The questions and answers in case studies are mixed together, so you need another person to omit the extra information until you ask for it.

Skills Necessary for a Case Study

Case studies require qualitative, analytic and diagnostic abilities:

*   Ability to structure problems quickly, precisely and logically

*   Ability to immediately identify critical issues and key factors

*   Ability to intuitively identify key points

*   Ability to identify the most important numbers and eloquently explain why they are important

*   Ability to use the above skills to quickly form a concise and compelling hypothesis

*   Interpersonal skills including professionalism, a genuine demeanor, clear verbal communication and overall likeability

*   Ability to exude confidence while not seeming condescending, pretentious or a know-it-all

- Ability to communicate all logic using multiple mediums, including quick sketches, legible notes and tree-diagrams

The following Case Interview Tips will assist in mastering case interview skills, provided that you are not a superhuman management consulting rock star already. After reviewing the tips, review the Ten Step Plan to learn how to apply the tips as you practice the case studies. To be best prepared, integrate the steps that make sense in your particular situation. *Note: For case interview novices, refer to Chapter 17 to get an overview of the case study basics.*

Ten Must-Do Case Interview Tips

1. *Hypothesize*

Earlier in the book, we covered how to structure your approach to the case. Once you have determined your framework and approach to the case interview question, you will need to decide where to go. Your approach is like a road map – it is a plan on how to get there, but you still need to drive.

Let's return to the example of the profits tree to illustrate how to hypothesize.

When starting out, you can look at either revenues or costs first. To determine which to start with, hypothesize which is more likely to be the problem based on the case description.

Suppose you were helping a newspaper company, and their profits were down. You may hypothesize that declining subscriptions is lowering revenues, so that's what you state to your interviewer. Then, you ask questions to determine if that's the root cause or not.

Don't let an incorrect hypothesis discourage you. An incorrect hypothesis is beneficial, because you have learned what the problem was not. You have shrunk the possible solution space, and you have made progress.

If your hypothesis is wrong based on the data, simply adjust your hypothesis. In the newspaper example, let's say that the data shows that the number of subscriptions has actually increased. Since you discover that revenues have still declined, you say "Ok, so volume is not the problem. I think revenues could still decrease if people are trading down subscriptions, perhaps by dropping to Sunday-only deliveries. Or maybe in this economy, many more people are late in paying their bills. Let's look at those areas."

The interviewer will hint if your hypothesis is off in the interest of time. If the interviewer suggests looking at costs instead, then move to costs and start to hypothesize there.

A common mistake is to cling to a hypothesis in the face of contrary data. It may give you a feeling of security, but it's going to waste your time. When you find that subscriptions increased, don't keep thinking of ways that volume could be the issue. Instead, adjust your hypothesis and reference the data that drove your adjustment.

You can also use your hypothesis to help you move through the case more quickly. It is important to identify the high priority items. Forming a hypothesis prioritizes which branches of your approach to examine first. How you prioritize reveals how you think, which is exactly what the interviewer wants to see.

When you're hypothesizing, don't merely ask a question: ask a question and offer your suggestions on the answer. For instance, rather than saying, "So I'd like to ask about costs, what are they?" instead, say something along the lines of, "So I'd like to ask about costs. I think the three biggest cost areas are materials, labor, and transportation. Does that sound right?" Once you have the final list of cost items, ask the interviewer if he has any numbers related to these costs. The goal is to capture as much data as the interviewer has available. Getting the cost numbers would suggest that you are moving in the right direction. Cost numbers will also help inform new hypotheses and drive the case forward.

Finally, hypothesizing comes in handy when the interviewer presents you with multiple data slides. Each data slide usually has one or two key points, such as "volume is decreasing," or "material cost is rising faster than other costs." After you see multiple slides, state a hypothesis on what the overall trend could be.

For example, imagine that one graph shows that profits are declining, and another graph shows that volumes of product A are growing while volumes of product B are declining. With this information, you could hypothesize that product A has a lower profit margin than product B. If that were true, the shift mix from B to A could cause the profits to decline. This is a great way to stand out, because not all students can form such a story.

2. Draw Pictures

Drawing pictures may sound juvenile, but it can help you by jump-starting your thinking process and communicating insights.

When developing your approach, you may get stuck. Let's say you have two branches, but you feel they're not collectively exhaustive. You can draw a picture to visualize the situation. Let's say you were asked to determine if a new drug should be released to the market, but weren't sure of the costs involved. You could draw out the value chain to help determine some of the areas of costs.

Whenever you see an insight, you can also draw it out. Pretend your notebook paper is a PowerPoint slide, and from a table of data you just determined costs are rising faster than revenues. How would you communicate that point graphically? Sketch a graph, and show it to the interviewer while you explain the data shows costs are rising faster than revenues.

By viewing your pieces of paper as PowerPoint slides, you turn the dialogue into an interaction. It is important to engage the interviewer as much as possible. If the interviewer is very clear on what you're thinking, they will be much more willing to help you.

Quick Tip

Drawing line charts, data tables, notional pie charts, value chains (such as a supply chain), and tree diagrams will help you "draw conclusions" and impress your interviewer.

3. *Use Your Notes to Interact with the Interviewer*

Begin the case by writing your objectives at the top of the paper. One way to lose big points is to answer a different question from the one the interviewer asked you to answer. As you proceed through the case, re-visit those objectives every few minutes in your head to ensure you're on track. If you get lost, share your thoughts out loud on what you know, and how you think you should proceed – otherwise the interviewer can't help you.

Secondly, engage the interviewer by showing your notes. After you determine your approach, flip the paper around and ask the interviewer if it looks good. When walking the interviewer through numbers you've computed, go through your computations with the interviewer.

Make sure your notes are structured and neat. If your notes are messy and unstructured, an interviewer may chalk up your structured approach to luck rather than a consistent skill. Offer visual evidence of structure so the interviewer cannot question whether your approach is structured or not.

It should be a habit of structuring everything: approach, notes, data collection, recommendations, summary, etc. Sometimes firms collect your notes after the interview to evaluate your work!

4. *Gut Check Your Answers*

When you reach a final answer, your case is not over. Perform a quick gut check on your answer to see whether it makes sense. The reason is that your interviewer will certainly perform a gut check as well, and you will get dinged if the answer doesn't make sense. By performing a gut check, you will increase the probability that your answer makes sense.

How do you gut check? One common way is to translate numbers into more comparable numbers. So, for example, let's say you estimated the number of owned dogs in the United States at 100,000,000 dogs. Is that a reasonable answer? Try seeing how many dogs that implies per person. If you assume there are 300,000,000 people in the U.S., then that's one dog for every three people: that might seem reasonable.

However, is number of people truly driving the number of dogs? It may be that number of households is a more relevant driver – most households probably have just one dog.

If we assume that there are 100,000,000 households in the U.S., assuming 3 people per households, then suddenly 100 million dogs looks a little high. So you'd go back to your assumptions and adjust downwards. BTW: the Humane Society estimated in late 2009 that there were ~78M owned dogs in the United States.

Always think about what metric may be the most relevant to the situation, and gut check your numbers based on that.

Gut check your qualitative recommendations as well. If product A has a lower profit margin than product B, you might hypothesize that the company should try to sell more of product B. Before finalizing this recommendation, gut check your answer. Maybe product B needs to be phased out over the next few years to comply with new industry policies. Maybe product A is projected to outperform product B five to one, and regardless of the lower profit margin, it makes for sense for the company to focus its resources on product A. To gut check your answers, you can refer to the information that the interviewer has provided or, better yet, have a dialogue with the interviewer.

5. *Practice Breadth Thinking*

Breadth thinking is your ability to think widely and "out of the box." This is an essential skill for mastering a collectively exhaustive approach.

Interviewers may describe a situation and ask you to identify the root causes. After you've listed a few root causes, they'll ask, "Ok good, what else?" And that's when your brain freezes. Panic sets in because you've already thought of everything, right? You wildly grasp for a few more root causes, until you cannot think of any more, and you say, "that's it." All the while, you are left wondering if you could have thought of more.

How can you avoid this potentially panic-filled situation? There's no way to know the case ahead of time, so you need to develop your ability to engage in breadth thinking. There are two components of breadth thinking: your general business acumen and your ability to connect the dots. When faced with the "What else?" question, you'll be able to think through your business background, and connect the current situation with a situation you've seen before.

Spend some time reading articles, books and cases (ABCs) to develop your general business acumen. It is time consuming, but it should be interesting to you. It relates directly to the line of work that you're applying to!

When you read cases or articles in *The Wall Street Journal*, take a few minutes to develop a framework to address the situation referenced in the article. Once you've done that, ask yourself, "What else could be important here?" Re-evaluate your approach, and see what other areas might be relevant to the issue at hand. Consider the same article or case after taking a break. Keep asking "What else?" until you have no more ideas. Then, discuss the article and approach with a friend. They may have different insights and perspectives which will help you to expand your breadth thinking.

When it comes time for the interview, even when you're sure you considered everything, spend a little more time: Review what led you to the answers you had already given, and see if there is anything you are missing. If you find yourself with no more ideas, or you are confident that you have covered your bases, indicate that you have touched on all of the relevant areas. You want to reach this conclusion before the interviewer asks you to move on in sake of time.

Another incentive to practice breadth thinking: you will receive major points if you think of a root cause that the interviewer hasn't heard before.

6. *Practice Depth Thinking*

Depth thinking is your ability to mine for data. How many levels can you make your issue tree, while ensuring it's Mutually Exclusive and Collectively Exhaustive (MECE)? To practice this, take some of your approaches from Tip #5 (Breadth Thinking), and choose a branch. Then, see how far you can break it down. For example, revenue breaks into price and quantity. But then what areas can you explore in pricing? How about quantity? To dig deeper on price and quantity, consider driving forces behind price and quantity (supply, demand, competition, costs, market expectations, etc.). What questions would you want to ask in these subcategories to answer your hypothesis?

7. *Structure Your Math Calculations*

Take the same rigor that you use to structure your case approach, and pass it to your equations. When asked to calculate anything numerical, first identify your variables. Then, figure out how to properly relate the variables. Make sure to talk through everything you're thinking.

It's less about rote memorization of formulas, and more about thinking through the equation logically. What result do I actually get by calculating this? By missing the units consumed by each customer per year, one student's calculation read, "X customer dollars/unit," instead of "X dollars." Check your units. Units will shed some light on whether you're missing an essential part of the equation.

To practice structuring equations, practice break-even analysis and calculating market sizes. These are common tasks asked in case interviews. The equation for breakeven is:

Volume * (Price – Variable Cost) – Fixed Cost = 0.

Try variations on this: give yourself a list of variable costs to add up, or different products with different prices/variable costs, and situations where you calculate time to breakeven rather than quantity.

The generic way of calculating annual market size is:

- [Total Market Size] = [Units consumed per customer per year] x [Average price per unit] x [Total number of customers]

    - Note that the units end up being $/year

If you're calculating how much money a boot company makes from their work boots in the USA, you could set it up like this:

- [Total number of pairs of work boots sold in USA] x [Client's percentage of this total number] x [How many pairs of work boots do each customer type purchase a year] x [Average price they pay per pair]

- 100,000,000 pairs of works boots are sold annually. Your client has 10% of this market. Each customer buys 2 pairs of work boots each year, and each pair costs $150.

- [100,000,000] x [10%] x [2] x [$150]

Before you do any calculations, make your numbers as neat and structured on the page as possible. As you calculate, repeat them to the interviewer. That way, if a number is off, it's very easy to look back, see which number is wrong and re-calculate.

Take this advice to heart – many students simply sprawl numbers all over the page in their mad rush to get to an answer, which may work if they get the right answer, but will cause them to lose a lot of time investigating if they don't get the "right" answer.

Tips For Success

Remember these principles for market share:

- A company can gain market share by growing faster than its competitors. Three primary scenarios that create this are:

  1. Growing sales faster than competitors' sales are growing

  2. Increasing sales when competitor sales are stagnant

  3. Increasing or maintaining sales when competitor sales are declining.

- A company can lose market share and still grow if competitors outpace them.

- Likewise, a company could lose sales, but still gain market share if they lose sales slower than the market as a whole.

8. *Brush Up on Mental Math*

We have cheated with calculators and Excel spreadsheets for most of our lives, but calculators and Excel are not allowed in a case interview. They want to see that you have some facility with numbers and are able to crunch numbers in your head and on paper. You need to learn what calculations you can do it your head, and what calculations you need to do on paper. Your chance of making a mistake is lower on paper, but it costs more time.

To practice mental math, get into the habit of doing it in everyday tasks. For example, you buy something and get a receipt: what's ½ of your total? What's 5x your total? What's 1/3 of your total? It's unlikely to be an even number, so it will help you practice working with less-than-ideal numbers.

One helpful mental math tip is to bound the potential answer using simple equations you do know, and then estimate. A student of mine once had some trouble performing the following equation in her head:

$$43 \div 12 = ?$$

First, assign bounds to the answer by identifying numbers that are close to 43 and easily divisible by 12. You know that $36 \div 12$ is 3, and $48 \div 12$ is 4, so the answer must be between 3 and 4. Is the resulting number likely to be closer to the lower or upper bound of your range?

In this case, take $43 - 36$ to get 7. 7 goes into 12 is a little more than 0.5. 0.6 is a fair estimate, because $0.5 + 1/12$th is more than 0.55, because $1/12$th > $1/20$th. So I would round the answer up to 0.6. The actual answer is 3.58, which is reasonably easy to estimate in your head as halfway between 3.5 (42) and 3.66 (44), but it is unlikely the interviewer would expect you to get that precise. Rounding is acceptable, but aim for at least two significant figures, so in this case, 3.6.

Another great place to practice mental math is at restaurants – What would a 15% tip be? To calculate, take 10 percent of the number by shifting the decimal point to the left, then find ½ of that result, and add together. For example, suppose your dinner was $18.28. 10% of this is roughly $1.83, and half of $1.83 is about 92 cents, so a 15% tip would be about 2.75 (the exact value is 2.742).

This begs another example – How would you quickly add $1.83 and $0.92? Like above, I'd break it down into easier numbers: In this case, 92 cents is the same as $1 minus 8 cents. So add $1 to $1.83 to get $2.83, and then subtract 8 cents to get $2.75.

Furthermore, one of my favorite things to do in a case interview is convert numbers to percentages or fractions to demonstrate my ease with numbers. Suppose I get revenue numbers for the last five years: I'd say, "Well, it looks like our client's revenue has decreased from $10 million to $6 million. That's a 40% decrease." This helps demonstrate the "So what?" to the interviewer: the percentage allows an easier relative comparison.

Quick Tip: Remember your Zeros

One of the most common mistakes that candidates make during a case interview is mess up the number of zeros while doing mental math. What's 20x10000000? Did you add your zeros correctly? A great way to avoid making this simple mistake is to take your time, write down numbers, use commas, and use M (millions) or B (billions) to make counting the number of zeros more manageable. What's 100 x 4,000,000? Simple – just add two zeros to $4M. Now you have $400M. Sadly, interviewees constantly make mistakes with the number of zeros.

9. *Practice Cases with Alumni in Consulting Firms*

After you are feeling comfortable with cases, it's time to practice some cases with the experts. Find a consultant in industry and ask them to help you practice a case study. The reason for this is twofold. Not only do you get to learn more about their firm and make a connection, but you get valuable feedback from someone who has seen both sides of the interview table.

The best way to find contacts in consulting is through your school's alumni database. These people, in my experience, are very willing to help you out. Practice a case with one or two alumni in each of your favorite firms. Be wary of over-doing it at any given firm, though!

10. *Relax and Turn the Interview into a Conversation*

As you will hear in case workshops and private conversations with consultants, the most frequently mentioned tip is to relax. It's very easy to become so focused on your paper, numbers and ideas that you forget to engage the interviewer. Never speak into your paper.

More importantly, display interest in solving the problem! If consulting is truly something that interests you, the problem should interest you. Be enthusiastic and smile. Lean forward and engage the interviewer: it makes it apparent that you want to solve the problem.

Have fun with the case, and joke if you can. It puts you and the interviewer at ease.

Also, work on language. No one wants to work with a robot! For example, if you are studying a coffee shop, instead of saying, "I'm going to look at price and quantity," say, "I'm going to look at how many cups of coffee our client is selling, and how much they're selling each cup for." Which one sounds more natural?

One associate at BCG summed up the idea of relaxing nicely with the following advice:

"I know it's weird advice, but I wouldn't try too hard to impress. At the end of the day, in my experience, the interviewer wants a genuine person who's upbeat, excited about the problem at hand, can give a cogent, thoughtful answer to the question and is just generally pleasant to be around."

Imagine you were running the interview – what would you be looking for? You can tell when people are trying a little too hard and are just giving canned answers ("Why consulting? Oh because I love problem solving"). That's not to say if that's the honest answer you shouldn't give it, just qualify it with proof, smile a bunch, and just generally try to be relaxed. I'm sure that's easier said than done, but it's the truth. They want you to succeed as much as you do."

Case Evaluation Criteria

How do these tips stack up against what interviewers use to evaluate candidates? Below is a comparison of the criteria typically used by consulting firms to the ten must-do interview tips:

1. Evaluate a candidate's qualitative, analytic, and diagnostic abilities:

    a. Structured the approach to the problem logically (Covered earlier in book)

    b. Identified critical issues and key factors (Tips 1, 5, and 6)

    c. Displayed accurate, creative, or insightful thinking (Tips 1, 5, and 6)

    d. Demonstrated good business judgement and reasoning skills (Tips 1, 5, and 6)

    e. Consistently drove towards answer and recommendation (Tip 1)

    f. Got every key point (Tips 1, 5, and 6)

2. Evaluate a candidate's quantitative and analytic abilities:

    a. Identified which numbers were important and why, and used those numbers to draw a hypothesis (Tips 1, 6, and 7)

    b. Demonstrated facility with numbers and calculations (Tips 7 and 8)

3. Evaluate a candidate's soft skills (Tips 2, 3, and 10):

   a. Acts professional

   b. Communicates well

   c. Was confident

   d. Was likeable

10 Step Plan to Ace Your Interviews

Now that we have gone over 10 tips to ace your case interviews, here's a 10-step plan to help you practice these tips. Think of the tips section as your case strategy, and this section as the implementation plan.

1. Read, read, read (*College2Consulting*, the news, *Good to Great, Say It with Charts*, the *Vault Guide*, etc.). Start reading business books. Some good ones may include books by management consulting firms, as well as articles freely available on their websites. This is to build your general business exposure, so that you can begin inventing your own frameworks.

2. While reading *The Wall Street Journal*, lay out a structure of how to approach the situation in each article. When you have laid out your structure, ask "What else should we consider?" Repeat until you can't think of anything else. Do three articles a day.

   Note: This step also builds your general business acumen, in addition to practicing your breadth thinking!

3. Practice at least 10 case interviews with trusted friends or mentors. Have them give feedback not only on how close you were to the "answer," but how structured you were, how confident you seemed and how excited you sounded. Practice like you play!

4. Now that you have a couple of cases under your belt, go back and skim through the reference books again, to focus on more advanced tips you may have missed before.

5. Practice advanced techniques in everyday life. Creating unique frameworks to daily problems, hypothesizing, remaining confident when asked difficult questions in class, mental math, etc.

6. Reach out to people in consulting firms with whom you can practice a case. As mentioned in the "Pre-recruitment Networking" chapter, start with one person. Meet them and practice a case with them before you ask to meet with someone else at the firm. Of course, get feedback after your case. Feedback from a person in industry is insurmountably more valuable than feedback from peers.

7. Form a case-interview group with your peers, where you simulate actual interview situations, complete with the obligatory small talk.

8. Pick a consulting firm, read some articles on their website, and debate the articles with your case-interview group. What do you like about their solution? How do you think they could have approached the problem better? The point of this exercise is to develop your ability to hold an intellectual discussion on strategy topics, which can be a huge benefit in interviews.

9. Remember that preparing for your fit interviews, researching firms and developing good questions to ask the interviewer can be just as important. Don't put all of your metaphorical management consulting eggs in the case interview basket. Make a schedule that takes your other necessary preparation into consideration.

10. Finally, interview with every consulting firm you can! Each interview can be seen as practice for the ones you really care about. I once took this to the extreme while looking for an internship. There was one big day where employers came to campus, and you could sign up for interview time slots. Most

students signed up for 2 or 3 interviews. I signed up for a dozen. That's right, 12 interviews in one day. This was great practice in all aspects, and exposed me to several firms that I seriously considered.

Case interviews are overwhelming for everyone at first. The interview format is foreign, there's significant pressure, and you're being judged by someone with far more experience. Remember that with enough practice, you will come to tolerate case interviews, and perhaps even enjoy them!

So start today: as the cliché goes, a journey of 1000 miles begins with a single footstep. If you follow and stick with these 10 tips and 10 steps, you will eventually reach the point of mastery. Once you have mastered cases, you can invent your own frameworks to suit the situation without training wheels like the solutions to cases in this book. Your ticket to management consulting is to blow away interviewers with unique perspectives and frameworks, developed through lots of practice.

24

How Do I Practice Framework Creation?

Members of the elite military force, U.S. Navy SEAL Team 6, practiced the assault on Osama Bin Laden's compound over and over again prior to the President giving the go ahead to commence the mission. No matter how many times they rehearsed the assault, SEAL Team 6 would never be able to practice the exact performance – there were simply too many variables and unknowns. They trained so that they could improvise within the context of the situation.

Likewise, in preparing for the case interview, you will never be able to know what to do ahead of time. The path to success in case interviewing is to know what kind of variation you are likely to see, and practice enough cases so that you can improvise flawlessly within the context of a 30-45 minute interview every time. You will know when you are ready when you have the confidence to improvise when a difficult roadblock is thrown in your path: most other students will panic.

For most students, building a unique framework is a daunting process at first. But it doesn't need to be: with practice, you will get better at generating a structured approach, developing a corresponding hypothesis, and tackling cases confidently. The goal is to be able to improvise and impress your interviewer by developing a unique,

MECE framework that specifically addresses the problem, rather than relying on an overused, canned framework from a book.

To get you started on your path to mastery, here are nineteen sample strategy questions that touch on common case interview types, along with a sample framework and discussion. Read each question and pause. Draw out your own structure before reading the sample solution. Then, compare your solution to the one provided. These are not complete case studies; rather, they are exercises to improve your case interview framework creation abilities.

There are limitless solutions, so if the framework that you develop does not match the solution in the book, it does not mean that you are wrong – just make sure that your framework gets to the same place as the suggested framework. If you think of something that isn't included, bonus points!

Do not memorize these frameworks, or any other frameworks for that matter. It hurts your ability to improvise. The example framework gives you one of many ways to approach the problem. By comparing your answer to the one provided, you can evaluate for yourself which elements make the most sense. You can also determine which framework (yours, the sample solution, or a combination of both) is the most elegant way to solve the problem.

19 Common Case Interview Types:

1. Company assessment
2. Capacity constraint analysis
3. Desire to grow number of customers
4. Pricing implementation
5. Grow core business
6. Barriers to entry
7. M&A synergies
8. Portfolio management

9. Substitute analysis

10. International expansion

11. Due diligence

12. Profitability

13. Adjacent market growth

14. Options for new market entry

15. Organizational scaling

16. Branding

17. M&A post merger integration

18. Pricing analysis

19. Competitive response

Quick Tip

How to effectively practice framework development:

Once you understand the objective of the strategic question, ask yourself, "What's most important here?" List out what could impact the answer (e.g., market dynamics, competitive landscape, customer concentration, etc.). Organize this list in a logical manner and prioritize or hypothesize what might be most relevant. Then, consider how to simplify the framework.

Also note that case interview questions are not mutually exclusive; most case interview questions rely on an understanding of multiple types of questions. Entering a market could involve M&A; going to market with a new product will involve pricing; increasing your profits will involve reducing costs and increasing sales. The point is that designing a framework for one category of case questions will augment your ability to dive deeper on a different case question.

1. *Company Assessment*

Everyone seems to be talking about an amazing new company. Your mom likes their products, your uncle wants to invest in it, your professor says it's the next iPod. Because you were born a skeptic, you decide to do your research. There has got to be something wrong with this company, right?

How do you categorize your research to make sure that you are both efficient and exhaustive in your search for dirt on this company?

One possible framework: The 5 C's – this novice framework should not actually be used in a case study because it has been used far too many times already and lacks originality. That said, it's such a fundamental framework, that you need to be familiar with it in order to develop your own frameworks. You can incorporate the same ideas as the 5 C's, because they are good ideas. Just don't say, "I'd like to look at 5 C's…," because the interviewer may penalize you for lack of originality.

---

5 C's

- **Customers** – Who are they and what do they want?

- **Competition** – Who are the competitors and how well are they positioned?

- **Costs** – What are the fixed and variable costs?

- **Channels** – What are the sales & distribution channels?

- **Company** – What are the products/services offered? What is the competitive advantage? What is the financial positioning? Etc.

Another possible framework – The 4 P's:

```
┌─────────────────┐
│      4 P's      │
└─────────────────┘
```

- **Product** – What is the product, and what's special about it?

- **Price** – What's the selling price, demand elasticity, and cost of development?

- **Place** – What are the distribution channels and geographic footprint of the company?

- **Promotion** – What is the sales & marketing strategy?

Another possible framework:

```
                    ┌──────────────┐
                    │ New Company  │
                    └──────────────┘
                   ╱                ╲
        ┌──────────────────┐   ┌──────────────────┐
        │ Internal Factors │   │ External Factors │
        └──────────────────┘   └──────────────────┘
```

Manufacturing Processes   Pricing   Suppliers   Competitors

Financials   Management & Organizational Structure   Market Variables   Customers

There is no right or wrong in framework development. The point is that by structuring your thoughts, you can more easily hone in on the relevant points. It also makes it easier for your interviewer to track your train of thought.

2. *Capacity Constraint Analysis:* The largest bottling facility in Buenos Aires has maxed out its output capacity. Limitations are such that the firm cannot increase its output even though customer demand is strong and growing.

Create a list of the possible constraints, categorize those constraints, and hypothesize which are the most likely culprits.

One possible framework:

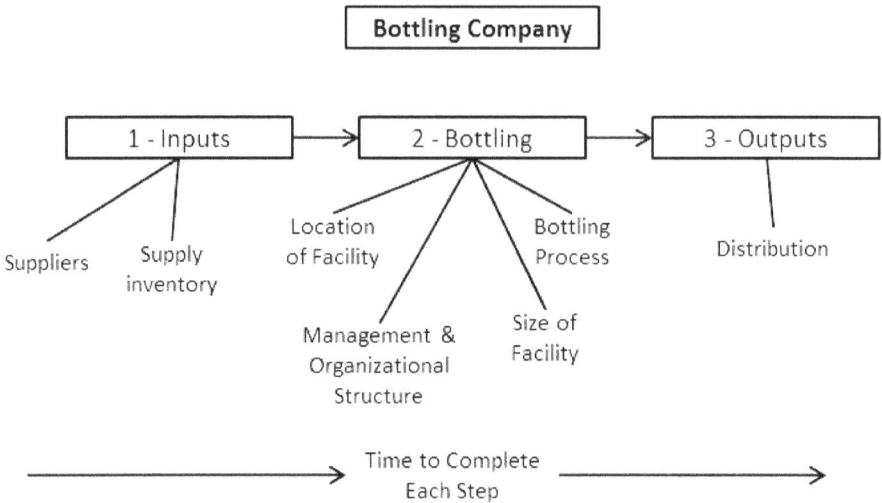

Discussion – The bottling company is strategically located in a large city, so it is unlikely that location of facility and distribution would be a primary constraint. The downside of the location is that it may be far from necessary inputs such as raw materials. I'd like to look at the inputs first. Then, let's investigate if the bottling process needs to be upgraded and try to eliminate any process "bottle necks."

3. *Desire to Grow Number of Customers:* Your local gym has a capacity for 1500 members, but membership has been about 500 since the opening of the gym 9 months ago. The gym is impeccably clean and known in the area for having good prices, amazing personal trainers, clean equipment, and even towel service. The manager of the gym is constantly folding towels because he has nothing to do. Eventually you become friends with him and he learns that you are a strategy consultant.

He's becomes very excited and asks you to help him think about how to improve membership at the gym. What do you say?

Introduction – "I've been going to this gym for a few months now and I love it. Your facilities are in perfect condition, and I believe that anyone who walks into this gym would want to join. Other gyms have strong current membership implying that it is not a market problem.

I suspect the problem is that not enough people are coming to visit the gym. You obviously have a great reputation, but for some reason that doesn't appear to be driving people to come visit the gym. What would you guestimate the membership sign up rate to be versus the number of people who make first time visits?"

Manager: "Hmmm, tough question, but probably about 10% - way better than any of the other gyms in the area though."

One possible framework: The goal then is to motivate more potential customers to come visit the gym. To do that, let's first compare the gym to the customer alternatives.

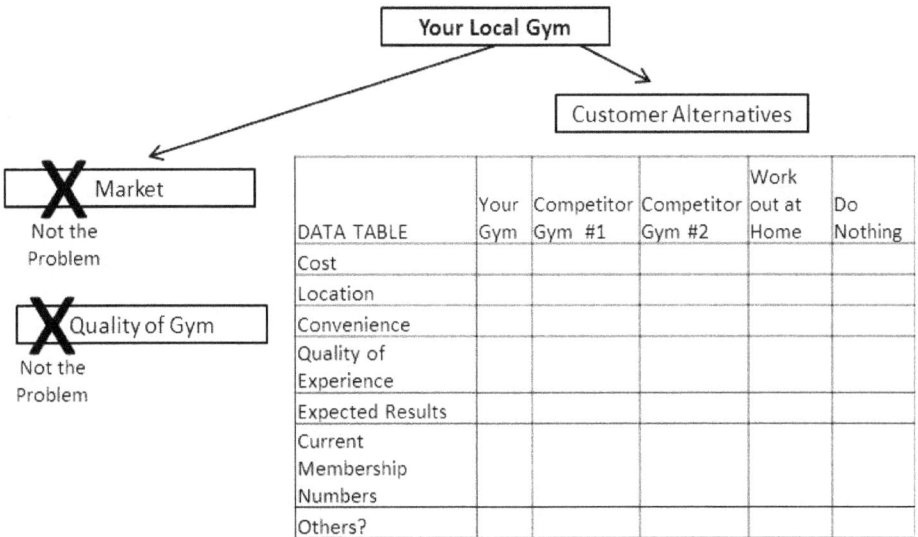

Your Local Gym

Customer Alternatives

X Market — Not the Problem

X Quality of Gym — Not the Problem

DATA TABLE	Your Gym	Competitor Gym #1	Competitor Gym #2	Work out at Home	Do Nothing
Cost					
Location					
Convenience					
Quality of Experience					
Expected Results					
Current Membership Numbers					
Others?					

Discussion – There could be many levers we could pull to boost membership: free training sessions, discounts, access to classes, etc. However, we should first understand the relative strengths and weaknesses of the customer alternatives (e.g., other gyms, working out at home, etc.) to understand how we are relatively positioned. I'd like to start with consumer awareness. My guess is that since we are a relatively new gym, we still have low awareness among consumers: we may be poorly positioned among most consumers on that attribute.

4. *Pricing Implementation:* A popular gum company has been selling its gum for $0.25 for the last decade, but inflation, increasing material costs, and increasing distribution costs have caused the company to reassess its pricing strategy. They are worried that since the $0.25 price point is so engrained in their customers' heads that increasing the price could be catastrophic for business.

What is your recommendation for the company if the goal is to maximize profits?

One possible framework:

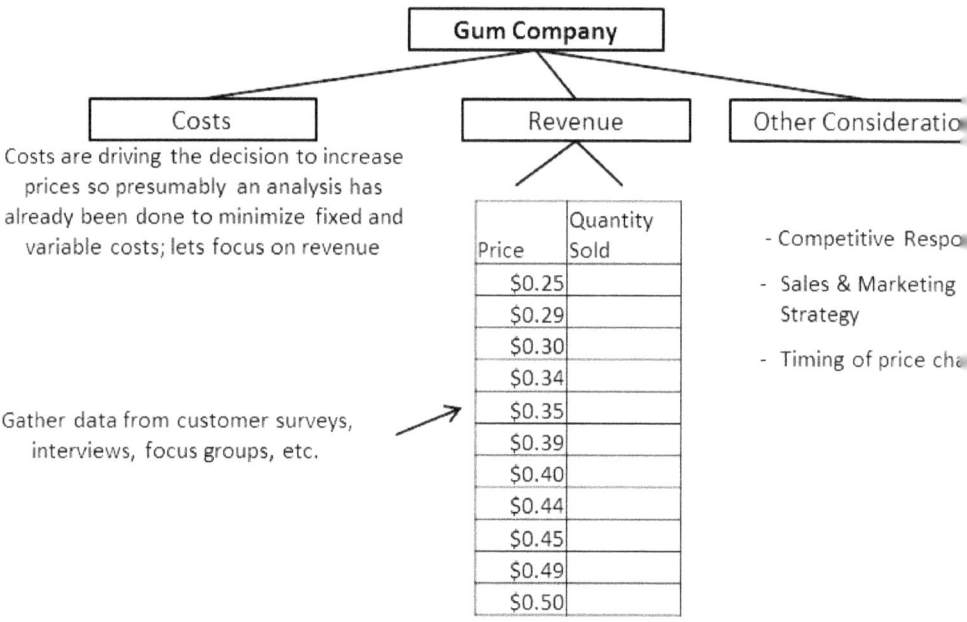

```
                           ┌─────────────────────┐
                           │    Gum Company      │
                           └─────────────────────┘
                ┌────────────────────┼──────────────────────┐
┌───────────────────────┐  ┌──────────────────┐  ┌──────────────────────┐
│        Costs          │  │     Revenue      │  │  Other Consideratio  │
└───────────────────────┘  └──────────────────┘  └──────────────────────┘
```

Costs are driving the decision to increase prices so presumably an analysis has already been done to minimize fixed and variable costs; lets focus on revenue

Price	Quantity Sold
$0.25	
$0.29	
$0.30	
$0.34	
$0.35	
$0.39	
$0.40	
$0.44	
$0.45	
$0.49	
$0.50	

Gather data from customer surveys, interviews, focus groups, etc.

- Competitive Respo

- Sales & Marketing Strategy

- Timing of price cha

Discussion – An increasing price will almost certainly have a negative effect on the number of gum packages sold. Using the data from the completed table, I would dentify the revenue that maximizes price (recall that revenue = price x quantity sold). The downside is that gathering data through surveys and focus groups is notoriously unreliable. To mitigate the risks associated with increasing prices, I would consider how to modify the sales and marketing strategy to minimize a negative customer response. I would also consider rolling out the price change at different times depending on the geographic location and our understanding of the local customer base.

Recall that profit is revenue minus costs. For example, the gum costs $0.20 to make and is sold for $0.30. There are also other expenses associated with selling that gum including taxes and general administrative costs. If these other expenses are $0.04, then the profit or net income per sale is $0.06. This means that your net profit margin is $0.06 ÷ $0.30 = 20%. Net profit margin equals net income divided by revenue.

5. *Grow Core Business:* An information technology services provider for the United States Government has experienced decreasing market share. The IT firm wants to improve growth within its core markets.

What are the considerations and how should the firm recover its market share?

One possible framework:

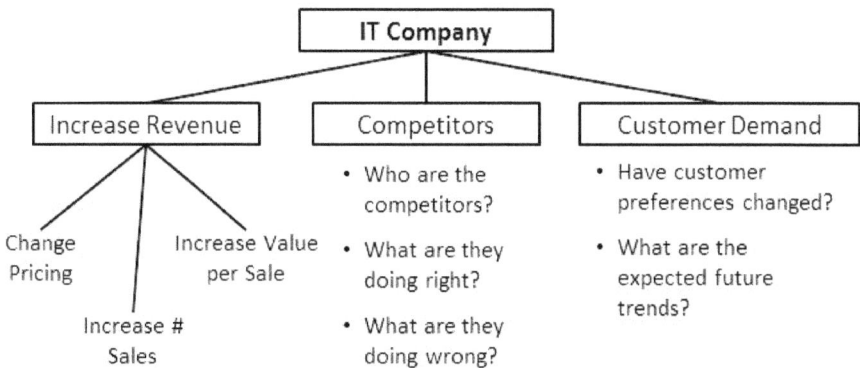

Discussion – To understand what the IT company can do to increase its market share, I need to investigate its own value proposition and if there is an opportunity to drive new sales. I also need an understanding of what the competitors have been doing such that they have successfully stolen share. Conducting a benchmarking study may be in order. Finally, a deep investigation of the customer needs, funding sources, and stakeholders will be vital.

Quick Tip

What is benchmarking?

Benchmarking is the process of determining who is the best, identifying their best practices, and then implementing those practices with a different organization

General Rules for Benchmarking

- Look for examples of success everywhere
- Do not reinvent what others have already discovered; borrow ideas and imitate others
- Adapt those ideas for your own organization
- Constantly monitor progress
- Repeat

The Benchmark

Sample Benchmarks

- Profit margins
- Delivery time
- Units/day output
- Growth rate
- Customer satisfaction

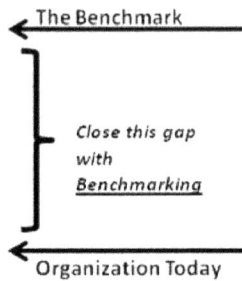

Close this gap with

Benchmarking

Organization Today

6. *Barriers to Entry:* A predominantly European shipping company wants to expand its operations into the Middle East and North Africa.

What are the barriers to entering these new markets?

One possible framework:

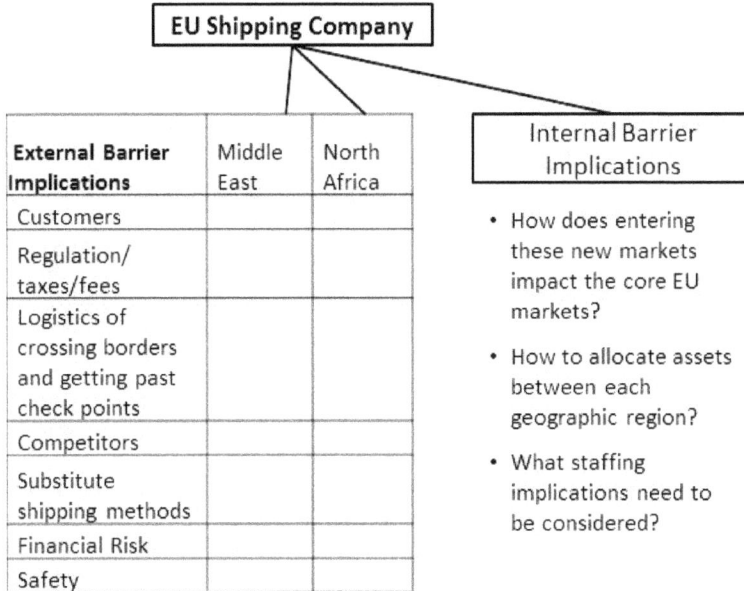

```
                    ┌─────────────────────────┐
                    │   EU Shipping Company    │
                    └─────────────────────────┘
```

External Barrier Implications	Middle East	North Africa
Customers		
Regulation/ taxes/fees		
Logistics of crossing borders and getting past check points		
Competitors		
Substitute shipping methods		
Financial Risk		
Safety		

Internal Barrier Implications

- How does entering these new markets impact the core EU markets?

- How to allocate assets between each geographic region?

- What staffing implications need to be considered?

Discussion – Internal barrier implications are relatively standard hurdles to new market entry. They should not be considered primary barriers to entry, although we should keep them in mind. That said, there are some notable barriers to entry including entering a new regulatory environment and selling to an entirely new customer community. Due to the expected complexities in entering either the Middle East or North Africa shipping market, I would consider focusing on one geographic region at a time. It may even reduce the risk of entry substantially if you establish a pilot program where you target one country at first.

7. *M&A Synergies:* SouthNorth Airlines just placed a preliminary bid to acquire WestEast Airlines in an all cash transaction. A large team of analysts was put together to determine synergies between the firms as a key input to a Return on Investment (ROI) analysis.

What synergies do two airlines have in common? Help the team of analysts think through a comprehensive list of synergies to improve the ROI argument. How do you bucket those synergies?

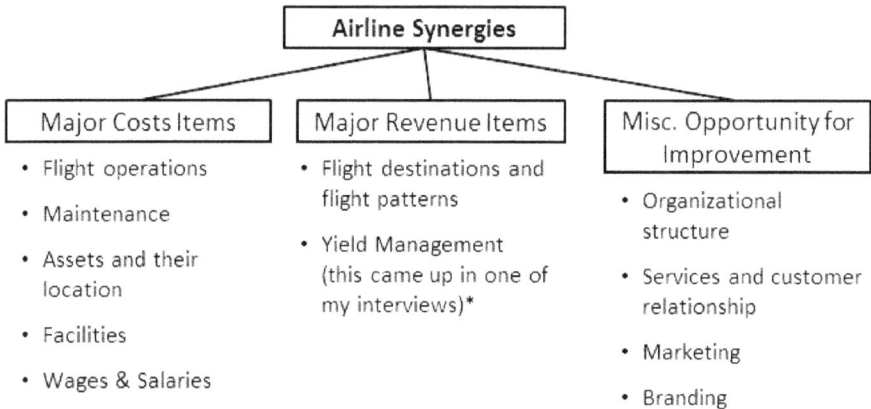

```
                        ┌─────────────────────────┐
                        │     Airline Synergies   │
                        └─────────────────────────┘
```

Major Costs Items	Major Revenue Items	Misc. Opportunity for Improvement
• Flight operations	• Flight destinations and flight patterns	• Organizational structure
• Maintenance	• Yield Management (this came up in one of my interviews)*	• Services and customer relationship
• Assets and their location		• Marketing
• Facilities		• Branding
• Wages & Salaries		

Yield Management

Yield management is a process of maximizing profits from perishable goods, including airline seats, by anticipating and modifying customer behavior. For example, if an airplane holds 210 people, the airline will probably book more than 210 seats, but exactly how many more seats depends on the outputs of algorithms that were developed using mountains of historical data. Yield management also includes modifying prices to influence a customer's decision to buy.

Discussion – The goal is to identify synergies between two large airlines. The best place to start is to look at the largest revenue generating sources and largest drivers of cost. A company's 10-k has this type of information. I would then bucket those revenue and cost items into what needs to be optimized and consolidated. I'd also consider how a change in branding or marketing could impact longer term revenue projections.

My hypothesis is that the most notable synergies will come from optimization of flight patterns.

8. *Portfolio Management:* A large conglomerate makes washing machines, sells breakfast foods, transports coal in North America, publishes books in Canada, and makes radar for the Ministry of Defense in the United Kingdom.

The CEO has hired you to do an analysis of their portfolio. What recommendations would you give the CEO?

One possible framework: consider using the Growth-share matrix also known as the BCG Matrix attributed to Bruce D. Henderson.

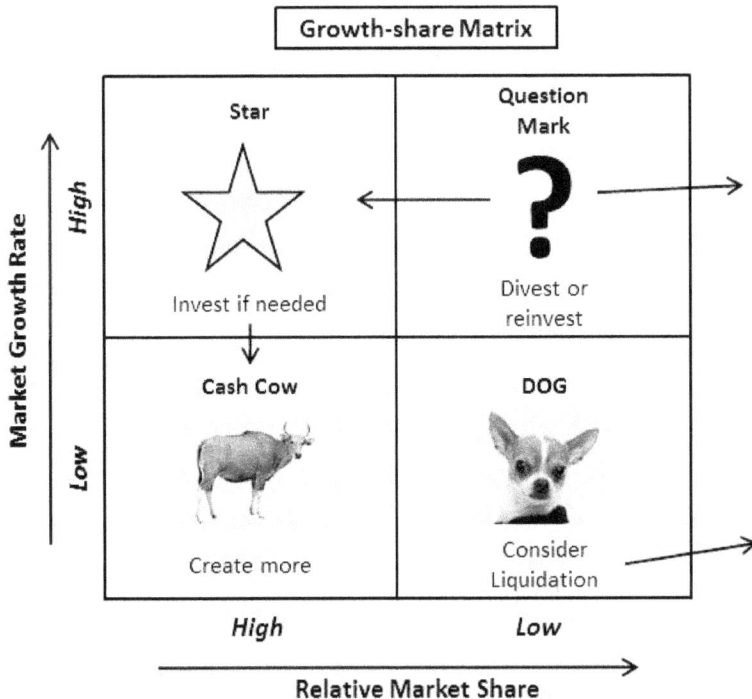

Growth-share Matrix

	Star	Question Mark
High	Invest if needed	Divest or reinvest
Low	Cash Cow — Create more	DOG — Consider Liquidation

Market Growth Rate

Relative Market Share — High / Low

Image Source: FreeDigitalPhotos.net

Cash Cow: Businesses with high relative market share within a low growth market. Create more cash cows.

Dog: Businesses with low relative market share within a low growth market. Consider liquidating dogs.

Question Mark: Businesses with low relative market share within a high growth market. Divest or reinvest.

Star: Businesses with high relative market share within a high growth market. Invest if needed, this is where you want to be. Stars have a tendency to turn into cows in the long run.

Discussion – I would start by categorizing the various pieces of the business as either being a dog, question mark, star, or cash cow. Ideally, we would create a portfolio of cash cows with a few stars and question marks. I would also like to look into a variety of other considerations prior to making a final recommendation. Financials and market projections would be at the top of my list in addition to an analysis of untapped synergies.

9. *Substitute Analysis:* A substitute is something that is interchangeable. For breakfast, eggs are a substitute to cereal. For movies, Redbox is a substitute to Netflix. For sun protection, a hat is a substitute to sunscreen.

How would you help an egg company address the competitive threat from cereal? What are some other substitutes to Netflix, and what can Netflix do to avoid erosion of market share? How do you continue growth in the hat industry, when the price of sunscreen just dropped 10%?

One possible framework:

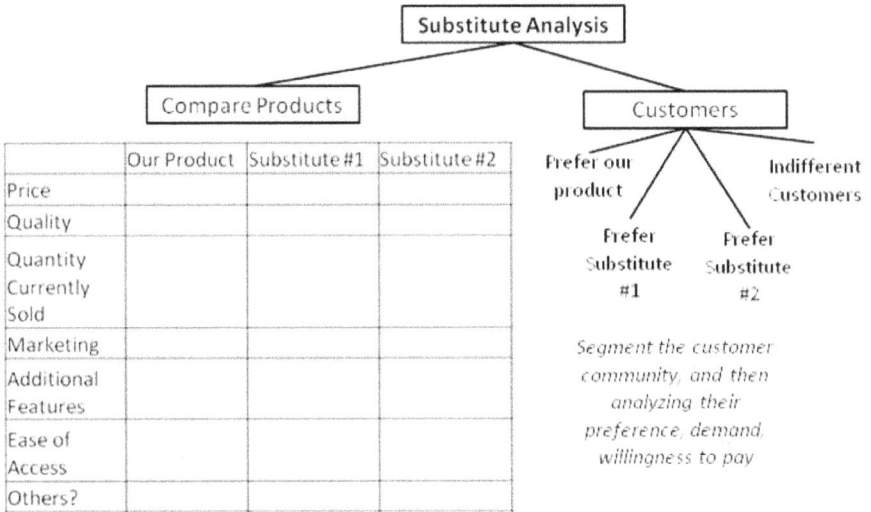

Discussion – I'd like to start out by comparing our product (or service for that matter) against its substitutes along a variety of metrics including price and quality. I'd then investigate customer preferences. Segmenting the customer community into groups such as those who prefer our product, those who prefer substitute #1, and those who prefer substitute #2 would help in analyzing customer demand. It might be helpful to also look at the customer community that does not have a preference between our product and the substitutes, because this might be the community that is most easily swayed. This information should provide a sufficient knowledge foundation from which to construct a strategy to mitigate the competitive threat of substitutes.

10. *International Expansion:* A reputable premier beer company from Wisconsin has had relatively stable sales over the last decade. The firm has enjoyed its comfortable ride during the peaks and troughs of a troubled economy. It has a strong distribution network set up in the United States. Wino Consulting has carved out a niche in the alcohol industry over the last few years and has become the go-to consulting firm in the industry.

The Wisconsin Beer company has hired Wino Consulting to help figure out how to sell its beer internationally.

One possible framework:

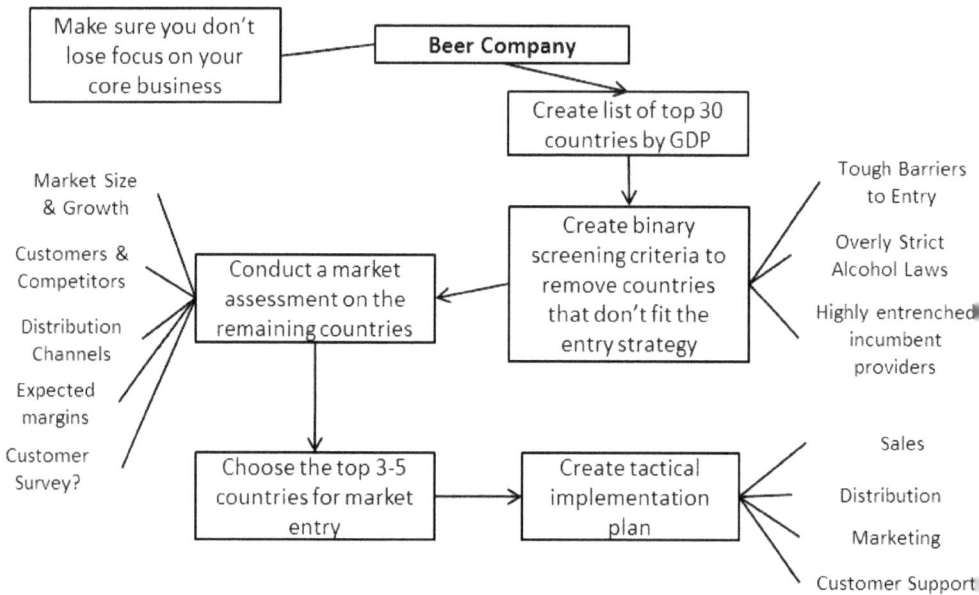

Discussion – The world is a big place, so we need to neck down the scope of opportunities to identify the best geographic locations to enter, then develop the tactical implementation plan. I would start by looking at the top 30 countries by GDP or another metric such as population size. I would then remove countries from the list that are obviously bad choices. Strict barriers to entry or regulatory measures would create enough of a reason to remove the country from the original list of 30. I would then conduct a typical market assessment of the remaining countries. A market assessment would include size and growth the local beer market, customer or competitor trends, existing distribution channels, etc. Using these qualitative and quantitative metrics, I would choose 3-5 countries with the best chance for success. Finally, we would need to create a tactical implementation plan.

11. *Due Diligence:* Defense contractors have been buying a lot of small cyber security companies to gain access to the growing market driven

by defensive measure to protect against the threat from Chinese hackers. One of these defense contractors calls up a partner at your consulting firm and says, "although we have been making tanks for the past 50 years, we want to enter the cyber security market because we need to diversify out of our current flat market."

The tank company hires your consulting firm to perform due diligence on a medium sized cyber security firm based in Virginia. What are the types of things you need to consider to determine the selling price of the cyber security firm?

One possible framework:

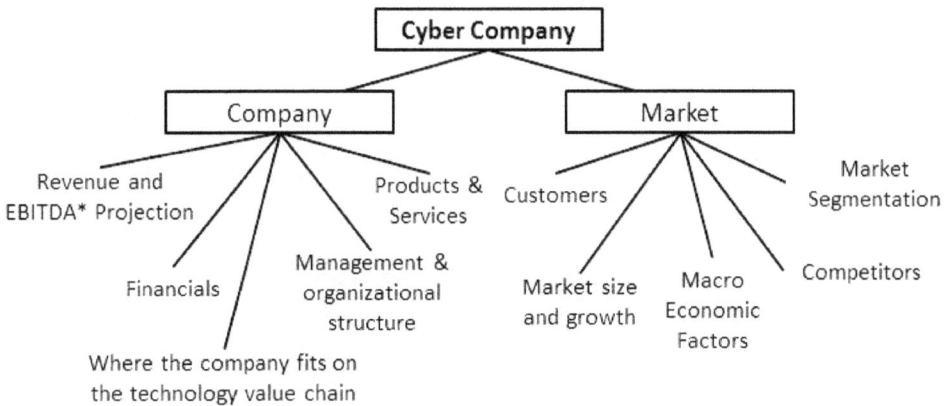

Discussion – Aside from performing a standard due diligence which includes the various factors mentioned in the framework, I would also want to consider synergies, post acquisition integration implications, how the state of the market will impact the acquisition price, and the longer term return on investment (ROI).

12. *Profitability:* A global leader in wind turbine design and manufacturing based in Germany has just released a massive new wind turbine to the market which incorporates permanent magnets. Recent increases in costs have really hurt the company's profitability.

Q1 and Q2 Segmentation of Costs

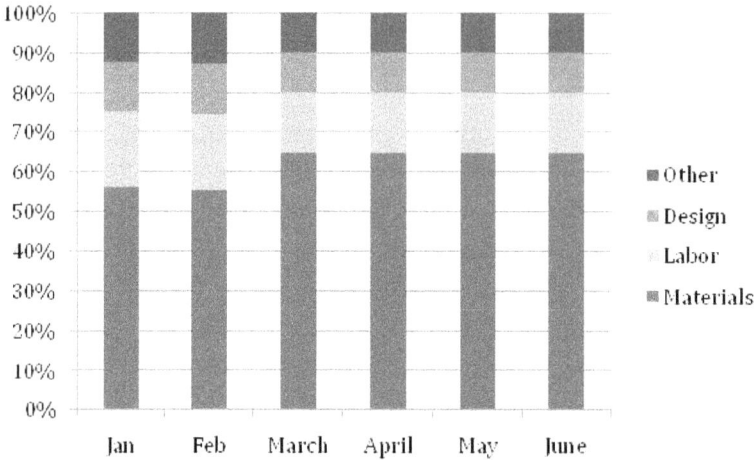

Unfortunately, due to a Chinese near-monopoly of permanent magnets, the price of this material just increased by 400%, resulting in a massive relative increase in the cost of materials.

Help the wind turbine manufacturer maintain profitability and minimize the margin compression as a result of increasing material costs.

One possible framework:

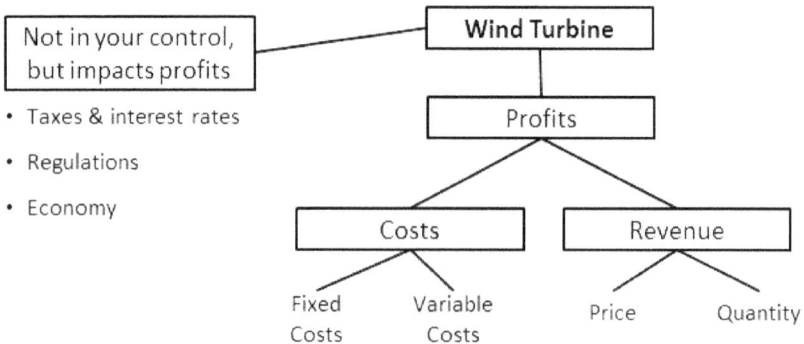

Discussion – The permanent magnet 400% cost increase must have happened in March, according to the bar chart. As a percentage of total costs though, materials increased by less than 10%, implying that the bulk of material costs are not associated with the permanent magnets.

Looking at variable costs, we may be able to find enough cost cutting opportunities to offset the increase in the permanent magnets. First, is there a way we could avoid using permanent magnets? What would the resulting impact be on customer demand or re-design costs? Assuming we must use permanent magnets, we might be able to reduce other material costs. Can we consolidate our buying power with fewer vendors for other components? Could we use a lower grade metal in any non-critical areas? Finally we could reduce costs outside of materials: labor, design, and other. For example, maybe some components could be outsourced to a manufacturer with a lower cost base (e.g., manufacturer in Mexico or China).

Beyond costs, an interesting idea would be to increase prices to absorb the hit. Key competitors who also incorporate permanent magnets will face the same changes in material costs. As long as the price is not increased too dramatically, the company should be able to maintain margins without losing market share.

However, the client should think carefully about this: another competitor could just keep their price the same, damaging their margin but perhaps picking up volume to compensate from all of the players who did raise their costs. So it could depend on our share: is our client a market leader or a niche player? They may have more latitude to raise prices if they're the market leader than if they are not.

13. *Adjacent Market Growth:* A big 4 telecommunications provider in the United States has been involved in a pricing war with its largest competitor, and as a result, their customers' monthly phone bills have been reduced by an average of 25%. The telecommunications provider has decided that if it wants to continue growing at projected rates, it will need to investigate adjacent markets.

Help your telecommunications client identify new markets that they could plausibly enter in the next 12-18 months.

One possible framework:

Adjacent Market Map

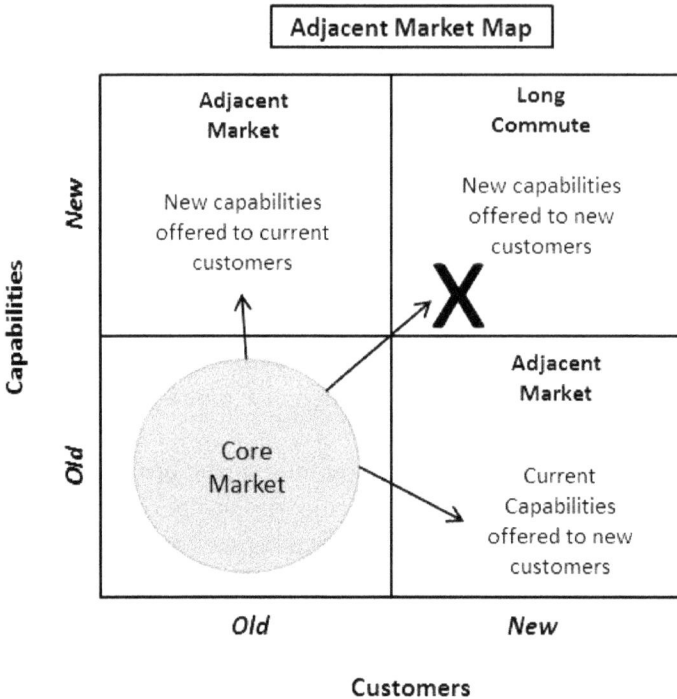

Additional information necessary before market entry:

- Size and growth
- Customers & Competitors
- Macro economic factors and market trends
- Sales & distribution requirements
- Customer service requirements
- Other synergies with core markets

- Costs of market entry

- Barriers to entry

- Others?

Discussion – To start, let's create a list of adjacent markets. Since we need to enter the market in the next 12-18 months, it probably doesn't make sense to look at new capabilities and new customers. We should instead focus on shorter commutes like selling current capabilities to new customers or selling new capabilities to our current customers. After creating a list, I would prioritize that list of adjacent markets to identify the markets where we have the best chance for success.

14. *Options for New Market Entry:* GenerateMe designs generators for a variety of applications. They make small generators that typically power flood lights, but they also make massive generators that are installed in dams across North America. The company decides that they want to sell generators to the Federal Government and the Department of Defense in particular, but they are not quite sure how to offer their products to this new customer community.

What are the avenues to new market entry and what is your recommendation?

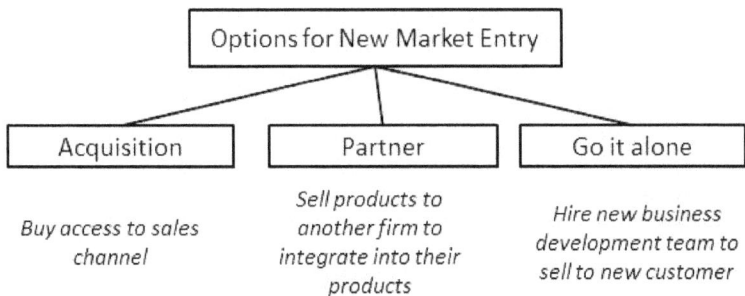

```
                    ┌──────────────────────────────┐
                    │ Options for New Market Entry │
                    └──────────────────────────────┘
                      /             │            \
          ┌──────────────┐  ┌──────────────┐  ┌──────────────┐
          │ Acquisition  │  │   Partner    │  │  Go it alone │
          └──────────────┘  └──────────────┘  └──────────────┘
```

	Acquisition	Partner	Go it alone
Discussion:	*Buy access to sales channel*	*Sell products to another firm to integrate into their products*	*Hire new business development team to sell to new customer*
Pros:			
Cons:			

Discussion: An acquisition would require substantial upfront investment, and attractively priced targets may not be available. Partnering, or selling products to another firm, means less market share. My recommendation would be to enter the market organically. Assuming the quality of the products is strong relative to the competition, I would suggest hiring high caliber business development personnel. These recruits would be familiar with selling products to the government, with a history of closing the deal. Hiring the right people can gain access to the Federal customer community. We should also think about hiring new customer service personnel to specifically address the needs of the new customer.

15. *Organizational Scaling:* A friend of yours just started a headphones company where the ear buds never actually fall out of your ears when you go running. An article about the headphones is about to be published in a popular technology magazine. Your friend has only sold 500 pairs so far, but everyone is expecting the product to take off.

How do you help your friend scale up the company so that it is prepared to receive orders of thousands of headphones?

One possible framework:

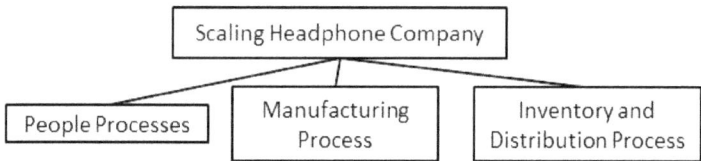

	Scaling Headphone Company		
	People Processes	Manufacturing Process	Inventory and Distribution Process
Considerations:	•Roles & Responsibilities	•Time to manufacture •Costs	•Size of inventory •Optimize distribution
Near-term Ramp Up:			
Long-term Sustainability:			

Map to customer demand; also be cognizant of potential for new market entrants and other competitors

Discussion – Scaling a business to prepare for a substantial increase in sales can be quite tricky. The first thing we need to know is a projection of how many orders are expected. An optimistic, pessimistic, and most likely projection of customer demand is ideal. Next, develop a near-term plan to manufacture and distribute headphones to meet this demand. Since headphones are small and light, I expect inventory costs to be quite low. So it might be smart to stock up on inventory to prepare for a large increase in orders. Thinking about scaling the people process, the manufacturing processes, and the inventory and distribution process will be vital. In the long run, once customer demand stabilizes, minimizing inventory and focusing on reducing manufacturing and distribution costs will be important to maximize profits while meeting customer demand. In short, stock up on inventory now to get you through a few months based on projections of customer demand.

I would stock up to meet the most likely projection of customer demand. The idea of exclusivity can be quite attractive. If the optimistic scenario actually happens and demand is greater than supply, the backlog will start to increase. As long as backlog can be met within a reasonable amount of time – say a few weeks – then using the scarcity of the product to your advantage could be smart.

16. *Branding:* Your local internet provider has a reputation for horrible customer service. In fact, all of your friends say, "if there was another option, I would switch in a heartbeat." Now, a second internet provider finally opened shop in your area. Your current internet provider was obviously aware that the new entrant was on its way in. To improve customer service, they fired the majority of their customer service staff and outsourced the work to a variety of regional staff augmentation firms. They also decided that rebranding would help disassociate their name from bad customer service.

When rebranding the company, what types of things need to be considered?

One possible framework:

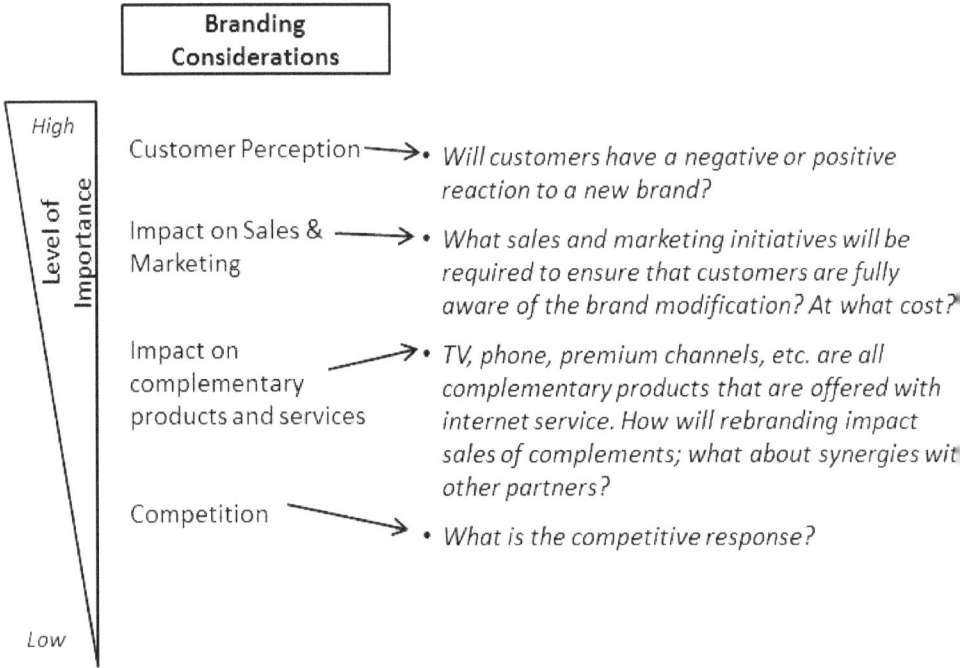

Discussion – At first glance, rebranding appears to be a fantastic decision, but let's consider a few things - most importantly customer perception. Rebranding has been very successful in the past with other companies, so let's assume that rebranding succeeds in overcoming a reputation for bad customer service. Unfortunately, there is limited awareness of the new brand. This could negatively impact sales. There are a few other things to consider in order of importance: sales and marketing, complementary products/services, and competitive response.

17. *M&A Post Merger Integration:* A large hotel chain, HolidayOut, has just acquired a motel chain, Motel 7. Management at HolidayOut wants to integrate the two chains, optimize operations, and maximize profitability.

They have hired your consulting firm to put together a post merger integration (PMI) strategy.

One possible framework:

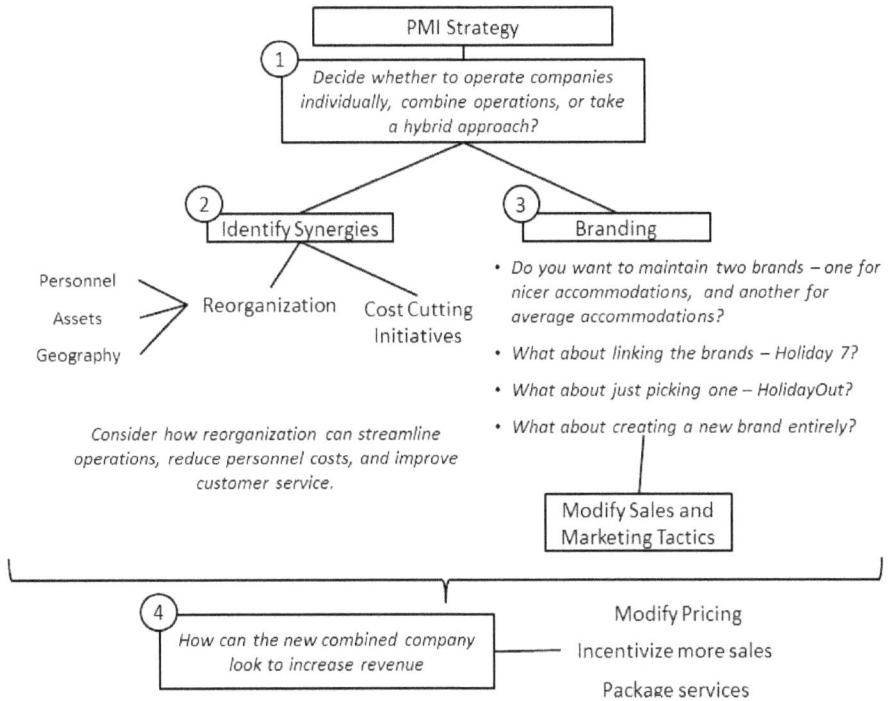

Discussion – The primary goal coming out of the acquisition is to maximize profits. To do this, I would start by determining what is most profitable - operate the 2 companies separately, completely combine operations, or take a hybrid approach. Given that there are notable synergies yet the companies have successfully operated independently, I would take a hybrid approach. In other words, integrate the companies in certain areas such as vendors, partnerships, customer service, and rewards programs while keeping certain day-to-day operations separate. This separation could simplify the PMI, ensure continuity of operations, and help maximize profitability. I would then look to at synergies to determine where are the best cost-cutting opportunities. A reorganization of assets, management, and headquarters is necessary. I would also want to look into how to brand the new combined company. Finally, I would like to consider how a new integrated organization can look to increase revenue.

18. *Pricing Analysis:* Mircrohard, a major software development firm, has just developed a new cloud computing, social networking, customer relationship management software tool. Microhard has hired your consulting firm to determine a selling price for the software.

What are the considerations that you need to think about prior to
setting a selling price of a new product?

One possible framework:

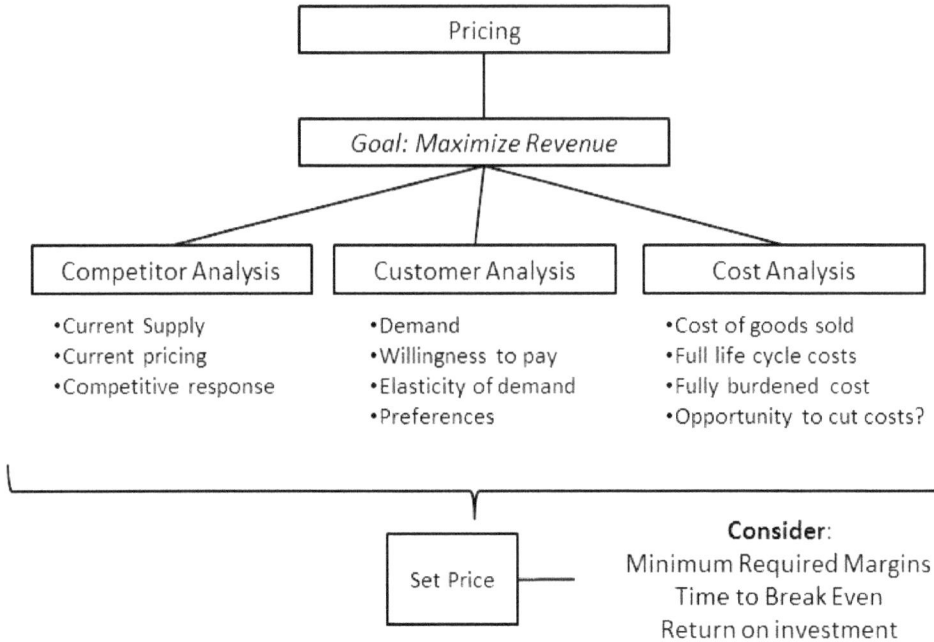

```
                          ┌─────────────────────┐
                          │       Pricing       │
                          └──────────┬──────────┘
                          ┌──────────┴──────────┐
                          │ Goal: Maximize Revenue │
                          └─────────────────────┘
```

Competitor Analysis	Customer Analysis	Cost Analysis
•Current Supply	•Demand	•Cost of goods sold
•Current pricing	•Willingness to pay	•Full life cycle costs
•Competitive response	•Elasticity of demand	•Fully burdened cost
	•Preferences	•Opportunity to cut costs?

Set Price

Consider:
Minimum Required Margins
Time to Break Even
Return on investment

*Remember: Set price to maximize revenue
regardless of cost – if the margins are not
sufficient, or the ROI is too long, then consider
dropping the project*

Discussion – Since Microhard is combining product offerings into an
all-in-one package, a notable challenge will be determining supply and
demand. Supply likely comes from a variety of sources currently, and
demand for individual products is different than for an all-in-one product.
An understanding of the supply and demand is crucial for pricing because
the goal is to maximize revenue and minimize dollars left on the table. As
a software product, the cost per sale should be minimal, and our margins
should be great, so it definitely does not make sense to price by adding
a margin on top of the per-unit cost. Instead we should be cognizant of
payback time for the research and development costs that went into the
creating the all-in-one product.

Let's start by analyzing the customer and competitive landscape to get a better understanding of supply and demand. We could benchmark the competition based on their pricing and match that with our understanding of the customers' willingness to pay.

19. *Competitive Response:* MyRobot has a 75% market share in its core market of robotics for consumer applications. A new company, Mr. Roboto Inc., just received an influx of $50M in private equity to complete the development of an all-in-one robot that will compete directly with MyRobot's suite of robots.

Help MyRobot develop a competitive response to mitigate the competitive threat of Mr. Roboto Inc.

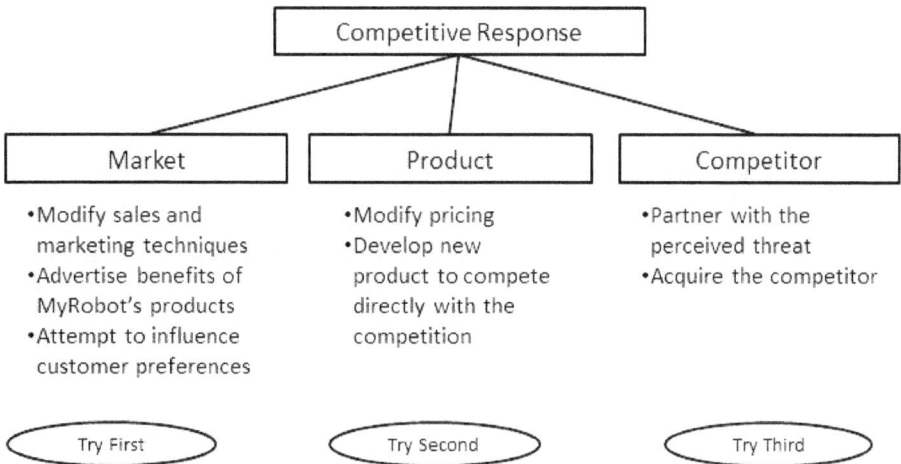

```
                    ┌──────────────────────────┐
                    │   Competitive Response   │
                    └──────────────────────────┘
        ┌───────────────────┬───────────────────┐
┌───────────────┐   ┌───────────────┐   ┌───────────────┐
│    Market     │   │    Product    │   │  Competitor   │
└───────────────┘   └───────────────┘   └───────────────┘
```

Market	Product	Competitor
•Modify sales and marketing techniques •Advertise benefits of MyRobot's products •Attempt to influence customer preferences	•Modify pricing •Develop new product to compete directly with the competition	•Partner with the perceived threat •Acquire the competitor
(Try First)	(Try Second)	(Try Third)

Discussion – Let's assume $50M is actually sufficient to finalize the development of the competitor's product and take it to market. First, I would like to ask how much time we have before their product goes on sale. I would expect a new robot design to take quite some time, which is good news for us. This gives us time to solidify customers' preference for our products. If that is not enough to mitigate the threat, we could look at our own products and decide if modifying our prices could undercut a competitor's more expensive product. Another option is using $50M in our own IR&D (internal research and development) funds to develop a competitive product. As a last resort we could look at either partnering or acquiring the competition.

Conclusion

In conclusion, getting comfortable developing a framework is initially quite challenging. But what's even more challenging is answering one of these case questions without an organized approach to solving the problem.

"First this, then that, finally this."

"Break this into four distinct buckets."

"Although there are many considerations, only 2 really matter."

Reading the news and quizzing yourself of the facts of the article, practicing cases, and responding to day to day questions in a structured manner will help engrain this approach to problem solving and enable you to successfully improvise during a case interview.

Extra Credit

Go back and "bucket" these 19 case types into logical groups.

One possible framework:

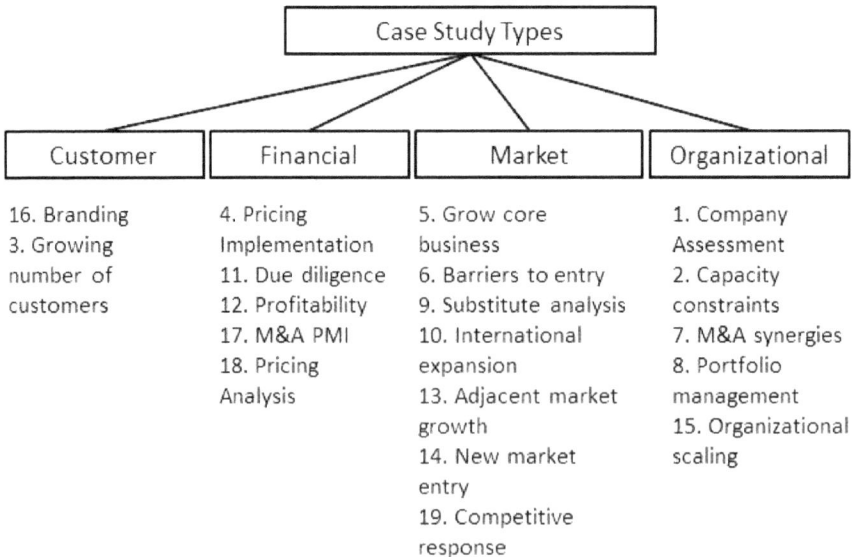

Customer	Financial	Market	Organizational
16. Branding	4. Pricing	5. Grow core	1. Company
3. Growing	Implementation	business	Assessment
number of	11. Due diligence	6. Barriers to entry	2. Capacity
customers	12. Profitability	9. Substitute analysis	constraints
	17. M&A PMI	10. International	7. M&A synergies
	18. Pricing	expansion	8. Portfolio
	Analysis	13. Adjacent market	management
		growth	15. Organizational
		14. New market	scaling
		entry	
		19. Competitive	
		response	

(Case Study Types)

25
Practice Cases

The following pages include practice case interview questions. Should you practice with a friend or on your own? Practicing with a friend offers numerous benefits over practicing by yourself:

Benefit 1: In a real case, the interviewer has extra information on hand that is available only if you ask for it. On your own, you are unable to see all of the answers to additional questions, providing you the chance to think of the follow-up questions on your own. When you practice alone, and you ask a question, you have to look through a substantial portion of the answer sections to find your answer. As a result, you inadvertently see additional facts outside of the scope of your question.

Benefit 2: The interviewer can re-route you – interviewers often have a critical piece of the case they want you to focus on. When you practice with a friend, he is able to guide you to the appropriate place to focus as needed. This is not only more realistic, but it also saves time.

Benefit 3: You get feedback on "soft" skills. A friend is able to not only give you feedback on your "hard" skills (i.e., did you crack the case?), but your "soft" skills as well (e.g., communicating thoughts, body language, enthusiasm, effective summary at end of case, etc.).

It is strongly recommended that you practice every case with another person, and always try to simulate an interview setting. Practice like you play, so that you play like you practice.

If you must practice on your own (e.g., the interview is tomorrow and you haven't practiced yet), there are still benefits to gain. Just write out all of your questions before you look at any data or answers, in case you inadvertently see other facts that you weren't supposed to know, then you can compare to see if you were planning to ask about that or not.

A note to the mock-interviewer:

There are lots of possibilities for each case. If the interviewee asks for data not included in the case, make up data to give to the interviewee if appropriate. *Only provide information to the interviewee as he or she requests it.*

In general, the interviewee needs to identify the key points of each case instead of immediately presenting a single "answer." Primarily, look out for whether the interviewee structures the key points of the case logically. Then confirm whether the interviewee proposes creative solution and a concise summary.

A note to the interviewee:

Identify whether each branch of your framework is a key point in order to determine where to focus your approach. Do not take a framework and blindly check every branch. Some points may not make sense in the context of the problem, and the interviewer will wonder why you're asking about it!

Good luck!

Disclaimer – All of the following cases, include fake names to describe companies, and made-up numbers as data points. Any similarity in names or numbers to real companies is purely a coincidence.

Don't Drink This Pop Slowly

Difficulty rating – 1/5 – A straightforward qualitative case to see how the candidate thinks.

Question: Recently, Pop A has been advertising that consumers should drink it slowly to enjoy it. The consumer response has been very positive, with general awareness of the pop in the U.S. raising from 70% to 80% and sales rising from $25,000,000 annually to $30,000,000 over the course of the campaign. Pop B, the main competitor, has hired you to determine a competitive response strategy for Pop B. What would you recommend, and why?

Data (to be given as interviewee asks for it):

Pop B Specifics:

- Nationally, consumer awareness of Pop B is 40%, given its availability in only a handful of states.

- Annual sales are $5,000,000.

- Pop B's main competitive advantage is that it's perceived by many consumers to be sweeter than Pop A, which is a trait desired by consumers. Both Pop A & B are produced by large companies.

- Surveys of pop-drinking consumers across the states show that, when faced with a description of Pop B, the majority express interest.

Sample Solution

Here is one way to structure an approach:

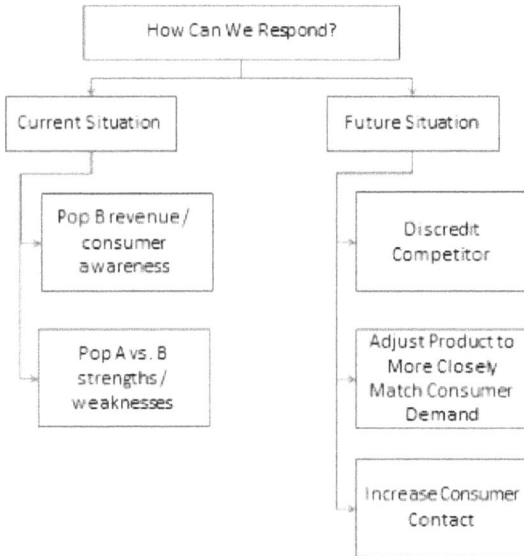

```
                    ┌─────────────────────────┐
                    │   How Can We Respond?    │
                    └─────────────────────────┘
              ┌──────────────┴──────────────┐
    ┌──────────────────┐         ┌──────────────────┐
    │ Current Situation │         │ Future Situation │
    └──────────────────┘         └──────────────────┘
              │                            │
    ┌──────────────────┐         ┌──────────────────┐
    │  Pop B revenue/  │         │    Discredit     │
    │     consumer     │         │    Competitor    │
    │    awareness     │         └──────────────────┘
    └──────────────────┘
                                 ┌──────────────────┐
    ┌──────────────────┐         │ Adjust Product to│
    │   Pop A vs. B    │         │   More Closely   │
    │    strengths/    │         │ Match Consumer   │
    │   weaknesses     │         │     Demand       │
    └──────────────────┘         └──────────────────┘

                                 ┌──────────────────┐
                                 │ Increase Consumer│
                                 │     Contact      │
                                 └──────────────────┘
```

In the "current situation," we learn that Pop B makes far less revenue, it's available in far fewer places, but it's considered sweeter than Pop A.

It's troubling to me that Pop B has only limited availability. Clearly there's demand in general for such a flavor of pop, otherwise Pop A would have limited availability as well.

Let's consider the future situation now. To discredit a larger competitor may be problematic, unless they use something such as rat poison in their creation process. Creating enemies is never a good business move. These days, companies discredit larger competitors by focusing on how large companies lack a focus on quality. For example, microbreweries are a terrific example of discrediting through a quality proposition: they sell lower volumes and have a reputation of higher quality. If you heard that Miller (a major manufacturer of beer) introduced a low volume/high quality beer, you would be suspicious – it's still made by a mass manufacturer. However, your product is just as mass-produced, so discrediting is not a viable option; we know that Pop B is produced by another large company.

Next, we can consider the product itself. Is it what consumers even want? It seems that yes, according to market research the company has conducted, the consumers do want a pop with the attributes of Pop B.

Lastly, we can consider how to increase consumer contact. This is beyond just increasing advertising: this could be hosting promotional events, increasing social media presence, etc.

One potential idea: Pepsi is perceived by many consumers to be sweeter than Coca-Cola. Pepsi took advantage of this in their "Pepsi Challenge" campaign, where they had people blind taste-test two samples of soda: one Pepsi and one Coca-Cola. This, in part, led Coca-Cola to its New Coke fiasco, where Coca-Cola tried to introduce a version of Coke that was sweeter than Pepsi and performed better in taste tests. It flopped and Coca-Cola didn't recover until it brought the original Coke back. I would suggest they conduct a "Pop B" challenge, and if their preliminary tests show that consumers do, in fact, prefer Pop B over Pop A, to advertise this fact heavily. The increased demand then could pull Pop B back into abandoned markets.

They could also have "soft" launches in states in which they don't have a presence, assuming there are no legal/logistical hurdles preventing entries into those states. Then, let consumer demand build by selectively advertising it, and roll the product out to the entire state as demand grows.

Super Airline

Difficulty Rating: 2/5 – Some numbers to crunch, and some high-level qualitative analysis thinking through next steps.

Question: A large U.S. airline has recently taken note of other transportation verticals where rides can be offered as low as $1. The idea is that the first ticket is $1, and then successive groups of tickets are more expensive and steadily climb in price as supply dwindles for that ride. They have hired you to look into whether this pricing strategy could be used at their airline. Would it make sense to price the first ticket at $1, and then sell successive tickets at more expensive prices? They are considering testing it on their New York to Washington D.C. route. If it does make sense, what other routes could they consider this pricing for?

Data (to be given as interviewee asks for it):

Current Airline Pricing

- Prices currently range from $130 per person to $250 per person for coach seats, depending on the expected consumer demand for that seat. Prices are for round-trip tickets.

- The jets the airline uses for this route have a maximum capacity of 210 coach passengers.

- While individual flights within the route vary, the long-run average coach capacity utilization is 180 people.

- There are 4 round-trip flights per day, every day of the year.

- Current pricing distribution in a flight:

  - 10% of passengers pay $130

  - 40% of passengers pay $170

  - 40% of passengers pay $230

  - 10% of passengers pay $250

Future Pricing:

- The proposed pricing distribution is expected to draw more attention to the airline, encouraging some passengers to check the airline before others. Long-run coach capacity utilization is expected to increase to 200 people.

- No other airlines currently have a pricing model like this.

- Expected pricing distribution with new pricing scheme:

  - 1 passenger pays $1

  - 19 passengers pay $50

  - 10% of passengers pay $130

  - 30% of passengers pay $170

  - 40% of passengers pay $230

  - 10% of passengers pay $250

- Increased costs from processing additional passengers are negligible.

Key Risks:

- Surveyed consumers indicated that generally they would not think less of the airline under the new pricing scheme; on the contrary, most consumers indicated they would be more likely to check an airline first with a pricing scheme similar to the one they're proposing.

- Surveyed consumers indicated they would be confused if the same airline advertised a pricing scheme on only some routes.

Sample Analysis

The crux of the first objective is to determine whether the new pricing scheme increases long-term profits. To do so, calculate the revenue per flight.

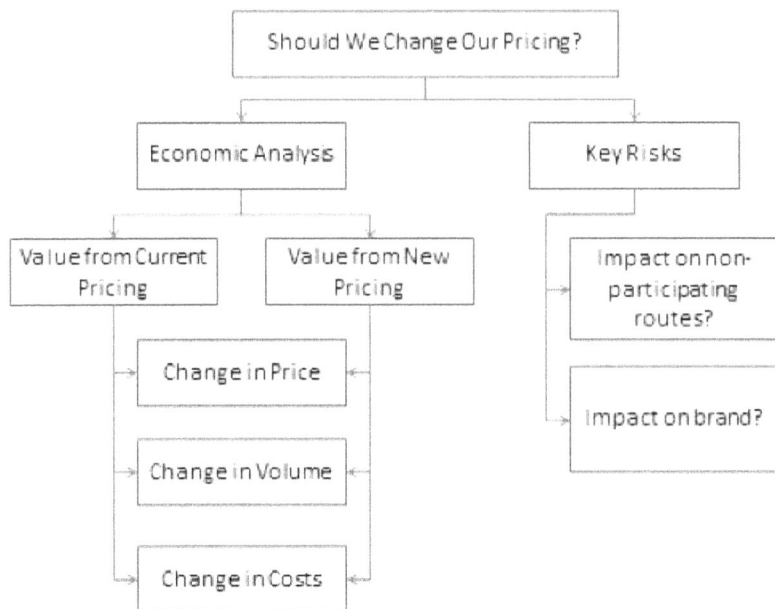

Current Revenue per Flight:

Passengers	Avg. capacity	Price Bucket	Passenger	Contribution
10%	180	18	130	2,340
80%	180	144	200	28,800
10%	180	18	250	4,500
Total		180		35,640

New Revenue per Flight:

Percent of Passengers	Total Passengers	# of Passengers in Price Bucket	Price per Passenger	Revenue Contribution
N/A	N/A	1	1	1
N/A	N/A	19	50	950
10%	200	20	130	2,600
30%	200	60	170	10,200
40%	200	80	230	18,400
10%	200	20	250	$5,000
Total				37,151

This new pricing scheme is expected to increase route revenue by $1500. There are 4 round-trip flights per day, 365 days per year, which would bring in ~$2M in incremental revenue per year. Given this is a large U.S. airline, saving ~$2M is not a huge needle mover on its own, but if it's rolled out to other routes, this could hold significant incremental revenue potential for this airline.

Regarding the second objective (What other routes could they consider?) this is an open-ended question for the interviewee. Some points to consider are below.

Future Routes:

- Routes with more leisure passengers may be more attractive than routes with more business customers, because business consumers have deals or loyalty programs with various airlines, so the gimmick may attract fewer business consumers. Also, business customers on the whole tend to be less price sensitive than consumers.

- Routes with fewer flights per day and lagging capacity utilization may be more attractive, because cutting flights is not as viable an option without cutting the route. If you have a route with 4 flights round trips per day, and they're all running at 60%

utilization, and consumers are not tied to departure times, you could potentially cut a round trip to consolidate demand.

- All else equal, less expensive (i.e., shorter) routes may be more attractive, because longer routes may have too large of a jump from "gimmick" price to "market" price, discouraging consumers from acting on promotion. If the going market rate is $400, and you hear that tickets are $1, how likely are you to believe that those tickets aren't gone in 1 second after being released? However, if the going market rate is $80, it's easier to believe that those $1 (and other lower priced tickets) may be available a little bit longer.

- Additionally, lost incremental revenue from discounting tickets is substantially greater on these flights, so it's riskier to offer on more expensive flights – will offering discount tickets on these flights result in enough incremental expensive seats?

Implementation Considerations and Risks

- How easy will it be to market this pricing if it's only on certain routes? Will consumers be confused which routes the special pricing applies to? This may not be a huge risk if advertising was kept to a minimum – just advertise to people searching for that route, and let word of mouth take it from there.

- Assuming that "middle man" sites such as Expedia.com add to the cost of tickets, it may make sense to offer these "deep discount" tickets only through the company website to make the "real" price of the ticket as close to $1 as possible. That would also drive more traffic to their sites and away from "comparison" sites, something the airlines have been trying to do for years.

Cub Construction

Difficulty Rating: 2/5 – Some number crunching, and a mixture of obvious and less obvious data points the interviewee may ask for.

Question: A Chicago condo construction firm, Cub Construction, is thinking of entering the Minneapolis market. Before they enter, they want to ensure that they can at least match their Chicago performance within 5 years. Is this a good idea?

Data (to be given as interviewee asks for it):

Chicago Market:

- Construction of 50 condo buildings started last year that were over 5 stories

- Leader has 50% market share, Cub Construction is second largest with 30% of started buildings, rest of market is fragmented

- Yearly demand for new condo buildings has been stagnant for several years

- Average revenue from building a condo is $500,000 per floor, average cost is $400,000 per floor

- Average condo height is 40 floors and take on average 3 years to complete

Cub Construction Specifics:

- Specializes in condo building over 5 stories

- Has a reputation for finishing buildings on time, but usually isn't the cheapest

Minneapolis Market:

- 20 condos started last year that were over 5 stories

- Leader has 70% market share, rest of market is fragmented (from general contractors)

- Average revenue from building a condo is $400,000 per floor, average cost is $200,000 per floor

- Average condo height is 30 floors, and take on average 3 years to complete

- Yearly demand for condos has increased 10% a year for last 5 years, and is expected to continue doing so over the next 5 years.

- Our preliminary research indicates the market leader finishes buildings on time only 50% of the time. Customers don't have an equivalent choice with the expertise, knowledge, and competitive price to build condos.

- Our research found that 50% of the market would pay more for a construction firm that could be depended on to finish the building on time.

- Our research found that 100% of the market is willing to switch contractors.

- Our research also indicates that there may be animosity among developers toward a construction firm even loosely tied to the Chicago Cubs, in a town that is proud of their Twins.

Start Up Costs:

- Would need to be licensed by Minnesota to open shop, at a cost of $100,000

- Start up costs $500,000 would include advertising, hiring more talent, etc.

Sample Analysis

We can set the problem up in the following way:

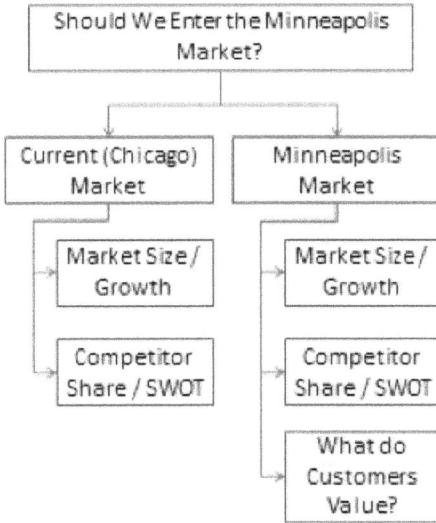

We will assess the market size and growth, our share, and our competitive advantages/disadvantages relative to others. If the Minneapolis market is large and growing, and there our key advantages line up with a gap in the market place, could be an attractive entry.

In order to evaluate "Chicago performance," we must estimate the Chicago market size. We know that 50 buildings were started last year, and we have 30% share, so we started 15 buildings. We make $100,000 per floor ($500,000 revenue - $400,000 costs), and the expected number of floors is 40, so that's $4,000,000 in gross profit per condo. With 15 buildings, that's $60,000,000. However, it takes 3 years to finish a building, so annual financial performance is thus $20,000,000 gross profit.

Average building gross profit in Minneapolis is expected to be [$200,000 profit per floor] x [30 floors] = $6,000,000. Cub Construction would need to secure 10 contracts a year to match their Chicago performance in terms of profit.

Gaining fifty percent (50%) is a tall order against an entrenched player. However, Cub has a significant competitive advantage over the existing market leader: finishing buildings on time. Cub could offer lower pricing to attract initial customers and begin building relationships with developers. Their on-time performance would then likely speak for itself.

But, only 50% of the market indicated a willingness to pay more for a contractor that could be depended on to finish on time. That means, at best, Cub could only gain 50% with its competitive advantage, which is the minimum it would have to gain to make this attractive. To gain the rest, it would have to beat the competitor's pricing, or develop another competitive advantage.

It appears this could be a viable growth opportunity for Cub, but due to the significantly smaller size of the market, it's unlikely that Cub will be able to generate the same total profit.

We Care Hospital

Difficulty Rating: 3/5 – Data inference, multiple angles, but nothing too difficult

Question: A large hospital's profits are down over past 5 years, what's wrong?

Data (to be given as interviewee asks for it):

*Product Group*s – For simplification purposes, suppose this hospital has four departments that are set up in the following way:

1. General Medicine – The "first line of defense," will treat and/or refer patients to one of three other departments.

2. Surgery – Any operation requiring anesthetic.

3. Diagnostic Medicine – Diagnoses and recommends treatment for cases that general medicine was unable to diagnose, or diagnosed incorrectly.

4. Rehabilitation – Regain original functionality after medical treatment.

All departments have existed for past 5 years.

Revenues over Time

- Overall Hospital Revenues: Please see Graph 1

- Revenue Generated by Department: Please see Graph 2

Prices

- The CEO of the hospital has set up affordable healthcare as a priority, so prices have remained fixed over the past 5 years.

Volume

- Ask interviewee to determine volume trends, based on given information

Collections (Accounts Receivable)

- For simplification purposes, assume all revenue is collected.

Competition

- There are a number of hospitals in the area, and informal conversations have indicated their profits are rising.

Market Share

- Assume market share has been fixed over the past 5 years.

Costs

- If interviewee asks for costs over time, see Graph 3

- If interviewee asks for costs broken down by product, see Graph 4

Diagnostic medicine variable costs (Ask interviewee to list out potential variable costs.)

- Potential variable cost sources: tests, medicine, use of procedure/ patient rooms, time of non-department staff, etc.

    - You can assume that all variable costs are given a standard markup, and that markup percentage has remained constant.

Diagnostic medicine fixed costs (Ask interviewee to list out potential fixed costs.)

- Potential fixed cost sources: salaries, any special subscription services, recruitment, etc.

    - One senior diagnostic specialist is paid $200,000 a year, and is given a 5% raise every year.

    - Each junior diagnostic specialist is paid $100,000 a year, and is given a 5% raise every year.

    - The senior specialist may hire or fire as many specialists as he needs to keep up with demand.

    - Utilization of junior specialists has historically been 20% (meaning 20% of their time is spent in their primary job function, diagnosing cases). The other 80% is split among paperwork, helping the general or surgery departments, and downtime.

- Assume 80% utilization is ideal in the eyes of management, to balance costs and responsiveness.

Graph 1: We Care Hospital - Revenues Over Time

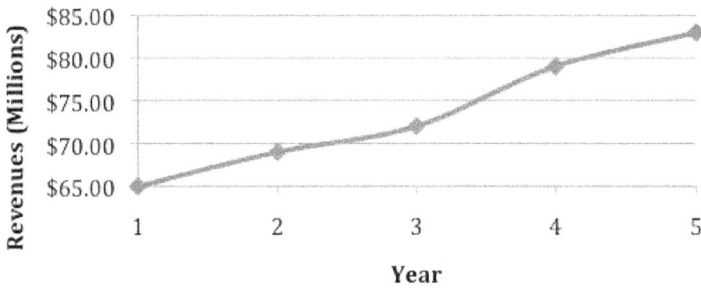

Graph 2: Breakdown of Revenues Over Past 5 Years

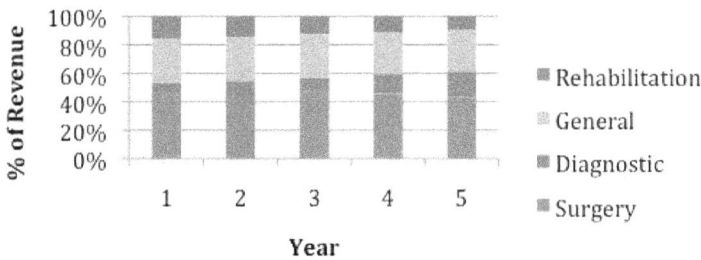

Graph 3: We Care Hospital - Costs Over Time

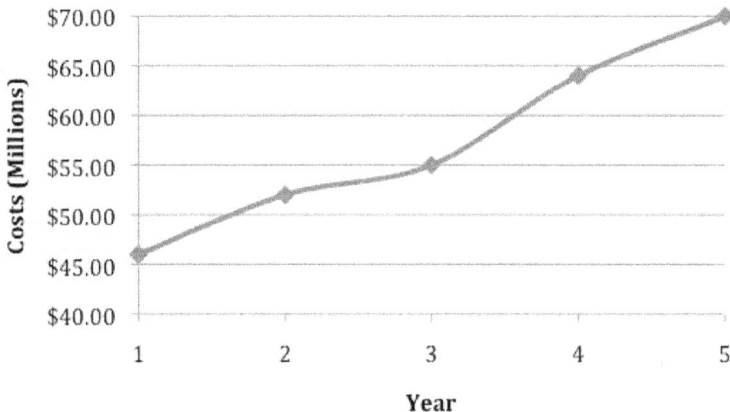

Graph 4: Breakdown of Costs Over Past 5 Years

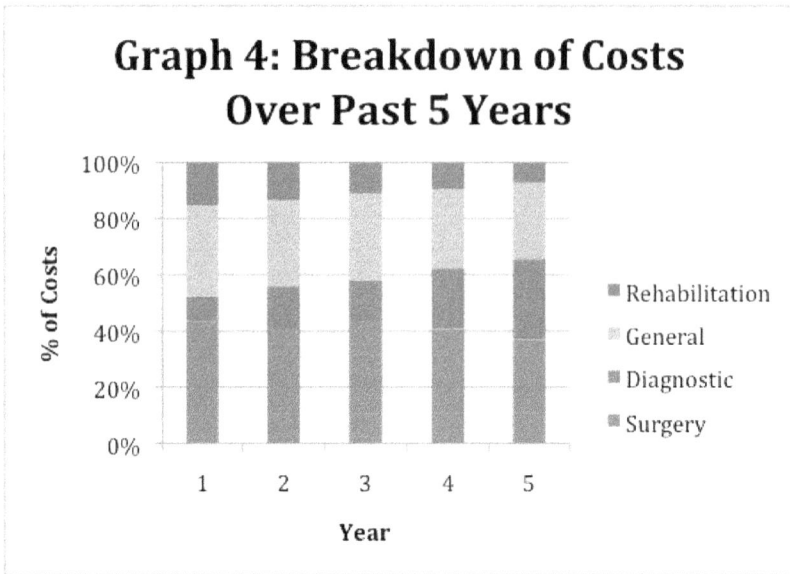

Sample Analysis:

Here is one way to structure this problem:

When we ask about revenue and costs, we get graphs on both, broken down by department. From the graphs, we can infer the volume of diagnostic medicine must be increasing, because of the following three facts:

1. Total revenue is increasing, so either price, volume, or some combination is increasing.

2. We are given prices are fixed, so volume of at least one product of the four is increasing.

3. Diagnostic medicine's percentage of total revenue is increasing.

From the overall revenue and cost graphs, we can see costs are increasing faster than revenues. Furthermore, we can see that the diagnostic medicine department costs are increasing much faster than any other department. Given the increase in volume, this makes sense. We are also told that variable cost margin has remained the same.

Now, we arrive at fixed costs. First problem I see is the 5% rise in salaries every year, while prices are fixed. The second problem is the over-hiring of junior specialists, as their utilization is only 20%. It would likely be bad to have a very high utilization (e.g., 95%), because then they wouldn't be available if multiple life threatening situations were to occur at once. But we could get closer to the 80% benchmark by automating steps in the paperwork and firing junior specialists, also a driver of reducing fixed costs.

Finally, looking at the product breakdown of revenues and costs, it seems that diagnostic medicine doesn't have as good of an overall contribution to profit as other departments do. Maybe diagnostic medicine's growth should be capped to free up resources for other departments with stronger profit contributions and growth prospects, such as surgery and rehabilitation.

Conclusion:

We Care Hospital's profitability has been falling over the past 5 years. Revenue has grown, thanks to growth in diagnostic medicine, but costs have grown faster. The cost increase is primarily due to over staffing in diagnostic medicine. I recommend they work to automate secondary tasks, and reduce staff levels so that each specialist in diagnostic medicine achieves the benchmark of spending 80% of their time on the primary task of diagnosing cases. Furthermore, the staff in the department has been receiving 5% wage increases annually, while prices have increased 0%. In order to protect profitability, I recommend matching price increases in the diagnostic department with annual raise percentages, such as 3% annually. This would enable both the specialists to maintain their lifestyle, and for the client to maintain profitability.

Quick Tip: Profitability

Here are some general tips for profitability cases:

- If sales are declining, check if it's industry-wide, an obsolete product, or substitutions are increasing due to faltering economy.

- If sales are flat, check change in client's market share to determine if it's an industry wide problem. If not, investigate revenues segments and benchmark the competition.

- If sales are increasing and profits are not, observe if prices have fallen, if overall volume has increased, if prices have remained constant while volume of lower margin products have risen, or if costs have risen. Also, check for any one-time large expenses.

In this problem, sales were increasing but profits were not. Prices were constant, but volume of lower margin products rose. Additionally, costs rose within that lower margin price, eroding that lower margin.

Bank Café

Difficulty Rating: 4/5 – Get ready to crunch some numbers! Includes a qualitative section as well for those students who are able to get through the quantitative portion within the time limit.

Question: ABC Bank, a large international bank, has recently opened a "bank café" branch with a coffee shop inside in the town of Whoville. This branch functions just as a normal bank does, but there is a separate counter that serves gourmet-style coffee. There is also free Wi-Fi, and plenty of seating.

If a standard branch makes $12,000,000 a year in profit, then how much more profitable is the Bank Café branch?

Data (to be given as interviewee asks for it):

Product

- The branch offers one type of coffee, a latte, which has a gross profit margin of $1 a cup.

- The branch offers three banking products: checking accounts, credit cards, and bank loans.

  - Checking accounts provide funding for loans – revenue comes from credit cards and loans

Pricing

- Each credit card account brings in $100 gross profit per year, and each loan brings in $5000 gross profit per year. These prices are the same at all branches.

Volume

- The Bank Café branch had a 20% higher daily volume of customers than the average daily volume of banks in similar locations last year.

- The average daily volume for branches in locations sharing characteristics with the Bank Café location was 500 people last year.

- Last year, in the Bank Café, 10% of the daily visitors only got a coffee, 50% got a coffee and conducted some bank business, and the remaining 40% conducted bank business only.

- Of the 50% of visitors who got coffee and conduct bank business, 20% were new (so 80% were repeat, not 30%). Of the 40% who conducted bank business only, 10% were new.

- You may assume each visitor that purchased coffee only bought one coffee.

- At both types of branches, 10% of new customers get a credit card, and 10% of new customers get a loan; the others get checking accounts or don't open anything on that day.

- Last year, at both Bank Café and normal branches, 2000 credit cards and 2000 loans on average were open at the beginning of the year and still open at the end of the year (i.e., didn't close).

Churn

- Last year, at the Bank Café, 520 credit cards and 520 loans were closed each year. Of those 520 loans, 100 defaulted.

- Last year, at the average branch, 600 credit cards and 600 loans were closed each year. Of those 600 loans, 100 defaulted.

Company information

- All of the company's banks were open 300 days a year last year (approximately meaning they weren't open Sundays and holidays)

Competitors

- No other banks offer a café, nor does it appear that any bank cafés are in the works

Costs

- The Bank Café incurred fixed costs of $1,000,000 last year (rent, salaries, security, etc). Normal branches incurred an average fixed cost of $800,000 last year.

- Assume the average cost to a bank of a defaulted loan is $100,000.

Sample Analysis:

Our first objective is to determine how much more profitable this branch is compared to other branches. We can lay out the following tree:

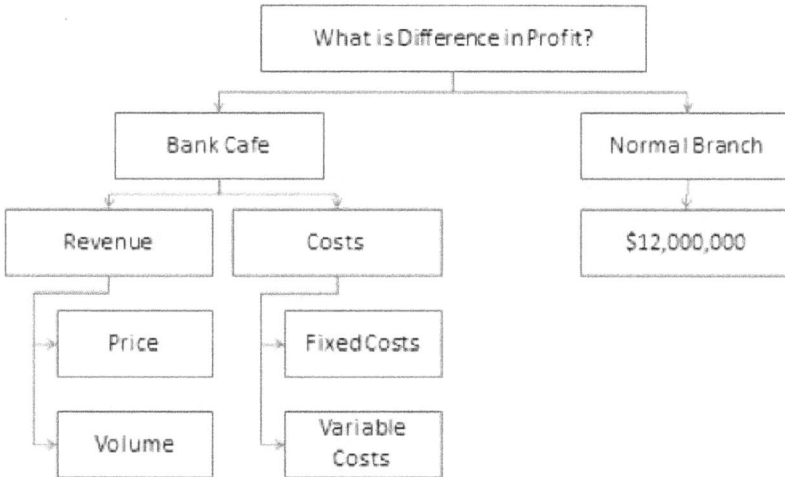

What's interesting is that as you start asking about their various products and the price of each, we're given all data points in terms of gross profit margin. So, we can combine price and variable costs into gross profit. We can use this equation to calculate profit:

Profit = Margin * Volume – FC

Margin:

- Coffee: $1
- Credit card: $100/year
- Loan: $5000/year

Now we need to determine volume for each of these products. Let's start off with the easy one: coffee. We know the average daily volume at a normal branch is 500 visitors per day. Therefore, we know that the new branch has 600 visitors per day. We know that 60% of customers buy a coffee, and that each customer buys 1 coffee, which means the Bank Café sells 360 coffees per day. Multiply this by 300 days (did you ask how many days in a year the bank is open?) to get 108,000 coffees sold annually.

Next, let's figure out the new customers each day. The tricky part is that the proportion of new customers varies by whether they bought a coffee or not, so we need to calculate each separately, then add together. Taking the 50% of customers who bought a coffee and conducted bank business, 20% of them are new, which means 60 customers are new and bought a coffee. On the other side, 40% of customers just conducted bank business, and 10% of those are new. This calculates to 24 visitors who are new and didn't buy a coffee. Total new customers per day = 84. This, per year, is 25,200 new customers.

We don't care about new checking accounts in this case – those don't bring in more revenue.

10% of new customers want a credit card = 2520 new credit cards per year

10% of new customers want a loan = 2520 new loans per year.

However, you must account for churn as well – those that close their accounts, pay off the loan, or default on the loan. We're given (if you ask):

- 520 credit cards close every year at the Bank Café.

- 520 loans close every year. Of those, 100 are defaults at the Bank Café.

- 2000 loans and credit cards were neither opened this year nor closed this year.

Using that information, we can calculate volume:

- Coffee: 360 x 300 = 108,000

- Credit Card: 4000 (2520 new – 520 closed + 2000 maintain = 4000)

- Loan: 4000

Now we can calculate Margin * Volume:

- Coffee: $1 x 108,000 = $108,000

- Credit Card: $100 x 4000 = $400,000

- Loans: $5000 x 4000 = $20,000,000

- Sum: $24,508,000

What are the fixed costs? We're given fixed costs are $1,000,000. But remember that clue about loan churns, those that default? We're given the average default cost is $100,000, and if there are 100 defaults, that's a cost of $10,000,000.

Profit = $24,508,000- $11,000,000 = $13,508,000

You may be tempted to give this as your answer, but the question was how much more profitable is a Bank Café than a regular branch?

We're given the profitability of an average branch: $12,000,000.

Difference in profit: $13,508,000 - $12,000,000 = $1,508,000.

Conclusion: Clearly, the Bank Café is more profitable. One interesting thing to note about the numbers is the sheer number of new loans and credit cards. For the Bank Café, the total number of credit cards and loan accounts grew 100% over the course of the year.

Bonus question if time: These are real branches of ING called ING Direct Cafes. They seem to be fairly successful for a new initiative. The question is, will this concept be successful in the long run, and create a sustainable completive advantage for ING? (Open discussion)

Some possible talking points…

- Possible Advantages?

    - Kill two birds with one stone: Get your coffee and banking business done before work at one location

- Could it convince people who don't like "stiff" (i.e., traditional) banking environments to switch their banking business to ING? Which segments of "people" do you think this may include?

- Possible Disadvantages?

  - Will people want to think about finances while relaxing over coffee and free WIFI?

  - How easily can the concept be copied by competitors?

- Other Considerations

  - Assume for a minute that coffee place can known for either cheap-tasting coffee or delicious but more expensive coffee: it cannot be known for both. The delicious coffee would necessarily cost more, assume 2x as much. Which type of coffee do you think ING Direct Café should brew?

Brown Co

Difficulty Rating: 2/5 – Growth strategy evaluation

Question: Brown Co is a large public cardboard manufacturer. Their growth has been less than satisfactory, how can they increase their growth?

Data (to be given as interviewee asks for it):

Current Initiatives

- Brown Co has been doing a lot to grow. Their traditional strong point has been heavy duty commercial packing. However in the last 5 years, they've introduced boxes for people moving and shipping items, as well as boxes for commercial producers that are thinner (like beer cases). Another consulting firm told them these would be great markets to enter, as these markets are all fairly fragmented.

Growth Rates

- Assume we're growing at 1% a year

- The industry is stagnant (0%)

- Dura Co, our main competitor, is growing at 5% a year

Competition

- Brown Co's main competitor is Dura Co. Although smaller, Dura Co's stock price has consistently grown more than Brown Co's over the past 5 years, 10% annually vs. 1% annually.

Market Size/Share

- See following graphs. The categories correspond to the ones listed below:

  1 = Consumer Shipping

  2 = Consumer Moving

  3 = Commercial Packaging – Thin

  4 = Commercial Packaging – Medium

  5 = Commercial Packaging - Heavy Duty

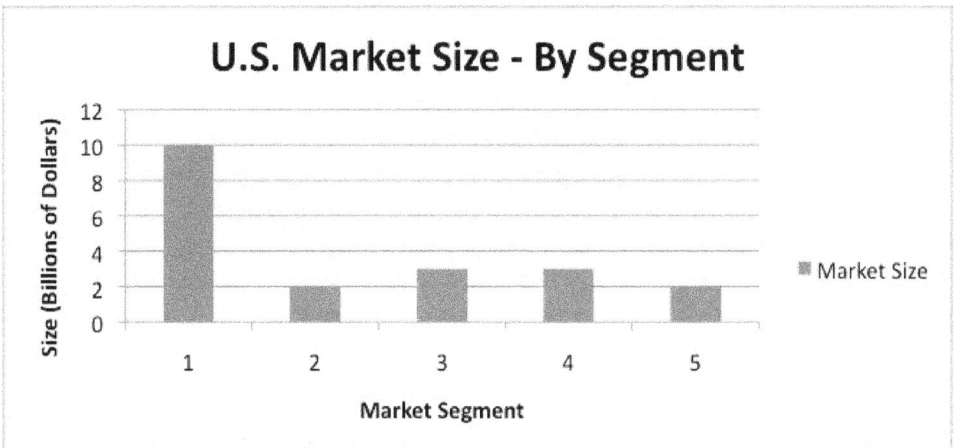

U.S. Market Size - By Segment

Market Share of Brown Co vs. Dura Co

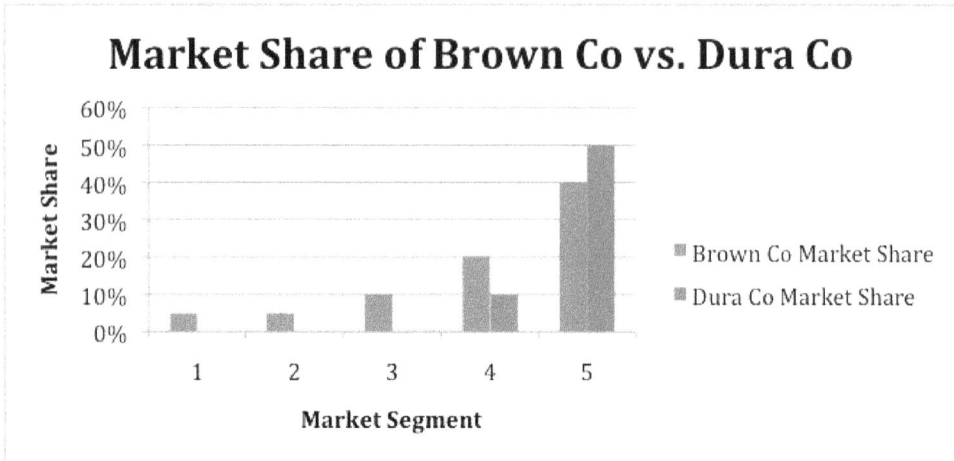

Revenues:

See following graph

Revenue of Brown Co vs. Dura Co

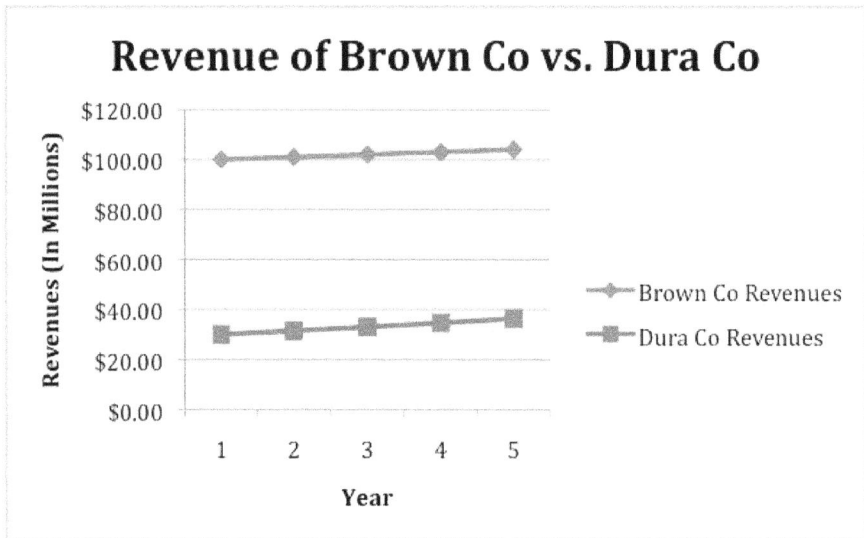

Sample Analysis:

This is an interesting case, because it appears Brown Co has several growth strategies: diversify product offering, increase product line, and broaden (presumably) their distribution channels to reach new customers interested in their new products. So what's going on here?

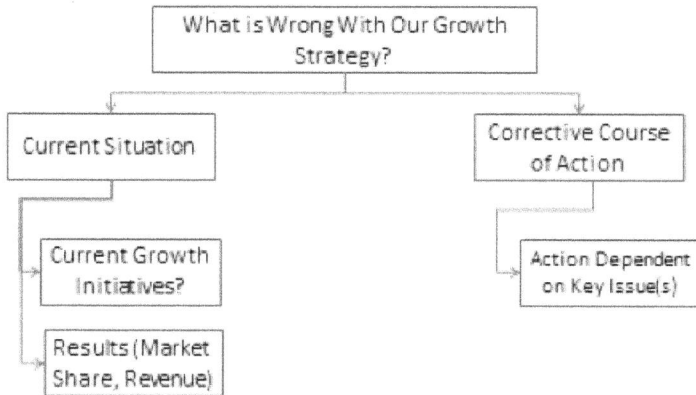

We learn that they've diversified, but that results haven't matched up. The revenues graph doesn't add that much value (except to tell you that Dura Co is smaller) the key is the market share graph.

Calculate a weighted market share for both Brown Co and Dura Co for the markets they are in, and you find that Dura Co has an overall stronger position.

Brown Co Weighted Market Share = $(10*5\%+2*5\%+3*10\%+3*20\%+2*40\%) \div (10+2+3+3+2) = (0.5 + 0.1 + 0.3 + 0.6 + 0.8) \div (20) = (2.3) \div 20 \sim = 10\%$

Dura Co Weighted Market Share = $(3*10\% + 2*50\%) \div (3 + 2) = (0.3 + 1.0) \div 5 = 1.3 \div 5 \sim = 25\%$

Having ~25% market share is certainly better than ~10%.

Basically what all this means is that Brown Co has likely spread themselves too thin. They're pouring capital into new markets, and not realizing much of a return on their investments because they're a small player in each. They're not realizing scale benefits and can't be a market leader. Each market, while utilizing some of the same raw materials, likely uses different types of cardboard, manufacturing processes and/or distribution channels. Meanwhile, Dura Co is focusing on a few markets they can do well in, and realizing a much better growth rate as a result of this focused effort. This is all confirmed in their individual stock performances as well.

I would want to see Brown Co's weighted market share above Dura Co's. To do this, they should pull out of markets 1, 2, and 3. That will lead to a new weighted market share of 30%. They then can focus their capital into increasing their market share in their two best markets.

Of course, the industry is stagnant, so it may be hard to snag much new market share. I'd suggest they do research to find out what really matters to consumers in their two best markets (commercial packaging; medium and heavy duty) – Price? Durability? Delivery time? Variety of sizes? Once they determine this, they can compare their products on these attributes to their competition, and determine how they can best deliver a strong value proposition to snag new customers.

If they're already the best on durability, but they already have all the customers who care about durability, they could consider introducing a new product that is in alignment with what the other customers care most about it, for instance price.

One final note, they may have a better chance for growth in the medium thickness segment than the heavy duty segment, because of fragmentation. In the heavy duty, 90% is already captured by Brown and Dura Co, whereas in the medium, only 30% is captured.

Iron-Surf

Rating – 1/5 – A simple market estimation case, with some simple numbers.

Question: A surfboard company produces surfboards that they sell through specialty surfing shops. They have recently developed an ironing board that functions well as a surfboard. It's a little bizarre, but your client is excited about it to appeal to occasional surfers, and has hired you to evaluate it. How would you determine if there's such a market for such a contraption?

Data (to be given as interviewee asks for it):

Competition

- No one else currently makes an ironing board that doubles as a surfboard.

Product

- The product is judged to be a medium-quality surfboard in focus groups, and works well as an ironing board.

- It is highly resistant to breakage and wear.

- It does not look like an ironing board, rather it looks like a surfboard, and can be attached to legs when needed for ironing. Focus groups have indicated this process is very easy.

- The material is highly resistant to heat, which is how the company came up with the idea in the first place.

- The company has a patent on the product.

Costs

- At 0-1000 iron-surfs, each costs $100 to produce. At 1000-5000 iron-surfs annually, each one costs $80 each produce. At 5000+, each one costs $60 to produce.

- Assume $10 per surfboard distribution cost.

- Assume it would cost $1,000,000 to bring to market – this includes advertising, development costs, operation setup, etc. Ongoing annual fixed costs would be $500,000.

- Assume that specialty retail shops will charge a 100% markup on the product.

Market

- This company has operations just in California, which you may assume has population of 40 million.

- Occasional surfers make up 10% of the California total (not surfer) population – your client wishes to prioritize this population over hard-core surfers.

- Focus groups and surveys indicate that 10% of occasional surfers expressed interest in this product, and that 1-2% of occasional surfers would be willing to buy right now if available, depending on if it cost $100 or $200.

Pricing

- Assume an ironing board costs $20, and a surfboard of comparable quality costs $250.

Sample Analysis

Here's one way to break the problem down:

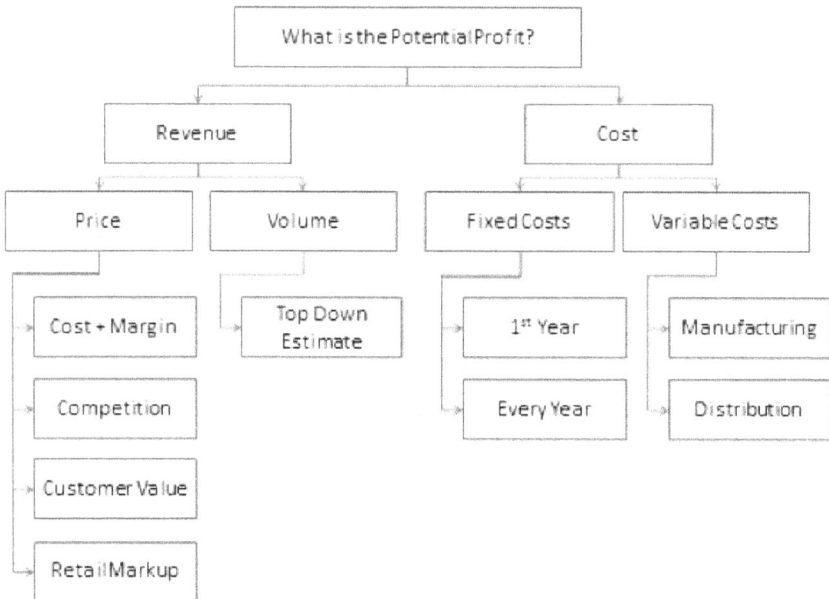

First we should estimate volume to estimate our price. In some cases, you'll find that the interviewer doesn't have market estimation figures. As such, it is necessary to estimate it, and a top-down approach would make sense here. However, you can continue to ask if the interviewer has various assumptions, and in this case, the interviewer does.

- What's our total population?

- What's the portion that is "occasional surfers"?

- Of the occasional surfers, how many would be interested in our product?

- Of those interested how many would buy, and how does that vary by price point?

I'm going to assume most surfing is concentrated in California to keep things simple. Serving a relatively small area first will help us roll out the product anyway. We know that California has a population of 40 million, and that 10% of the population likes to surf occasionally, or 4 million people. These people might be interested in a medium-quality board that costs less than average.

However, it's still a little strange that it doubles as an ironing board; questions about quality would naturally come up. We know that 10% of the potential market, or 400,000 people, would be willing to try it on their own or if a friend tried it. Finally, we know that 1-2% of the potential market would try the surfboard this year, depending on whether the price was $200 or $100. Our volume could vary between 40,000 and 80,000. So which price should we choose?

Basically our volume doubles at a $100 price point, so how does our margin compare at both price points to determine profitability?

We know that is costs $60 to produce at the highest volume levels, and up to $100 at the lowest volume levels. Both scenarios would qualify for the highest volume level, or $60. Both scenarios incur a $10 distribution cost per board, so our variable costs under both scenarios is $70.

But we must keep in mind: the price consumers are willing to pay is based on the retail price as opposed to our price. It's likely that we would try to sell our product through our existing distribution channels, given the customer relationships we presumably have. We learn that retail markup is 100% in this case. So for a price point of $100, we'd earn $50, and at a price point of $200, we'd earn $100.

Based on this analysis, we have to charge $200, as we'd lose money on $100. $200 end-revenue - $100 markup - $70 cost = $30 margin. $40 x 40,000 = $160,000. That's our gross profit.

But what about our fixed costs? We learn that it's a $1,000,000 first year cost, and $500,000 ongoing.

So annual gross profit would not exceed our startup costs, so I would recommend the company further research the market to determine how much traction they can ultimately achieve. If 1% of the potential customers buy now and are happy, what do we think year 2 will look like? Is there a maximum penetration, that is, a certain percentage of the occasional surfer population who would never buy?

One key thing working in their favor is that they also have the advantage of being an established company, and so would likely have access to necessary distribution channels and have experience in successfully bringing a surf board to market.

In conclusion, the company is currently not poised to turn a profit on this product. They need to think carefully about future adoption, as well as whether they can reduce any of their costs, or whether they can increase first-year adoption.

C.N.A. Dispatch
Guest Written by Kiran Pookote

Note: This is an example of a more interviewer-driven case. While the interviewee kicked off the discussion with laying out a very basic structure, the interviewer drove the interview by asking various questions. You should always still be prepared with a structure.

Rating – 3/5 – A primarily-qualitative case testing ability to segment customers

Question: Your client is C.N.A Dispatch, a taxi car service. They serve as a dispatch for all drivers that join their umbrella. They have two options for the drivers: either C.N.A will provide the car or the drivers will provide their own car. C.N.A recieves a cut of the drivers' fares. Over the past 3 years, the client has seen declining revenues and limited growth in profits (hand interviewee Figure 1). The CEO has contacted you to find out what is going on and if he should be worried about long-term profits declining.

Data:

- Revenue and gross profit – Figure 1 (provided to interviewee)

- Number of taxis in service – Figure 2 (interview should ask for)

- Cost structure per taxi – Figure 3 (interview should ask for)

Sample Answer:

Interviewee: Alright, let me make sure I understand. We are serving a taxi dispatch service that has drivers who own their own cars and drivers who drive company owned cars. The revenues are decreasing and the profits are up-and-down. The CEO wants to see why the revenues are decreasing and if he should be worried long term.

Interviewer: Yes, that is correct.

Interviewee: Can I have a few minutes to collect my thoughts?

Interviewer: No.

Interviewee: Um…

Interviewer: Just kidding. Go ahead and take some time.

<Interviewee takes a minute>

Interviewee: Alright, so I'd like to look at revenues and costs. Let's look at revenues first, so I can understand where the money is coming in. Revenues are price times quantity. Do we have information about the different types of cars and how much money they make?

Interviewer: Actually, we have this information on the number of taxis in service. Take a look at FIGURE 2.

Interviewee: This is very interesting. The total number of drivers has gone up. But, I can see that the driver owned number has increased while firm owned has decreased. Based on FIGURE 1 and FIGURE 2, I would hypothesize that the driver-owned cars make less money.

Interviewer: So why do you think firm-owned cars are decreasing?

Interviewee: It could be a number of things: company strategy, capital constraints, limits on medallions, etc.

Interviewer: Good answer. Now, we do have information about how much each car makes. Take a look at FIGURE 3.

Interviewee: I see that the driver gets a much larger cut when they own the car, thus decreasing our revenues. So, as I was thinking, our decrease in revenues is driven by the shift towards driver-owned cars.

Interviewer: Alright. That's very interesting. Should I be worried long term?

Interviewee: Well, the profit margin for the driver-owned is 7% and the profit margin for the firm-owned is 21%. This tells me that we need approximately 3 driver-owned cars to replace 1 firm-owned car. And, driver-owned cars are increasing at 30% while firm-owned cars are decreasing at 15%. In order to replace the profit of losing firm-owned cars, driver-owned cars would have to grow at 45%. Thus, the firm is in trouble of decreasing profits long-term.

Interviewer: That's very scary to hear. What recommendations do you have to fix the problem?

Interviewee: The firm should try to attract more firm-owned cars as opposed to driver-owned cars. Maybe they should give a larger cut to drivers of firm-owned cars, since the profit margin on firm-owned cars would still be bigger than on driver-owned cars. The firm should also try to increase the cut they get from the driver-owned cars, perhaps by investigating potential value-added services. Additionally, given these economics, it certainly makes sense why drivers are shifting to driver-owned cars. However, I wonder why they didn't do this earlier,

Did something positively impact the cost structure on the driver-owned side recently, or did financing become easier?

Interviewer: Actually, yes. Recently, C.N.A. started a program that helped drivers who were driving firm-owned cars easily buy the car from C.N.A. The reason behind this is that C.N.A. thought their portfolio was too risky and wanted to have a safer profile. But you're recommending they go the opposite direction, and have more firm-owned cars. Are there any risks associated with having more firm-owned cars?

Interviewee: Yes, the firm has more liabilities and risk associated with letting people drive cars that the firm owns. The firm must think carefully about increasing the firm-owned cars.

Interviewer: Considering that, what might an optimal portfolio for C.N.A. in the long run?

Interviewee: First, if they feel like they have reached their optimal risk balance, they should end the easy financing to stop the shift from their existing base of company-owned cars to driver-owned cars. They then could use the growth of the driver-owned model to fund outreach efforts to attract more drivers, perhaps through developing a network of partnerships. Or, if they feel as if they have been too cautious, they could invest in more firm-owned cars and reap the higher gross margins. They have a lot of options.

Interviewer: Alright, please sum up.

Interviewee: For C.N.A., long-term profits are in danger because of the shift from firm-owned cars to driver-owned cars. This shift is driving decreasing revenues and could lead to decreasing profits if the current growth rates stand. We would recommend stopping the shift of drivers to the driver-owned model through making the financing less attractive, and then attracting more driver-owned cars, because through both actions, we can grow profits without increasing risk for the company.

Interviewer: Thank you.

Key takeaway: Segmenting properly

Distinguished candidate: Understands risks associated with firm-owned model.

Figure 1: C.N.A. Dispatch Revenues vs. Gross Profit (2007 – 10)

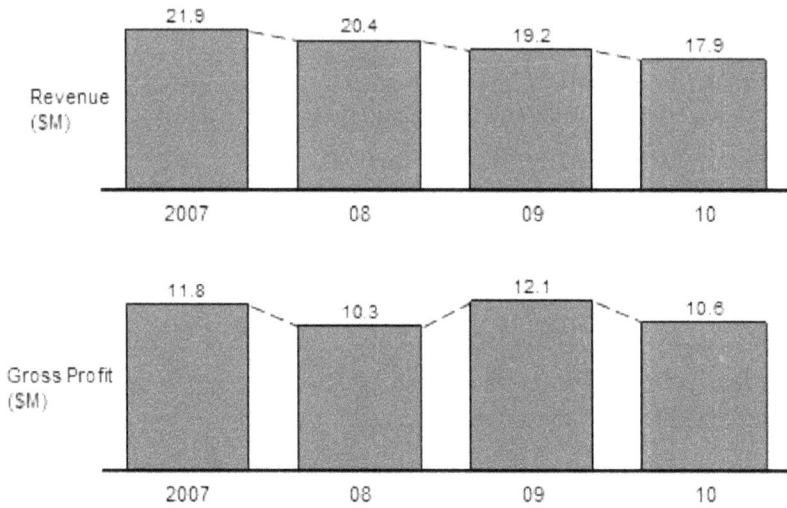

Figure 2: C.N.A. Dispatch Number of Taxis in Service – By Ownership (2006 – 10)

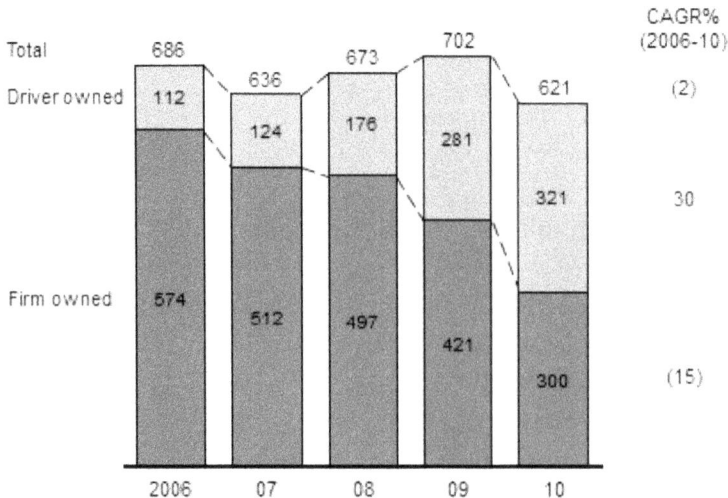

Figure 3: C.N.A. Dispatch Profit Break-down by Car Type (2010)

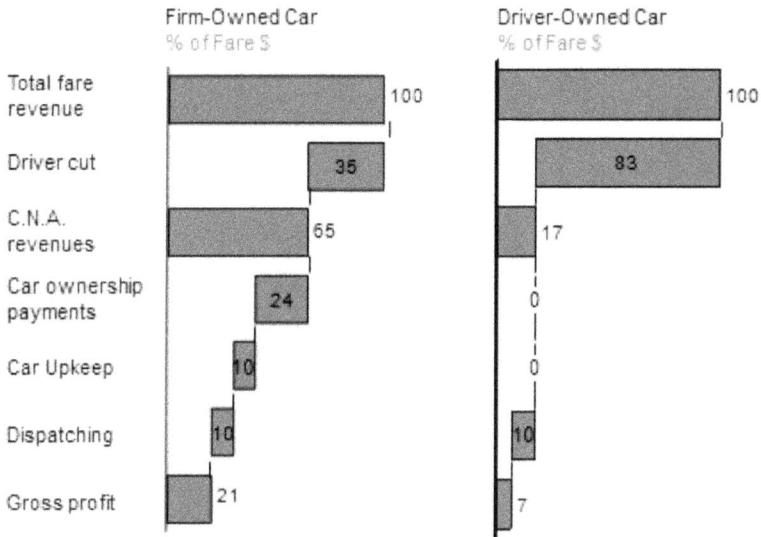

Mow & Grow

Rating – 2/5 – A qualitative open-ended question to ask how a company should grow

Question: Your client, Lion Mowers, makes a walking lawn mower. They have done well in this space, but they want to grow. What do you tell them?

Data (to be given as interviewee asks for it):

Core Competencies

- Low cost manufacturing – Lion mowers is one of the cheapest mowers on the market, due in part to their low cost base in China. In the "good," "better" and "best" view of the market, they are the low cost player in "good."

- Customer service – consistently highly rated by end customers with prompt and informative service

- Strong relationships with lawn and garden retail stores

Opportunities Management is Considering

- Riding mowers

- Other power lawn equipment (e.g., leaf blowers)

Markets

- Walking mowers

  - U.S. Size (equipment, parts and service): $2B, growing at 1% per year

- Riding mowers

  - U.S. Size (equipment, parts and service): $3B, growing at 2% per year

- Other Lawn Equipment

  - U.S. Size (equipment, parts and service): $2B, growing at 3% per year

Competitors

- Riding Mowers & Other Power Lawn Equipment: Most players established players in these markets are the same as are in walking mowers. There is no player with over 20% of market.

Customers

- Customers of riding mowers and other lawn equipment are the same as walking mowers, and include "big box" stores such as Home Depot and Sears, as well as smaller independent stores.

- Similar to walking mowers, riding mowers and other lawn equipment can be segmented into "good," "better," and "best" categories.

- Customers are overall fairly price sensitive, particularly in the "good" category.

- Lion Mowers estimates they could offer a riding mower at a 5% discount to current market prices in the "good" category.

- Lion Mowers estimates they could only match going market rates in other lawn equipment, due to the lower overall prices.

- Focus groups indicate that customers trust a brand, and would be likely to buy a riding mower or other power lawn equipment from the same company that made their walking mower.

Sample Analysis:

This is an interesting problem, in that it's so vague. Where can this company grow to? The answer lies somewhere between "everywhere" and "walking mowers," so we need to narrow the field of possibilities down. I would structure in the following way:

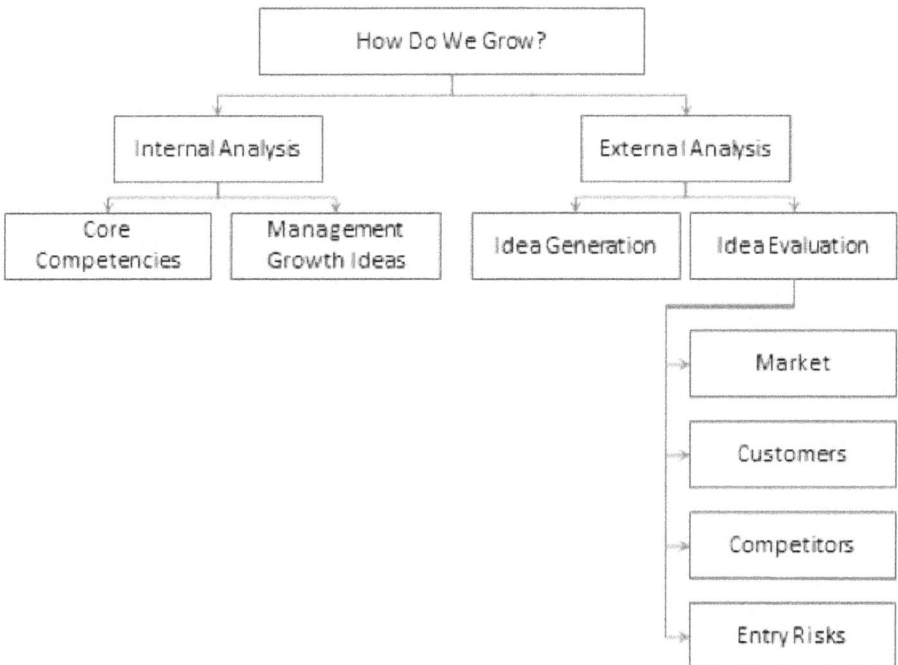

Core Competencies

First, we should get management's perspective on what they think
they are best at (i.e., core competencies), and where they have
thought to grow. This is because they know their business, and there
is value in including their ideas (and if you don't take their ideas
seriously, they may be more reluctant to listen to yours).

In this case, they are great at providing a cheap "good" product, have
great customer relationships and provide excellent end-customer
support. Management has considered expanding within the lawn
equipment vertical to riding mowers and other lawn equipment (e.g.,
leaf blowers).

This is a good start. Using these core competencies, we need to
consider whether there are other opportunities to evaluate. This is
completely up to the interviewee: there won't be back-up data for
these other opportunities that the interviewee thinks of, but the
interviewer should feel free to make up data.

In this case, they're good at making small motorized equipment
for consumers. They might want to consider other items that may
be sold in their same distribution channel, such as power tools, air
compressors, etc. They could also consider non-motorized lawn
equipment, such as trailers you can pull behind a mower or fertilizer
spreaders you can push around your yard. All of these items would
leverage at least 2 of their 3 core competencies.

Opportunities That Management is Considering

Now let's analyze the ideas we know management wants to consider:
riding lawn mowers and other power lawn equipment.

First we can ask about the market: what is the size and what is the
growth? Both new markets are growing faster than our current
market, though all three are fairly mature and stable industries, so
growth rates are not high relative to say, medical devices. Riding
mowers is the largest, but growing a little slower than other power
lawn equipment.

At this moment I'm thinking riding mowers is the most attractive, given the relative size increase for a small growth decrease, but I want to look at customers and competitors.

How do the individual customers differ? How are they segmented? How price sensitive are they? And ultimately, could we match customer's expectations on prices?

We learn that both of these categories appeal to the same end-customers and are generally sold through the same distribution and retail locations. We also learn that, from a customer perspective, their needs are fairly similar. That is, some customers just want a "good" riding mower, while others want the "best." Our client plays well in the "good" space, so it was important to determine whether that segment exists.

We also learn that customers are price sensitive and that customers trust a brand, which is great for Lion Mowers. Finally, we learn that Lion Mowers could gain a price advantage in riding mowers but not other power lawn equipment.

Competitors

At this point, riding mowers is certainly emerging as the more attractive choice, but let's look at competitors to make sure.

How fragmented is the market with respect to competitors? Are there any competitors that dominate the market? How familiar are we with the competitors?

In this case, we learn in both markets that the same players are present, and that no player dominates any given market.

Competition situation does not favor other power lawn equipment, so at this point I would summarize for the interviewer that riding lawn mowers appears to be the more attractive idea for Lion Mowers based on market attractiveness. However, at this point I want to consider risks.

Risks

One key risk they face is that a riding mower involves several more components that they have no experience with: different engines, more complexity, etc. They've obviously considered these additional complexities in being able to estimate that they could still come in 5% below market price when all is said and done, but that doesn't fully mitigate the risk. They could seek out another player to acquire: a "good" player who has some fat in their cost structure that Lion Mowers could help eliminate and get the price down. If they choose to develop internally, they could hire key design and operations people from competitors in the riding lawn mower market to help reduce risk.

So at this point, riding lawn mowers seems to be a great choice for Lion Mowers.

- The market is bigger and growing a little faster than their current market

- Customers and their needs are similar (and they trust walking mower brands to make riding lawn mowers)

- Competitors are the same as in walking lawn mowers: Lion Mowers would have some familiarity with competitors and their strategies

- An additional benefit is that entering consumer riding lawn mowers would allow a smoother transition to future verticals, such as commercial riding lawn mowers or even other small engine applications (e.g., golf carts).

Lion Mowers could always enter other power lawn equipment in the future, but for now, I recommend they prioritize riding lawn mowers, given management's ideas.

Extra Analysis – If You Have Time!

Now, let's consider other ideas: power tools and non-motor lawn equipment. We could go through the same analysis, but my hunch is as follows. Non-motor lawn equipment is probably growing similarly to overall lawn equipment, uses the same customers and has similar competitors.

Power tools, on the other hand, may be growing a little faster: there may be more innovations there, given small design tweaks could help a consumer get a job done faster (as opposed to mowers, where they can typically only drive so fast to effectively cut grass and not require additional safety equipment).

That said, power tools would require different industry knowledge, different customer needs, and different competitors. If it turns out the market is large and growing more quickly, and the same "good," "better," and "best" segmentation applies, the market could be attractive if Lion Mowers acquired someone in the market to jump start their efforts. Similar to riding lawn mowers, it would make sense to look for someone who plays well in the "good" category but has some fat in their cost structure that could be reduced through synergies or Lion Mower's efficiency-know how.

At this point, I don't see either opportunity being more attractive than riding lawn mowers, which leverages Lion Mowers' core competencies. I maintain my original suggestion they prioritize riding lawn mowers, and then they can consider these additional growth verticals at a future point in time.

APPENDICES

Appendix 1: Sponsor Profiles

AVASCENT

Who are we?

Avascent is the leading provider of business consulting services to firms operating in industries at the intersection of business, technology, and government policy. Avascent combines the analytic rigor and breadth of the large general management consultancies with the sector depth of a boutique firm to deliver sophisticated, fact-based and pragmatic solutions for our clients.

Avascent has advised global aerospace and defense primes, Fortune 500 OEMs and integrators, mid-tier systems and service providers, diversified global businesses and technology firms and leading private equity and investment firms for more than 25 years. Avascent's clients are active in a wide variety of markets where government is a key customer or influencer, including defense, commercial aerospace and aviation, space, homeland security, and transportation.

Seasoned professionals with diverse backgrounds are the key to Avascent's success. Our project teams bring a broad mix of business, policy, and government experience and insight to our clients. Additionally, our Washington, DC-based team of 80 full-time professionals is supplemented by a worldwide network of subject matter and regional experts.

By fusing our analytic talents with a deep understanding of the industries we serve and their broader political and policy context, we have earned a reputation for providing business leaders with actionable recommendations and solutions to pressing challenges. Avascent is set apart by our dedication to quality, timeliness, and pragmatism.

What is the role of an entry level analyst?

Analysts comprise the core of our entry-level hires and provide the critical research and analysis that drive our conclusions and recommendations for clients.

Analysts at Avascent:

- are active, integral members of our project teams

- provide thoughtful, informed insights and information critical to client engagements

- interact with senior staff across the firm

- take part in client meetings and presentations

Candidates join the firm directly after graduation, although some may bring 1 to 2 years of relevant work experience and degrees in fields such as economics, international affairs, engineering, or business.

"...As a new analyst I was quickly expected to perform in leading roles on projects and given direct client exposure..." – Senior Analyst

"... What makes the day-to-day experience of an Analyst so rewarding is that I am challenged to take on meaningful responsibilities alongside an intellectually stimulating team...."– Analyst

How do I apply?

Go to *http://www.avascent.com/Join-Avascent* to find our application form. You will also find additional helpful resources on applying, such as:

- Attributes we look for in candidates

- How we assess applicants

Additionally, review our recruiting calendar, *http://www.avascent.com/Join-Avascent/Campus-Recruiting*, to determine if we will be recruiting at your school.

AIESEC has 60 years of experience in developing high-potential youth into globally minded responsible leaders.

Present in over 110 countries and territories and with over 60,000 members, AIESEC is the world's largest youth-run organization. Focused on providing a platform for youth leadership development, AIESEC offers young people the opportunity to participate in international internships, experience leadership and participate in a global learning environment. What makes AIESEC unique is the youth driven impactful experience that it offers to its members. AIESEC is run by young people for young people, enabling a strong experience to all its stakeholders.

- Our members are part of an exciting, driven global network. They are able to contribute to societal change while exploring their own vision for a positive impact on society.

- We are supported by thousands of partner organizations around the globe who look to AIESEC to support the development of youth and to access top talent through our global internship program.

- Our alumni are leaders within their organizations and communities. They use the experience, skills and inspiration AIESEC has provided them to be agents of positive change within today's society.

We currently have 60,000 members and over 945,000 alumni. Learn more at *http://www.aiesec.org*.

85 Broads

85 Broads is an exclusive global women's network whose mission is to generate exceptional professional and social value for its members. Through regional events and our online, password-protected community, members engage in a rapid, high-powered exchange of ideas and information which is what makes 85 Broads unique.

From 1997 to 2000, 85 Broads was a network founded exclusively for current and former Goldman Sachs women who worked at 85 Broad Street, the firm's NYC headquarters, and at other GS offices worldwide. In 2000, we realized that we were "too exclusive" and at the urging of women at Harvard Business School, we invited HBS women to join, along with thousands of women at other leading graduate business schools in the US and abroad, irrespective of chosen career path.

In 2004, we recognized the need to include women at the undergraduate level who were pursuing every career path imaginable and over the next 3 years, we created clubs on over 40 campuses in the US and abroad.

And in 2007, we extended membership in 85 Broads to all trailblazing women worldwide, irrespective of one's college or graduate school affiliation.

The women in 85 Broads are entrepreneurs, investment bankers, consultants, lawyers, educators, venture capitalists, hedge fund managers, philanthropists, athletes, doctors, engineers, artists, and rocket scientists.

Learn more about our exclusive global network and apply for membership at *www.85broads.com.*

Appendix 2: International Students

What if I'm an International Student?

US Citizenship – Unfortunately, if you are not a US Citizen, it may be extremely difficult to get a job in management consulting in the United States. If you are not a US Citizen or Permanent Resident, it is recommended to apply to the consulting offices in your home country. This is because you need a work visa to be employed, and there's no guarantee you'll get it. Thus, the company would be taking a risk by hiring someone that may not be legal to work here instead of a US Citizen or Permanent Resident. Luckily some firms sponsor international students.

The first step is to ask, "Do you sponsor international students?" Try e-mailing HR or talking to representatives at an industry day. There is no harm in asking. Regrettably, most firms will say no. So play the numbers game again. The more firms you ask, the better the probability of success. If nothing else, the question gives you an introduction to having a more substantive conversation that can make you look good and even land you an interview. I once heard a story of an international student that was so good, that even though the firm had a policy not to sponsor international students, the firm made an exception. Don't take 'NO' for an answer!

Another route is to simply apply to the offices in your home country (many major consultancies have a global presence) and then transfer back to the US in a couple of years.

Once you have identified which firms will sponsor you, the next step is to impress. Unfortunately, recruiters have an ongoing concern regarding international students: communication. Communication is an integral part of consulting from making presentations to informal talk with colleagues and thus an important part of the recruiting process. This can be summed up in the following e-mail. Katie, an international student was concerned about her application. So she posted her concerns to LinkedIn, and Tom, a headhunter, responded with some helpful advice:

Hi Katie,

I can speak to this from the vantage point of a headhunter. Unfortunately, I have seen MANY hiring managers simply pass up on EXTREMELY talented candidates because they did not want the "hassle" of having to repeat themselves or otherwise exert themselves in the area of communication. If I could share one thing with professionals from other countries, I would let them know that their written and verbal communication skills are absolutely just as important as their credentials. Too many foreign candidates believe that their expertise alone will win the day. The goal for them should be to master their communication skills to the extent that a hiring manger perceives them as fluent with a pleasant accent. Anything less won't cut it.

Best,

Tom

So, if you haven't already, brush up on your English. If you want to conduct business in America, this won't be a waste of time.

Appendix 3: Crucial Economic Concepts

Not everyone who applies to consulting has taken several (or even one) economics or business courses. If you fall in this camp, or would like a refresher, we have included a few crucial economic concepts for your benefit.

1. Objective of any company – The objective of any for-profit company is just that – to make profit. Whenever you are doing a case interview, always remember you are ultimately looking to increase the client's profits. It doesn't matter if they're looking to enter a new market, respond to a competitor, sell off a division, or launch a hotel into space – your objective is to always increase long-term profits for the company.

    Note the qualifier, "long-term." There could be a scenario where a company could increase short-term profits of a division at the expense of long-term profits. This is clearly not a good idea, unless they're planning to sell the division off, in which case it may be good to bring up ethical concerns!

2. Components of profits

    Profit equals revenues minus costs. Revenues refer to money that the company brings in, while costs are money that goes out of the company. Revenues can be further divided into how many items you sold, and the price of each of those items. Costs can be further divided into how many items you sold and the cost of each (variable costs), and your fixed costs.

3. Supply/Demand Curve

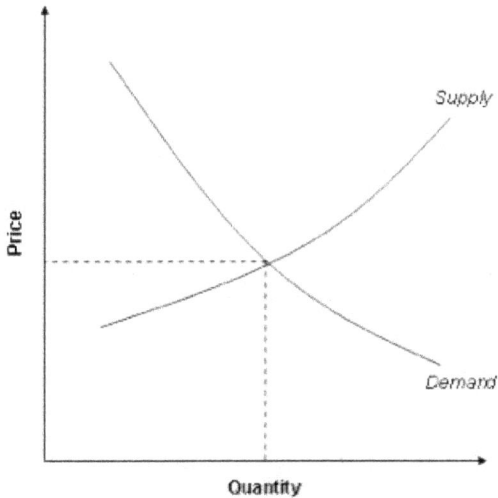

The Supply and Demand Curve indicates that as demand falls, or as supply rises, the price of a given item falls. Vice versa, if demand rises, or if supply falls, the price of a given items rises. Then there are price ceilings, price floors, demand and supply shifts, and all sorts of other cool things you can do with this graph. Google "Supply and Demand," or take some basic Economics courses for further information.

4. Elastic Demand vs. Inelastic Demand – How elastic is demand as price changes? In an economist's metaphor, if you exert "force" on the price, how far will the demand "stretch"? If it stretches (changes) a lot, then it has a high amount of elasticity. One good example of a highly elastic product is pop (soda for you non-Midwesterners). That's one reason why it's always on sale at the grocery store. Highly elastic items are generally less preferable to a company than inelastic items, because you have less ability to raise prices. That doesn't mean that you cannot succeed selling items with highly elastic prices: Coca Cola would like to have a word with me if I said otherwise. However, Coca Cola would most likely prefer the price of pop to be less elastic, because they would be able to charge more for each pop without demand going down.

High demand elasticity could be beneficial if your client can manufacture much higher quantities than their competitors. This way, your client can lower prices a little, and then meet the resulting surge in demand. If the competition tried to undercut your price, they would face shortages of supply.

On the other hand, low demand elasticity is generally a better situation for your client. You can raise prices without much loss in demand. Milk is a good (though not perfect) example of an item with low demand elasticity. Ask yourself, how many times have you seen milk on sale? If you have, it's probably a strategy to draw people into the store (since milk is one of the essential items many people buy).

5. Commoditized Items vs. Specialized Items – Commoditized items have few distinguishing features between brands. Bread, gasoline and napkins are commodities. One downside of offering a commodity is that you have less room to maneuver on price (the same problem as having high elasticity). If you raise prices, consumers will simply switch to the less-expensive brand with little to no utility loss or switching costs, and your sales will decline.

Specialized items have many distinguishing features between brands. Since your product is different in some important way, you have more room to move prices. For example, designer clothes are specialized items because they have a unique design. The clothing is made of higher quality materials and has high brand equity, which calls for a higher premium.

Note that commodity items tend to have higher volumes than specialty items. Ultimately, economic analysis is required to determine whether a commodity route or specialty route is the bottom line. Does the volume make up the lower margins? A general trend in different industries is that the big players make commodity products, and the niche players make specialty products. This is because the smaller firms can't effectively compete on commodity products. Seems logical right? Tidbits like these are indispensible during your interviews.

Appendix 4: References

Most of the information in this book came from experience and dozens of College2Consulting interviews. However, a few pieces of information came from secondary sources, and we are grateful to them.

Chapter 2

- Arthur Little History – *http://www.adl.com/fileadmin/user_upload/ Prism_2006_s2_3_history-1.pdf*

- Booz & Company history – *http://www.booz.com/global/home/who_ we_are/history*

- McKinsey & Company history – *http://www.mckinsey.com/About_us/ History.aspx*

- BCG history – *http://www.bcg.com/about_bcg/history/history_1965. aspx*

Chapter 8

- Percentage of job seekers who find job through referrals – *http:// www.quintcareers.com/getting_jobs.html*

Appendix 2

- Supply Demand Graph – *http://www.mikeonads.com/category/supply- and-demand/*